Microsoft Dynamics GP 2013 Cookbook

Over 110 immediately usable and effective recipes
to solve real-world Dynamics GP problems

Ian Grieve

Mark Polino

BIRMINGHAM - MUMBAI

Microsoft Dynamics GP 2013 Cookbook

First published: July 2010

Second edition: May 2013

Production Reference: 1170513

Published by Packt Publishing Ltd.
Livery Place
35 Livery Street
Birmingham B3 2PB, UK.
ISBN 978-1-84968-938-0

www.packtpub.com

Cover Image by Sandeep Babu (sandyjb@gmail.com)

Credits

Authors
Ian Grieve

Mark Polino

Reviewers
Vaidhyanathan Mohan

Jivtesh Singh

Joseph R. Tews

Acquisition Editor
Kartikey Pandey

Lead Technical Editor
Susmita Panda

Technical Editors
Prasad Dalvi

Worrell Lewis

Amit Ramadas

Varun Pius Rodrigues

Project Coordinator
Kranti Berde

Proofreaders
Lawrence A. Herman

Linda Morris

Indexer
Monica Ajmera Mehta

Production Coordinator
Aparna Bhagat

Cover Work
Aparna Bhagat

About the Author

Ian Grieve is a Microsoft Dynamics GP and CRM certified consultant specializing in the delivery of Microsoft Dynamics GP and CRM projects. He is a senior consultant at Perfect Image Ltd., a Microsoft partner and VAR in the North East of England.

Ian has worked with Microsoft Dynamics GP since 2003 and, over the years since, has dealt with all aspects of the product life cycle from presales, to implementation, to technical and functional training, to post go-live support and subsequent upgrades, and process reviews.

Alongside his work with Microsoft Dynamics GP, he has fulfilled a similar role dealing with Microsoft Dynamics CRM, with a special emphasis on project delivery and training of end users on the management of sales, marketing, and service.

In his spare time, Ian runs the *azurecurve | Ramblings of a Dynamics GP Consultant* (`http://www.azurecurve.co.uk`) blog dedicated to Microsoft Dynamics GP and related products and tries, often unsuccessfully, to squeeze in extra time for the Dynamics CRM-related blog *coralcurve | A Consultant's Dabblings in Dynamics CRM* (`http://www.coralcurve.co.uk`).

Acknowledgment

Thanks to my parents for their support through the years, especially my dad who got me into computers when I was young; it's turned from a hobby into a good career.

Thank you to Rob Hankin and William Morris at Perfect Image Ltd., for your openness to my writing this book; without your support this project would never have been started.

Thanks also to Dave Staples who, despite my initial reluctance, first got me working on Financial Management Systems and then working with Microsoft Dynamics GP; first on the helpdesk and then progressing into a consultant's role. Without you I'd never have been in a position to start this book.

Thanks must also go to Andrew Cooper (AGC, never AC) with whom I worked alongside on Dynamics GP for a number of years as we not only learned the system, its flaws, and imperfections, but also its depth, breadth, and capabilities.

Finally, thanks to the people at Packt Publishing who I worked with through the course of the project and, not least, to Mark Polino for the predecessor version of this book and for his efforts in the wider Dynamics GP community.

About the Author

Mark Polino is a Microsoft MVP for Dynamics GP, a Certified Public Accountant, and a Microsoft Certified Business Management Solutions Professional. He is the author of the premier Dynamics GP related blog, DynamicAccounting.net, and the creator and presenter of the successful series *Getting More Out of Microsoft Dynamics GP: 50 Tips in 50 minutes*. Mark has worked with Dynamics GP and its predecessor, Great Plains, for more than 10 years.

He works as a Principal Consultant with I.B.I.S., Inc. and spends his days helping clients implement Microsoft Dynamics GP.

Acknowledgment

To my wife Dara and my children, Micah and Angelina, thank you for your support in this project. You've patiently endured this obsession without complaining or killing me in my sleep. To mom and dad, thanks for the cheerleading even though you had no idea what this book is about.

Thank you to Andy Vabulas, Dwight Specht, and Clinton Weldon at I.B.I.S. for your support of this book. Without your openness to this project it never would have happened. To Abby, Troy, Ross, and all the other I.B.I.S. consultants who listened to me drone on about how the book was progressing, you have both my apologies and my thanks for your encouragement.

I owe a debt of gratitude to the kind folks at the Hampton Inn in Mt. Airy, NC. The majority of this book was written there while working on a Dynamics GP project. The hotel is staffed with some of the nicest people that you will ever meet and they were happy to fuel this book with great rooms and Diet Mt. Dew.

Much of this book was written on an Acer netbook. Without the small size and long battery life of the netbook, *Microsoft Dynamics GP 2010 Cookbook* would never have been finished on time.

To everyone else who has offered encouragement throughout this project, you have my thanks. To those who have been less than encouraging, I hope you someday decide to write a book.

About the Reviewers

Vaidhyanathan Mohan is a Microsoft-certified freelance Microsoft Dynamics GP consultant with expertise in Microsoft Dynamics GP and related technologies. Starting his career as a GP developer, he slowly and steadily enhanced his skills on Microsoft Dynamics GP, both on the product and technologies, and became a complete product consultant.

He has worked on various challenging customization developments and Dynamics GP implementations. He is an active participant on all Microsoft Dynamics GP community forums and Microsoft Dynamics GP technical blogger, namely *Dynamics GP – Learn & Discuss* (http://vaidymohan.com), which is listed on Microsoft's official Dynamics GP blog space. He is also one of the technical reviewers of the book, *Developing Microsoft Dynamics GP Business Applications* by *Packt Publishing*.

He is who he is now because of his devoted parents, his brother and family, his wife and his daughter. He is an avid photography enthusiast (http://500px.com/seshadri), music fanatic, coffee addict, and immensely fond of anything about Microsoft Dynamics GP.

Jivtesh Singh is a Microsoft Dynamics GP MVP, and a Microsoft Dynamics Certified Technology Specialist for Dynamics GP. Through his blog, which is widely read in the Dynamics GP community, he covers Dynamics GP tips, tricks, and news.

Jivtesh is a Dynamics GP Consultant and Systems Implementer, and has been associated with the Microsoft Technologies since the launch of Microsoft .NET Framework. Jivtesh has over 10 years of experience in development and maintenance of enterprise software using best coding practices, refactoring and usage of design patterns, and Test-driven development. Jivtesh recently built a Kinect interface to control the Microsoft Dynamics GP 2010 R2 Business Analyzer with gestures. Later, he built a part of the GP Future demo for Convergence GP Keynote.

Jivtesh has set up a custom search engine directory for Dynamics GP blog at www.gpwindow.com to help with easier access of Dynamics GP resources for the GP community. With MVP Mark Polino, he has also set up a Dynamics GP product directory www.dynamicsgpproducts.com.

Jivtesh's blog on Dynamics GP is www.jivtesh.com. Jivtesh's custom search engine for GP blogs is www.gpwindow.com. Dynamics GP Products website is www.dynamicsgpproducts.com.

Joseph R. Tews is a Microsoft Dynamics and SharePoint Professional, and Microsoft Certified Trainer, with experience as both a Microsoft partner and customer. Joe's experience is varied from implementations and upgrades, to product administration, support, and training delivery to end users and other Microsoft partners. He specializes in working with Microsoft SharePoint Technologies in Microsoft Dynamics GP, Microsoft Dynamics GP installation and administration, as well as working with Microsoft Dynamics CRM, Microsoft SQL Server, and Business Intelligence.

Joe teaches Microsoft Dynamics GP and other specialized classes across the country and the world for both customers and partners, and has also been identified as a Lead Trainer for the MCT program. In recognition for his work with Microsoft SharePoint and Microsoft SharePoint Technologies in Microsoft Dynamics GP, Joe has presented multiple sessions on these topics at Microsoft's Convergence, GP Partner Connections, and GPUG conferences. Joe has also been a contributing author to multiple courseware offerings from Microsoft learning.

I'd like to thank my family, most importantly my parents Bob and Nancy, and my sisters Corrie and Jenna, for all of their support throughout my professional career. I would also like to thank my friends and coworkers for all the help and support throughout the years. I wouldn't be where I am today without all of them.

www.PacktPub.com

Support files, eBooks, discount offers and more

You might want to visit www.PacktPub.com for support files and downloads related to your book.

Did you know that Packt offers eBook versions of every book published, with PDF and ePub files available? You can upgrade to the eBook version at www.PacktPub.com and as a print book customer, you are entitled to a discount on the eBook copy. Get in touch with us at service@packtpub.com for more details.

At www.PacktPub.com, you can also read a collection of free technical articles, sign up for a range of free newsletters and receive exclusive discounts and offers on Packt books and eBooks.

http://PacktLib.PacktPub.com

Do you need instant solutions to your IT questions? PacktLib is Packt's online digital book library. Here, you can access, read and search across Packt's entire library of books.

Why Subscribe?

- ▸ Fully searchable across every book published by Packt
- ▸ Copy and paste, print and bookmark content
- ▸ On demand and accessible via web browser

Free Access for Packt account holders

If you have an account with Packt at www.PacktPub.com, you can use this to access PacktLib today and view nine entirely free books. Simply use your login credentials for immediate access.

Instant Updates on New Packt Books

Get notified! Find out when new books are published by following @PacktEnterprise on Twitter, or the *Packt Enterprise* Facebook page.

Table of Contents

Preface

Tens of thousands of Microsoft Dynamics GP users keep the accounting functions of their firms running day in and day out. They ensure that vendors get paid, customer payments are tracked, and the financial statements balance at the end of the month. In short, they provide the information critical to corporate decision making.

Of the many tens of thousands of people using Dynamics GP, the majority of them only ever use a small subset of the available functionality. They may get basic training when Dynamics GP is implemented, or when they join the company, and learn enough to do their job but never look beyond this set of skills for ways to improve processes and become more efficient.

On top of this, many users start working with a particular version of Dynamics GP and continue to use the system in the same way as the years pass and upgrades are installed with many new features available.

The work gets done but good employees are left with a nagging feeling, an itch, that there must be a better way. This book is designed for those people who want to scratch the itch and learn how to get more out of Microsoft Dynamics GP.

Many of the ways to get more from Dynamics GP do not require extensive knowledge of the system, merely a desire to learn and make Dynamics GP easier, faster, and simpler. These features, tips, and techniques have been compiled into a set of recipes designed to let Dynamics GP users cook up solutions to their problems.

Like any good cookbook, the recipes are laid out into simple, sequential, steps optimized for quick application and be easy to follow and get right on the first attempt. This easy gratification is designed to draw users deeper into the recipes with the goal of improving efficiency, allowing the time saved to be put back into other finance activities, or the simple pleasure of wrapping up the day and going home early.

What this book covers

Chapter 1, Personalizing Dynamics GP, includes recipes designed to enhance the usefulness of Microsoft Dynamics GP by personalizing the look and feel of the application.

Chapter 2, New in Dynamics GP 2013, includes recipes demonstrating some of the key new features of Dynamics GP 2013 from the Financial and Supply Chain Management series.

Chapter 3, Organizing Dynamics GP, includes recipes that are designed to help administrators get more out of Dynamics GP for their users by changing the way Dynamics GP is organized.

Chapter 4, Automating Dynamics GP, includes recipes that focus on efficiency and automation, and are designed to be time savers across the system.

Chapter 5, Harnessing the Power of SmartLists, includes recipes to harness the power of Dynamics GP's ad hoc reporting tool and ways to leverage the reporting power of SmartLists.

Chapter 6, Connecting Dynamics GP to Microsoft Office 2013, includes recipes that help to connect Dynamics GP with Microsoft Office 2013 and ways to use Office to improve processes in Dynamics GP.

Chapter 7, Exposing Hidden Features in Dynamics GP, includes recipes on techniques that are often well-known to consultants but missed by users. It contains hidden settings that can help save a lot of time.

Chapter 8, Improving Dynamics GP with Hacks, includes recipes that are used to hack existing features in Dynamics GP so as to improve.

Chapter 9, Preventing Errors in Dynamics GP, includes recipes for administrators and users to help prevent errors in Dynamics GP. It also includes ways to fix erroneous transactions that managed to make it to the general ledger.

Chapter 10, Maintaining Dynamics GP, includes recipes for an administrator or power user to help maintain Dynamics GP.

Chapter 11, Extending Dynamics GP with the Support Debugging Tool, includes recipes that make use of the Support Debugging Tool to improve efficiency and error tracing in Dynamics GP.

Chapter 12, Extending Dynamics GP Professional Services Tools Library, includes recipes which use PSTL to ease company and data setup and to modify data in an existing Dynamics GP implementation.

What you need for this book

You will require the following software for this book:

- Microsoft Dynamics GP 2013 with the Fabrikam, Inc. sample company deployed and a second company without any configuration completed
- Microsoft SQL Server 2012 (or SQL Server 2008 R2)
- Microsoft Office 2013
- Windows Server 2012 (or Windows Server 2008 R2) with a domain controller available

Who this book is for

This book is for Dynamics GP users and Microsoft Dynamics GP partners and is primarily focused on delivering time-proven application modifications. This book assumes that you have a basic understanding of business management systems and basic knowledge of Microsoft Dynamics GP. All of these recipes are real-world tested and designed to be used immediately.

Conventions

In this book, you will find a number of styles of text that distinguish between different kinds of information. Here are some examples of these styles, and an explanation of their meaning.

Code words in text are shown as follows: "Save the sheet to the desktop as Segment3Import."

A block of code is set as follows:

```
Delete from SY01401
where coDefaultType = 13
```

New terms and **important words** are shown in bold. Words that you see on the screen, in menus or dialog boxes for example, appear in the text like this: "Click on **Redisplay** to run the inquiry."

Reader feedback

Feedback from our readers is always welcome. Let us know what you think about this book—what you liked or may have disliked. Reader feedback is important for us to develop titles that you really get the most out of.

To send us general feedback, simply send an e-mail to feedback@packtpub.com, and mention the book title via the subject of your message.

If there is a topic that you have expertise in and you are interested in either writing or contributing to a book, see our author guide on www.packtpub.com/authors.

Customer support

Now that you are the proud owner of a Packt book, we have a number of things to help you to get the most from your purchase.

Errata

Although we have taken every care to ensure the accuracy of our content, mistakes do happen. If you find a mistake in one of our books—maybe a mistake in the text or the code—we would be grateful if you would report this to us. By doing so, you can save other readers from frustration and help us improve subsequent versions of this book. If you find any errata, please report them by visiting http://www.packtpub.com/submit-errata, selecting your book, clicking on the **errata submission form** link, and entering the details of your errata. Once your errata are verified, your submission will be accepted and the errata will be uploaded on our website, or added to any list of existing errata, under the Errata section of that title. Any existing errata can be viewed by selecting your title from http://www.packtpub.com/support.

Piracy

Piracy of copyright material on the Internet is an ongoing problem across all media. At Packt, we take the protection of our copyright and licenses very seriously. If you come across any illegal copies of our works, in any form, on the Internet, please provide us with the location address or website name immediately so that we can pursue a remedy.

Please contact us at copyright@packtpub.com with a link to the suspected pirated material.

We appreciate your help in protecting our authors, and our ability to bring you valuable content.

Questions

You can contact us at questions@packtpub.com if you are having a problem with any aspect of the book, and we will do our best to address it.

1
Personalizing Dynamics GP

In this chapter, we start with recipes for users of Microsoft Dynamics GP where we will look at ways of:

- ▸ Improving visibility by setting required fields to bold and red
- ▸ Getting faster access to data with the shortcut bar.
- ▸ Reducing clicks with start-up shortcuts
- ▸ Personalizing the Home page by selecting the right role
- ▸ Further personalizing the Home page by customizing the layout
- ▸ Speeding access to data with Quick Links
- ▸ Rearranging navigation to make it easier
- ▸ Jumping to the right location with breadcrumbs
- ▸ Managing personal reports with My Reports
- ▸ Viewing open items with the Task List
- ▸ Visualizing information with Business Analyzer on the Home page
- ▸ Accessing accounts faster with favorites in lookups
- ▸ Cleaning up the mess by fixing AutoComplete errors

Introduction

This chapter explores recipes designed to enhance the usefulness of Microsoft Dynamics GP by personalizing the look and feel of the application. These recipes provide the first few steps in harnessing the full power of Dynamics GP. They are designed to improve productivity today so don't wait to put them to use.

In almost all cases, the recipes in this chapter do not require an administrator and are available to the average user. The ability of each user to tailor these items to their own needs is what makes them so powerful.

By personalizing Dynamics GP, users get the opportunity to fine tune the system to the way that they work. There is something incredibly satisfying about tailoring a system to make it more efficient and we'll cover some of those personalizing options here.

While the nature of these recipes makes them useful right away, it is strongly recommended that these items be attempted in a test environment first.

Improving visibility by setting required fields to bold and red

Microsoft Dynamics GP provides an option for each user to identify required fields on any form. By activating this setting, users can get an obvious visual cue indicating the minimum required fields on any form. This recipe shows how to turn Required Fields bold red and what the end result looks like.

Getting ready

Prior to changing the appearance of required fields, the feature **Show Required Fields** needs to be turned on. To activate this feature:

1. Select **Help** (the white question mark on a blue background in the upper-right corner) from the main Home page of Dynamics GP.

2. Ensure that **Show Required Fields** has a check mark next to it. If it does not, click on the **Show Required Fields** item to turn this option on.

How to do it...

To improve visibility of required fields, follow these steps:

1. The shortcut bar is the vertical bar on the top-left side of the screen when the **Home** button is selected on the left. From the shortcut bar, click on **User Preferences** then click on the **Display** button to open the **User Display Preferences** window; if you don't have **User Preferences** on the shortcut bar, click on the Microsoft Dynamics GP menu and then click on **User Preferences**.

2. On the bottom-right side, under the heading **Required Fields**, set the **Font Color** field to **Red** and **Font Style** to **Bold**.

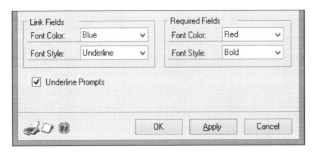

3. Click on **OK** to accept the changes and close the window, then click on **OK** to close **User Preferences**. Now any windows that allow data entry will show their required fields in bold red, as shown in the following screenshot:

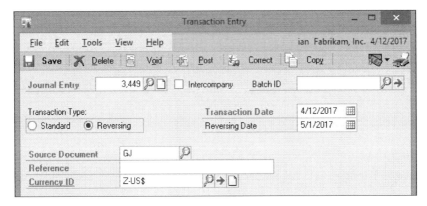

How it works...

Dynamics GP contains identifiers behind the scenes to mark fields as required. Dynamics GP uses these identifiers to change the color of the field name. Highlighting required fields provides a quick visual cue to ensure that at least the minimum amount of data is entered prior to saving a form. This will save hours of time by preventing annoying messages indicating that required fields have not been completed, especially since there is no indicator as to what field is missing.

There's more...

By default, activating **Show Required Fields** simply sets required fields to black and regular. That is, it doesn't distinguish them at all. This is important because if **Show Required Fields** is off completely, Dynamics GP 2013 will prompt users to turn it on but it won't appear to have any effect.

There are some areas in Dynamics GP where required fields are not marked in red and bold despite this feature being properly applied. In almost all cases, these required fields occur in the grid section of a transaction entry form. This area of a form has a heading at the top and a grid that allows multiple entries under one heading. The nature of the programming behind the grid format prevents Dynamics GP from properly highlighting these fields and, unfortunately, there is way to force a field inside the grid to reflect the **Show Required Fields** setting.

When a user receives a warning that a required field is missing but all required fields appear to be correctly filled in, they should examine the fields in the grid for missing information. The most common culprits are **Unit of Measure** (U of M) and **Site ID** fields.

Modifier with Visual Basic for Applications (VBA)

With the available **Modifier with VBA** utility for Dynamics GP, an administrator or developer can make additional fields required, and in most cases Dynamics GP will properly apply the red and bold formatting automatically. More information on Modifier with VBA is available from the manuals in Dynamics GP or from an authorized Microsoft Dynamics partner.

Getting faster access to data with the shortcut bar

The shortcut bar provides fast access to Dynamics GP's windows and SmartLists along with web pages and external applications. Often, external shortcuts are used for quick access to things such as currency websites, budget spreadsheets, shipping sites, or other applications. Almost anything used to improve a user's productivity can be linked to via the shortcut bar. In this recipe, we'll spend some time looking at how to get the most out of it.

Getting ready

The vertical area to the left side of the Dynamics GP Home page is known as the **Navigation Pane**. Select **Home** on the Navigation Pane to make the shortcut bar visible on the top left side.

Selecting other Navigation Pane sections makes other navigation options available. Only the **Home** selection makes the shortcut bar available.

There are six types of items that can be added to the shortcut bar:

- ▶ Dynamics GP windows
- ▶ SmartLists
- ▶ Macros
- ▶ Web pages

- ▸ External files
- ▸ Folders

How to do it...

The most common use of the shortcut bar is to add a Dynamics GP window for fast access. The simplest way to do that is as follows:

1. Select **Financial** from the Navigation Pane on the left side. In the center area page, select **General**. This opens the **Transaction Entry** window.

2. From the **Transaction Entry** window, select **File | Add to Shortcuts**.

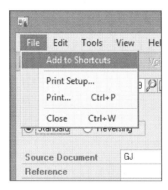

3. Click on the **Home** button to see the **Transaction Entry** window added to the shortcut bar.

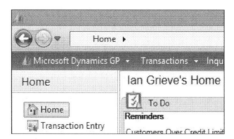

How it works...

The shortcut bar in Microsoft Dynamics GP works a lot like shortcuts on the Microsoft Windows desktop. Dynamics GP places a pointer to the window or file inside the shortcut and launches the appropriate selection when the shortcut is clicked.

There's more...

Typically, users simply accumulate shortcuts on the shortcut bar but to really get the most out of the Shortcut Bar requires are a few extra techniques.

Use external Shortcuts for greater flexibility

For web pages and external shortcuts, right-click on the Shortcut Bar. Then select **Add** followed by **Add Web Page** or **Add External Shortcut**.

Selecting **Add Web Page** provides the option to enter the location (URL) along with a button to test that the link works correctly.

Selecting **Add External Shortcut** provides an option to browse for the external file on your system. This can be an application file such as an Excel spreadsheet or a Microsoft Word document. It can also be a link to an application such as Microsoft CRM, budgeting software, or Solitaire for a much needed break.

Setting a keyboard shortcut allows the use of a set of keystrokes to launch a shortcut. For example, this means that *Ctrl + Shift + J* could be setup to launch the **Transaction Entry** window for a journal entry or *F2* to launch Microsoft Office Excel.

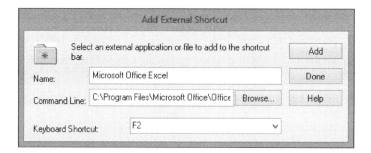

Organize with folders

Right-clicking on the Shortcut Bar and selecting **Add | Folder** provides an option to add a folder to the Shortcut Bar that can be used to organize entries. For example, a `Month End` folder can be used to hold links to windows, routines, and reports that are used as part of the month end closing process. This is a great place to start organizing shortcuts.

Complex shortcuts

Microsoft's Developing for Dynamics GP site provides additional information on dealing with complex shortcuts for scenarios such as launching an application and opening a specific file. More information is available at `http://blogs.msdn.com/developingfordynamicsgp/archive/2009/08/24/creating-external-shortcuts-with-parameters.aspx`.

See also

For information about activating shortcuts when Dynamics GP starts, look at the *Reducing clicks with start-up shortcuts* recipe. For more information about folders, take a look at the *Remembering processes with Ad Hoc Workflow* recipe in *Chapter 3, Organizing Dynamics GP.*

Reducing clicks with start-up shortcuts

For users who want the same set of features available every time Dynamics GP opens, the shortcut bar supports automatically opening a window, SmartList Favorite, web page, macro, or external file when Dynamics GP starts.

For example, someone with heavy accounts payable responsibilities would regularly use the **Payables Transaction Entry** window. Adding that window as a start-up shortcut would open that window immediately after Dynamics GP starts without the user having to do anything. In this recipe, we'll look at how to activate a shortcut automatically when Dynamics GP starts.

Getting ready

To use this recipe, users need a basic familiarity with shortcuts. Since that was covered in the last recipe, everyone should be in good shape.

How to do it...

To set **shortcuts** to open automatically, complete the following steps:

1. Open the **Payables Transaction** window in Dynamics GP by selecting **Purchasing** from the Navigation Pane and clicking on **Transaction Entry**.
2. Select **File | Add as a Shortcut** to add the shortcut to the shortcut bar.
3. Select **Home** to see the shortcut that was just added.

4. Right-click on the shortcut that was just created and select **Cut**. Right-click on the **Startup** folder and select **Paste**. Once Dynamics GP is restarted, the window represented by the shortcut will start automatically.

How it works...

The **Startup** folder on the shortcut bar is designed to open items when Dynamics GP starts, providing consistent, quick access to regularly used items in the system. These are unique for each user.

There's more...

The **Startup** shortcut folder is designed for more than just windows in Dynamics GP.

File example

Another option to add items to the **Startup** folder on the shortcut bar is to right-click on the folder and select **Add | Add External Shortcut**. Name the shortcut and select **Browse**. Find the external file in the menu system and click on **Open**.

Optionally add a keyboard shortcut then click on **Add**.

Drag and drop

Experienced users will comment that it is also possible to select the shortcut with the left mouse button and drag it to the **Startup** folder. That works as well except for a bug in Dynamics GP that prevents dragging and dropping the first shortcut onto the **Startup** folder. If there is already a shortcut in the folder, dragging and dropping works fine, but until the first one has been created, dragging and dropping a shortcut onto a folder is impossible.

Interestingly, dragging shortcuts to folders worked correctly in Version 9 and seems to have broken with Version 10 and has not been fixed in either version 2010 or 2013.

See also

For more information on how the shortcut bar works, refer to the *Getting faster access to data with the shortcut bar* recipe in this chapter and the *Improving consistency with shortcuts and user classes* recipe in *Chapter 4, Automating Dynamics GP*.

Personalizing the Home page by selecting the right role

Since Version 2010 of Dynamics GP, Microsoft has placed a strong emphasis on a user's role in both the organization and the software. Selecting the right role in the system presents many of the best Home page options by default.

A role is usually selected by default when a user is created and it's often wrong because at setup the focus is placed on job titles, not on tasks the user performs. Additionally, user's roles evolve and change over time. Fortunately, changing a user's role is easy, so we'll look at how to do it in this recipe.

How to do it...

To change a user's Home page role, complete the following steps:

1. On the Home page, click on the **Customize this Page** link in the upper-right corner.
2. Click on the **Change Role** button in the bottom-right corner.

   Changing the role resets any customizations that a user has made to their **Quick Links** or **Business Analyzer** settings on the Home page; the user is prompted with a warning that their customizations will be lost and given the choice of cancelling the change of role.

3. Click on **OK** to indicate an understanding of the consequences of changing a role.
4. Select an industry at the top. Changing an industry simply adds or removes available role options below. Selecting **Other** as the industry provides all of the role options.

5. On the left side, select the role closest to a user's responsibilities. As a role is highlighted, a description of that role's tasks is included on the right side. Click on **OK** to accept the role.

See also

▸ The *Managing personal reports with My Reports* recipe

▸ The *Further personalizing the Home page by customizing the layout* recipe

▸ The *Visualizing information with Business Analyzer on the Home page* recipe

▸ The *Speeding up navigation lists by disabling Business Analyzer* recipe in *Chapter 10, Maintaining Dynamics GP*

Further personalizing the Home page by customizing the layout

The customization possible on the Home page has been enhanced further in Microsoft Dynamics GP from the options that were available in Microsoft Dynamics GP 2010.

A default two column layout will be loaded when the Home page role is selected but can be customized by the user.

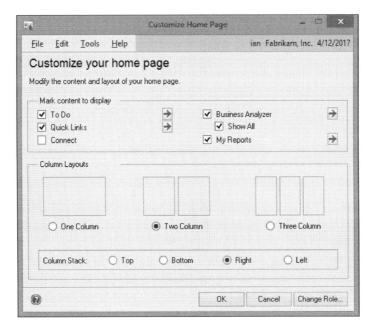

How to do it...

To change a user's Home page role, complete the following steps:

1. On the Home page, click on the **Customize this Page** link in the upper right corner.

2. The content being displayed can be amended in the top **Mark content to display** section. To disable a piece of content, such as **Connect**, unmark the checkbox and click on **OK** and this section will be removed from the Home page.

3. The expansion buttons, represented by horizontal blue arrows, allow additional criteria to be defined. Business Analyzer has an additional option, **Show All**, which will show all of the selected Business Analyzer reports on the Home page.

4. The three available **Column Layouts** can be selected by marking the required radio button.

5. The final customization option available is the **Column Stack** option, which controls the display of Home page sections when one is maximized by moving the remaining small windows to the top, bottom, right, or left.

6. A section is maximized by clicking on the **Maximize/Multicolumn Mode** button (a square containing four arrows pointing outwards from the center).

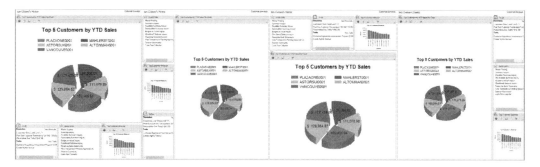

7. Once the desired customization options have been selected, click on the **OK** button.

There's more...

In Microsoft Dynamics GP 2010, sections on the Home page were reorganized within the **Customize this page...** window. In both the Microsoft Dynamics GP 2013 Desktop client and Web client, reorganization is accomplished on the Home page itself by using the mouse to drag and drop the section in the same way you would for a window.

The Home page will automatically shuffle the other sections around as the selected one is being moved. When placed in the required position release the mouse button and the section will click into place.

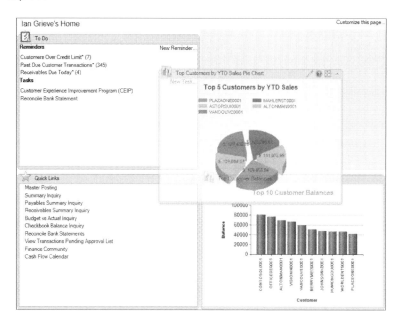

See also

- ▸ The *Managing personal reports with My Reports* recipe
- ▸ The *Visualizing information with Business Analyzer on the Home page* recipe
- ▸ The *Speeding up navigation lists by disabling Business Analyzer* recipe in *Chapter 10, Maintaining Dynamics GP*

Speeding access to data with Quick Links

Like the shortcut bar, Quick Links provides fast access to data both inside and outside of Dynamics GP. Though there is some overlap with Shortcuts, Quick Links provide some unique features. For starters, related Quick Links are provided based on the user's Home page role. Additionally, Quick Links also provide fast access to Navigation Lists, something that shortcuts can't do. In this recipe we'll select an included Navigation List and then add it as a Quick Link.

Getting ready

Navigation Lists provide another way to work with data in Dynamics GP and they aren't available to add to the shortcut bar. For our Quick Links example, we will look at adding a Navigation List as a Quick Link.

How to do it...

To add a Navigation List as a Quick Link, perform the following steps:

1. Click on the Home button on the Navigation Pane to the left. On the main Home screen, find the section labeled Quick Links.

2. Place the cursor in the Quick Links box and a pencil will appear in the upper-right corner. Click on the small pencil icon and select **Add | Dynamics GP Navigation List**.

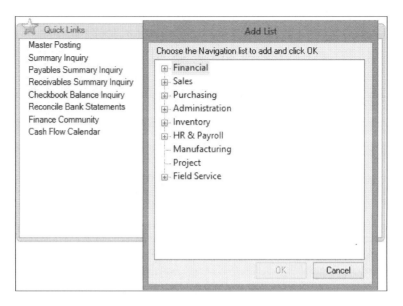

3. Click the plus (**+**) sign next to **Sales** to expand those lists.

4. Click the plus (**+**) sign next to **Accounts** and select **Customers**. Click on **OK** to finish.

5. In the open **Quick Links Details** box, find and select the **Customers** link. Click on the **Move Up** button repeatedly until **Customers** is at the top of the list and click on **OK**.

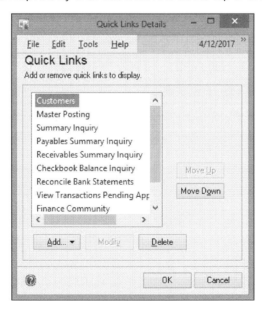

How it works...

This process put the **Customer Quick Link** at the top of the **Quick Links** area. Now, clicking on the **Customer Quick Link** will immediately open that Navigation List. Without this Quick Link, a user would need to select **Sales** from the Home page and find the **Customer** link every time they needed to add a customer. Simply selecting a Quick Link is a much faster way to get deep into Dynamics GP.

See also

▶ The *Personalizing the Home page by selecting the right role* recipe

Rearranging navigation to make it easier

The Navigation Pane on the left side of Dynamics GP is full of useful functions. Sometimes it is too full! For many users, it's beneficial to rearrange items on the Navigation Pane to better suit their role. We'll look at how to do that in this recipe.

Getting ready

Most users quickly discover that left-clicking and dragging the separator above the **Home** button on the left allows them to shrink and expand the space available for Navigation Pane buttons. This expands the room for lists and shortcuts above by transforming the large buttons into smaller but less intuitive icons. But there is so much more that can be done to personalize the Navigation Pane.

How to do it...

Cleaning up the Navigation Pane can provide faster and simpler navigation options. Let's see how by completing the following steps:

1. On the Navigation Pane, select the bottom-right corner of the pane and pick **Option**.

2. From here, select **Purchasing** and move it to the top using the **Move Up** and **Move Down** buttons at the right side.

3. Then select the **Sales** module and uncheck that selection. Click on **OK**.

Now the **Purchasing** choice has been moved to the top where a user can easily get at it and the **Sales** option not required for this user has been removed.

How it works...

In our example, a heavy user of the **Purchasing** module now has that Navigation Pane button immediately below the **Home** button and easily accessible. The **Sales** button, which wouldn't be used by a typical Purchasing employee, has been removed to clean up the interface.

Jumping to the right location with breadcrumbs

Dynamics GP 2010 and later has embraced the concept of **breadcrumbs**. Breadcrumbs provide a fantastic opportunity to ease system navigation. By showing the path through the system, new users gain an understanding of how to navigate within Dynamics GP. Experienced users learn that it's a fast way to hop through the system without accessing menus. In this recipe, we'll look at how to use breadcrumbs to improve navigating through Dynamics GP.

Getting ready

In Dynamics GP, select **Financials** from the Navigation Pane. On the **Financial** area page, select **Transaction Entry** in the **Transactions** area. This will open the **Transaction Entry** window for a General Journal Entry.

How to do it...

Let's now look at how breadcrumbs can improve navigation for a user by completing the following steps:

1. On the upper left of the screen is the breadcrumbs trail. It shows **Home | Financial | Financial**.

2. This is the path through the system to this window. It indicates that from the Home page the user is in the **Financial** area and has selected the **Financial** area page.

3. On the Navigation Pane to the left, select **Accounts**. This opens the Accounts Navigation List and changes the breadcrumb to show **Home | Financial | Accounts**. Select **Financial** from inside the breadcrumb trail to go back one step and return to the **Financial** area page.

Managing personal reports with My Reports

My Reports is a section of the Dynamics GP Home page designed to provide fast access to reporting options in Dynamics GP. Similar to Quick Links functionality, My Reports provides single click access to reports, replacing multiple clicks and drill downs with a direct connection.

In Dynamics GP, every prebuilt report (also known as a **Report Writer** report) requires an **option**. An option is simply a named group of settings for a particular report. For example, a user may have a `Receivables Aged Trial Balance` report with date and selection criteria designed for month end reporting. The report name is always `Receivables Aged Trial Balance` but the option name to describe those particular month end settings might be `Month End`.

The My Reports feature provides one click access to reports with saved options. In this recipe we'll look at how to add a report to My Reports.

How to do it...

To add a report to My Reports, we will need to complete the following steps:

1. Select the **Sales** button from the Navigation Pane on the left side. In the list on the left select **Report List**.

2. In the center section, scroll down to the report named **Aged Trial Balance** with the **Option** column value of **demo** and check the box to the left.

   Demo is a prebuilt, saved report option. Report options are saved report settings for items like dates and restrictions.

3. Click on the **Add to** button to add this to the **My Reports** section of the Home page. Accept the default name for the report by clicking on **OK**.

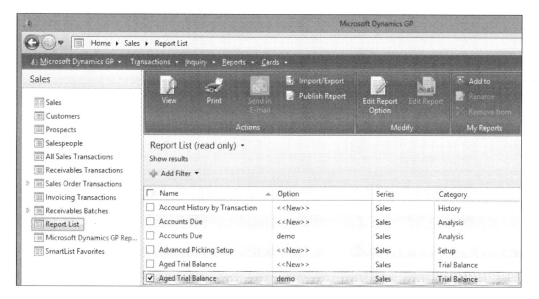

4. Click on the **Home** button on the Navigation Pane to return to the Home page. The **Aged Trial Balance-demo** report now appears on the Home page under **My Reports**.

5. Clicking on the **Aged Trial Balance-demo** link under **My Reports** now runs the report automatically.

There's more...

Other features and options are available to assist with managing reporting in Dynamics GP.

Reports without options

Reports without options cannot be added to the **My Reports** section of the Home page. Consequently, users need to create and save report options to make those reports available to the Home page.

Better dates in report options

A technique for setting up report dates for automatic reporting is covered in detail in the *Controlling reporting dates with Beginning and Ending Periods* recipe in *Chapter 4, Automating Dynamics GP*.

See also

- ▶ The *Personalizing the Home Page by selecting the right role* recipe
- ▶ The *Speeding access to data with Quick Links* recipe
- ▶ The *Viewing open items with the Task List* recipe
- ▶ The *Controlling reporting dates with beginning and ending periods* recipe in *Chapter 4, Automating Dynamics GP*

Viewing open items with the Task List

Dynamics GP provides a Task List for managing items to be accomplished within the system. While not quite as powerful as, say, Outlook's tasks, the Task List in Dynamics GP can provide direct links to the appropriate window, web page, or external file needed to accomplish the task. Even Outlook can't provide a direct link to the right window in Dynamics GP. In addition, tasks can be assigned to other users in the system to better delegate the workload. Let's look at how to use the Task List in Dynamics GP in this recipe.

Getting ready

Open tasks are displayed on the Home page in Dynamics GP under the **To Do** heading.

To get started, select **New Task** from the Home Page to see the full task list. Yes, that's not particularly intuitive but that is how it works.

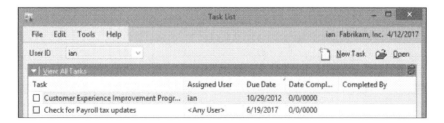

How to do it...

As an example, we'll look at adding a month end bank reconciliation task by completing the following steps:

1. To create a new task, select **New Task** from the Home page in the **To Do** section to open the full task list.

2. Select **New Task** on the **Task List** window. In the **Task** section enter `Reconcile Bank Statement`. Set the due date to the fifth of the next month and set the status to pending.

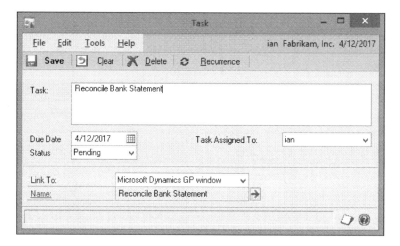

3. In the **Task Assigned To** box, select a user to assign this task to. In the **Link To** box, pick Microsoft Dynamics GP window.

4. To attach the **Reconcile Bank Statements** window, click on the blue arrow next to **Name**.

5. In the new **Add Command** box that opens, pick **Transactions** on the left side then click on the plus (**+**) sign next to **Financial** on the right.

6. In the right-side pane select **Reconcile Bank Statement** and click on **OK**.

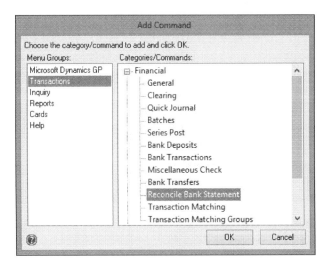

7. Click on **Save** to save the task. If the task was assigned to another user, it will now appear in that user's task list.

How it works...

The new task now appears in the **Tasks** area on the Home page. Checking the box next to a task marks it as complete and sets the user who completed the task as well as the date completed.

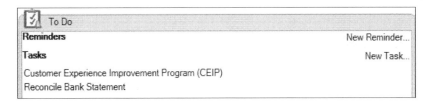

There's more...

Even better, tasks can be repeated, which means that they work great for regular processes such as month end or quarter end tasks.

Recurring tasks

To set a task as recurring:

1. Select the **Recurrence** button during task creation or double-click on an existing task and pick **Recurrence**.

2. From the previous example, select the **Reconcile Bank Statement** task and double-click the line.

3. Click on the **Recurrence** button. Set the recurrence pattern to **Monthly**, select **Day**, and enter values 5 and 1 in the appropriate fields, as shown in the next screenshot.

   This means the task will recur on the fifth of each month. That's about five days after a typical bank statement cut off.

4. Leave the range of recurrence set to **No End Date** and click on **OK**.

Now this task will repeat each month on the fifth day of the month, perfect for a calendar month end bank cut off. Obviously, if a company's bank statement cuts off at some other time during the month, these settings can be easily changed.

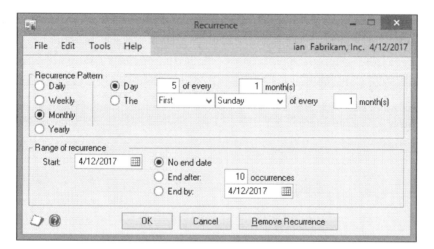

See also

▶ The *Using Reminders to remember important events* recipe in *Chapter 4, Automating Dynamics GP*

Visualizing information with Business Analyzer on the Home page

On the Home page, Dynamics GP provides a default set of reports via charts and graphs designed to provide better visualization of data based on a user's role. Individual users can include or exclude various charts from their Home pages and select default charts. In this recipe, we'll look at ways to tailor Business Analyzer reports for each user.

How to do it...

Business Analyzer reports provide charts for additional analysis. Let's see how to put them to use by completing the following steps:

1. On the Home page in the **Business Analyzer** section, move the mouse over the report title to expose additional options on the right side. Select the pencil icon that now appears on the title bar to the right side.

2. The left side shows all the reports available to a particular user. Selecting a report on the left and clicking **Insert** moves that report to the right and makes it available on the user's Home page. Selecting a chart on the right and clicking on **Remove** eliminates that chart from the Home page.

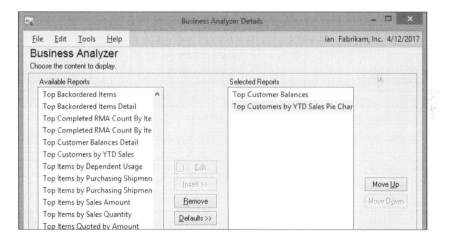

How it works...

The Business Analyzer functionality was added in Version 2013 and replaces Metrics from Versions, 10 and 2010. In Dynamics GP 2013, users can add multiple reports to their Home pages. Additionally, users can create their own reports using **SQL Server Reporting Services (SSRS)** and apply those reports to their Home pages. The creation of new reports is beyond the scope of this book but more information is available via the Dynamics GP manuals.

There's more...

Dynamics GP 2013 provides an option to view multiple reports on the home screen, open reports in a browser window, and drill back for more information.

Multiple Business Analyzer reports

Inserting multiple reports in the **Selected Reports** box can place all of those reports on the Home page.

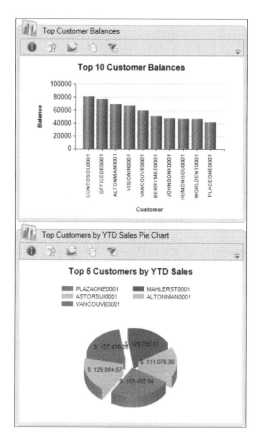

The option to display all of the selected reports is controlled by the **Customize this page** selection on the Home page. Once opened, the **Show All** check box under the **Business Analyzer** selection of the **Customize Home Page** window controls whether all of the reports appear or one report with an option to scroll through the others.

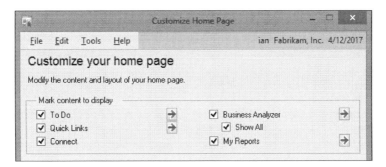

Full view

Clicking on the **Full View** option below a report opens the SSRS report behind that report in a web browser. Selecting individual items in the report drills back to reports with more information. For example, clicking on **Full View** below the Top Customer Balances report and then clicking the **CONTOSOL001** column drills down into that customer's balance detail.

See also

- ▶ The *Personalizing the Home page by selecting the right role* recipe
- ▶ The *Speeding access to data with Quick Links* recipe
- ▶ The *Managing personal reports with My Reports* recipe

Accessing accounts faster with favorites in lookups

In larger organizations it is common for users to only work with a subset of the chart of accounts. Often these accounts are limited to a certain division or department. To find a set of accounts fast, Dynamics GP provides a mechanism to lookup a more limited set of accounts and save them as favorites. This provides faster access when selecting accounts in transactions. In this recipe, we'll look at using favorites in lookups. Favorites are actually part of SmartLists, which are covered in detail in *Chapter 5, Harnessing the Power of SmartLists*.

This recipe showcases the power of integrating SmartLists into the application interface. It provides an unlimited number of ways to target account selection including selection based on department, company, account type, financial statement type, and more, all with just a few clicks.

Getting ready

To begin this recipe, we are required to set up a simple SmartList to setup the account limits:

1. Select the Microsoft Dynamics GP menu and click on **SmartList** to open SmartLists.

2. Click on the plus sign (**+**) next to **Financial** and select **Accounts**:

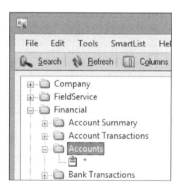

3. Now, select the **Search** button. Click on the lookup icon (it looks like a magnifying glass) and select **Account Number**. Click on **OK**.

4. Set the **Filter** dropdown to **begins with** and enter the value 000. Click on **OK** to close:

5. Select the **Favorites** button. In the **Name** box enter Segment 000 and click on **Add | Add favorite**:

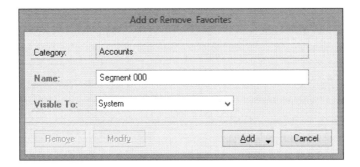

This process creates a specialized list based on a segment in the chart of accounts and then saves it to make it available for account selection.

How to do it...

The favorites list only needs to be built once. After that, the real fun starts.

1. First, select **Financial** from the Navigation Pane on the left side and pick **General** from the **Financial** area page.

2. Click on the **Account** field in the middle and select the lookup button. Click on the arrow next to **View** and hover over **Favorites**.

3. Pick **Segment 000**, the favorite created in the *Getting ready* section:

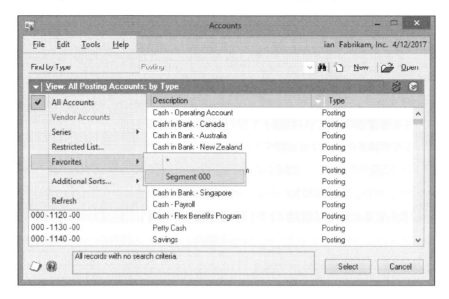

This presents a specialized list to users giving them a more targeted list of accounts to select from when creating a transaction.

There's more...

There are more options than just this recipe for limiting the selections from the chart of accounts.

Set as default view

New in Dynamics GP 2010 and improved in Dynamics GP 2013 is the ability to save a favorite as the default view. Once a favorite has been selected in the view, simply click **Set as Default View** from the **View** menu. Default views are per user and only available for master record lookup, not transactions.

Restricted list

If users only need to restrict the available accounts occasionally there is a temporary option. After selecting the lookup button and clicking on the arrow next to **View**, users can select **Restricted List** instead of **Favorites**. The **Restricted List** option provides similar functionality to **Favorites** but the search is not saved and restricted lists cannot be set as the default view.

Resetting

Selecting **All Accounts** resets the list, removing all restrictions.

Account security

Account security is a feature in Dynamics GP that limits a user's access to certain accounts in the chart. A user cannot even see an account that they don't have access to. This is another option to limit the selection of accounts available to a user but it requires an administrator and a lot of thought to set up correctly. Setting up account security is less like a recipe and more like a seven course meal so it's not covered here.

Activating account security without proper setup makes it appear as if the chart of accounts has been deleted. Deactivating account security returns users' access to the chart but not before triggering a gut wrenching fear that it's time to find a new job.

See also

▸   *Chapter 5, Harnessing the Power of SmartLists*

Cleaning up the mess by fixing AutoComplete errors

Dynamics GP includes a fantastic feature known as **AutoComplete** that remembers what a user has typed in a field and later makes data entry suggestions based on that information. This can significantly reduce repetitive data entry. However, if a user makes an error during data entry, such as a misspelled or incorrect word, that error will continue to be suggested over and over again.

There is a simple way to remove erroneous entries and we'll look at how in this recipe.

Getting ready

To demonstrate this feature, we first need to intentionally create an autocomplete error:

1.   Select **Sales** from the Navigation Pane on the left.

2.   On the area page for **Sales**, select **Customer** under **Cards** on the right to open up the **Customer Maintenance** window.

3. With the **Customer Maintenance** window open, type MISPELL in the **Customer ID** field and click on the *Tab* key. Press the **Clear** button to remove this customer entry.

How to do it...

Now that we have an error, let's see how to fix it:

1. Back in the **Customer ID** field type MIS. Dynamics GP will suggest **MISPELL**. Right-click on the suggested word MISPELL and select **Remove From List**.

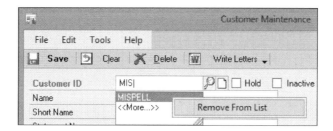

Now typing MIS in the **Customer ID** field doesn't provide the **MISPELL** suggestion.

How it works...

AutoComplete is controlled in **User Preferences**, which is accessed via the shortcut bar. The AutoComplete settings are defined for each user. This means that each user has a different set of AutoComplete entries so removing an errant entry doesn't affect other users.

There's more...

To better manage AutoComplete there are some other settings that can be adjusted on a per user basis.

Removed unused entries

The AutoComplete cache of entries can grow quite large and unwieldy, leading to a significant number of entries to sort through and reducing the effectiveness of this feature. A consistent way to manage the size of the AutoComplete list is by letting AutoComplete remove unused entries automatically. To set this up:

1. Select **User Preferences** from the shortcut bar and click on **Auto Complete**.

2. In the **Remove Unused Entries After** field enter 90 and click on OK.

3. This means that any AutoComplete entries will be removed after 90 days without any use.

Reduce the number of AutoComplete entries

Another option for managing the size of the AutoComplete cache is to limit the maximum number of AutoComplete entries. To accomplish this:

1. Select **User Preferences** from the shortcut bar and click on **Auto Complete**.

2. For the **Max. Number of Entries to Store per Field** entry, the default is `10,000`, which is a huge limit.

3. This can safely be lowered to 1,000 by changing the number in the **Max. Number of Entries to Store per Field** box to `1,000`.

Reset AutoComplete

If significant changes are made to a system, users can get a fresh start by completely resetting their AutoComplete entries. This is accomplished via the **Remove Entries** button available by clicking **User Preferences**, then the **Auto Complete** button.

2
New in Dynamics GP 2013

In this chapter, we will take a look at some of the new features introduced in Microsoft Dynamics GP 2013:

- ▸ EFT format enhancements
- ▸ Enhanced GL Year-End Closing
- ▸ Modifying the sales order's Ship To address
- ▸ Reason codes for inventory transactions
- ▸ Tolerance handling
- ▸ Tracking serial and lot numbers on drop ship POs
- ▸ Selecting multiple serial or lot numbers
- ▸ Relating or linking items for suggested sales
- ▸ Intercompany asset transfer
- ▸ Historical depreciation report
- ▸ Fixed assets batches

Introduction

This chapter explores the recipes covering the new functionalities introduced in Microsoft Dynamics GP 2013 and assumes some familiarity with the basic functionalities where Microsoft Dynamics GP 2013 has been extended.

In almost all cases, the recipes and new features in this chapter do not require an administrator and are available to the average user.

EFT format enhancements

The EFT for payables management and EFT for receivables management have been enhanced in Microsoft Dynamics GP 2013 to provide additional functionality for setting a settlement date in the EFT output.

Getting ready

This recipe assumes that EFT is already configured in Dynamics GP and the user making changes is familiar with the maintenance process.

How to do it...

To improve visibility of the required fields, follow these steps:

1. Open the **EFT File Format Maintenance** window in Dynamics GP by selecting **Financial** from the **Cards** menu and clicking on **EFT File Format**.

2. An EFT file can be composed of multiple lines. To add a settlement date to a particular line, select the line in the header and then in the **Maps To** column of the scrolling window select **Settlement Date**.

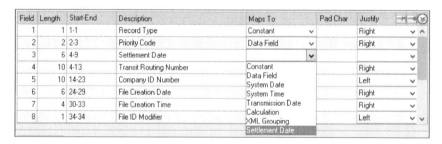

3. Save the EFT file format.

4. Perform the standard payment run process and in the **Generate EFT File** step, you can set a settlement date (different from the transmission date), which is output on the EFT file in the field specified in the template.

There's more...

In Dynamics GP 2013, EFT File Format Maintenance has been enhanced further to allow file types other than fixed format text files to be produced.

In the **EFT File Format Maintenance** window, a field delimiter can now be specified in the **Delimit Fields** section of the window.

Field delimiters can be set to the standard ones such as **Comma**, **Space**, and **Tab**. The **Other** option can be selected to use a user-specified delimiter. The text qualifiers, which can allow commas to be used in files that are comma delimited, can also be selected.

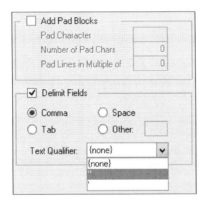

Enhanced GL Year-End Closing

Year-End Closing on the General Ledger is the only routine which must be performed at a year end. This process performs several actions, such as resetting the year-to-date figures, rolling the balances of balance sheet accounts forward to the new year, as well as closing off the profit and loss accounts to the retained earnings account.

Dynamics GP 2013 has seen an enhancement to the **Year-End Closing** window, which allows inactive accounts to be maintained on the system rather than automatically deleted.

The final and much appreciated addition of a progress bar that shows how far the Year-End Closing has progressed, serves to reassure the user that the process has not hung or crashed; this has been a regular concern due to the critical nature of the process.

How to do it...

To use the enhanced Year-End Closing routine, perform the following steps:

1. Open **Financial** from the navigation pane on the left. In the central area page, under **Routines**, select **Year End Closing**.

2. To keep inactive accounts on the system, mark the **Maintain Inactive Accounts** checkbox.

3. Either all inactive accounts can be retained by selecting the **All Inactive Accounts** radio button, or only those with budget amounts for the next financial year can be retained by selecting **With Budget Amounts**.

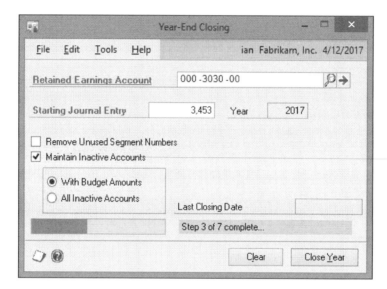

4. After clicking on **Close Year**, a green progress bar will be displayed along with the text that shows the steps, which progress from step 1 to 7.

How it works...

Leaving **Maintain Inactive Accounts** unchecked will have the Year-End Closing routines work as they always have and remove all inactive accounts from the system. Once the checkbox is checked, the selected inactive accounts will be retained on the system rather than being deleted.

There's more...

In Dynamics GP 2010 and earlier versions, the balance of a unit account used to continue to increase through the year end. A further enhancement to the Year-End Closing routine in Dynamics GP 2013, is the ability to have the unit account's balance cleared.

This is done by marking the **Clear Balance During Year-End Close** checkbox in the **Unit Account Maintenance** window.

To check this checkbox, open **Financial** from the navigation pane on the left and in the central area page, under **Cards**, select **Unit Accounts** and check the **Clear Balance During Year End Close** checkbox.

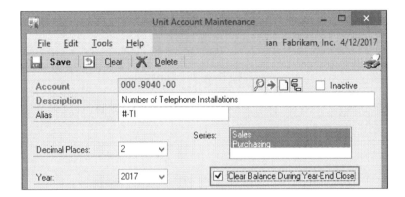

Modifying the sales order's Ship To address

Sales order processing has been enhanced to allow the **Ship To** addresses to be named individually and to have one of the phone numbers of the customer to be selected.

Getting ready

To use this recipe, users need a basic familiarity with the sales order processing and maintaining customers.

How to do it...

To set a name of the **Ship To** address, perform the following steps:

1. Open the **Customer Address Maintenance** window in Dynamics GP by selecting **Sales** from the navigation pane and clicking on **Addresses**.

2. Enter, or do a lookup and select, the **Customer ID**.

3. Enter, or do a lookup and select, the **Address ID**.

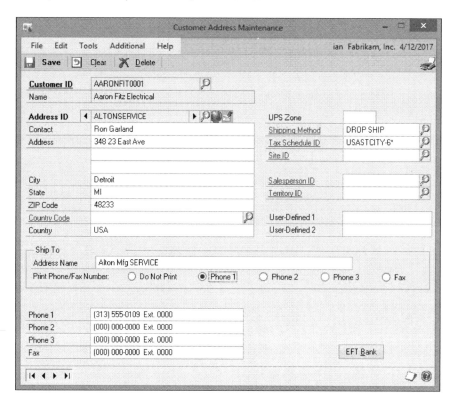

4. In the **Ship To** section of the window, enter the **Address Name**, which is to be included on the sales document.

5. Choose whether one of the three phone numbers, or the fax number, from the master customer record is to be printed, or you can choose **Do Not Print** if none are required for the loaded address.

How it works...

When a sales transaction is entered, the **Ship To** address is entered on each line as normal. When the transaction is printed, the address name and the selected phone number is printed along with the address itself.

Order

Page 1/1
Order ORDST2233
Date 4/12/2017

Fabrikam, Inc.
4277 West Oak Parkway
Chicago IL   60601-4277

Bill To: Aaron Fitz Electrical   Ship To:
           One Microsoft Way   11403 45 St. South
           Redmond WA   98052-6399   Chicago IL   60603-0776

Purchase Order No.	Customer ID	Salesperson ID	Shipping Method	Payment Terms	Req Ship Date	Master No.
	AARONFIT0001	PAUL W.	DROP SHIP	Net 30	4/12/2017	407

Ordered	Shipped	B/O	Item Number	Description	Discount	Unit Price	Ext. Price
1	0	1	2-A3284A	Dual Core Server	$0.00	$128,000.00	$128,000.00
			Deliver To:	Alton Mfg SERVICE Ron Garland 348 23 East Ave Detroit MI 48233 USA (313) 555-0109 Ext. 0000			
1	0	1	2-A3284A	Dual Core Server	$0.00	$128,000.00	$128,000.00
			Deliver To:	Alton Mfg PRIMARY Jennifer Rossini P.O. Box 3343 Detroit MI 48233-3343 USA			

There's more...

The same **Ship To** address functionality is used in drop ship orders in purchase order processing. When the order is printed, the address name and phone number will be printed in the same way as they are printed in the sales transaction.

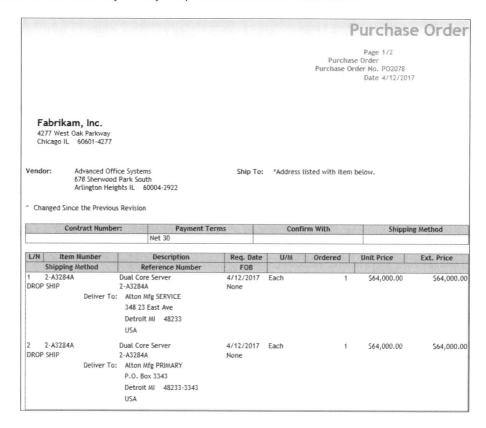

See also

▸ The *Relating or linking items for suggested sales* recipe

Reason codes for inventory transactions

Dynamics GP 2013 introduces a long-time requested feature, the ability to record the reason for inventory transactions. Reason codes can be used on both adjustment and variance transactions to give clarity as to why the transaction was entered.

Getting ready

The first step to using a reason code on an inventory transaction is to create the required reason codes:

1. Open the **Reason Code Setup** window in Dynamics GP by selecting **Inventory** from the navigation pane and clicking on **Reason Code Setup** in the **Setup** section.

2. Enter a new reason code, which can be up to fifteen characters long and is the only mandatory field on the window.

3. Enter a description giving a greater explanation of the reason.

4. Select whether the reason code can be used for adjustment and/or variances.

5. The **Type of Adjustments/Variances** field can also be set with available options of **Increase and Decrease**, **Decrease Only**, and **Increase Only**.

6. Select the **Default Offset Account**, which should be used to override defaults supplied from elsewhere in Dynamics GP.

7. The final options allow the reason code to be made available for use on item transfers, in-transit transfers, and item bin transfers.

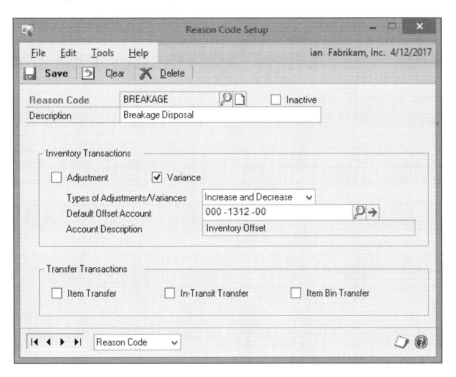

How to do it...

A **Reason Code** field has been introduced to each of the relevant windows. As an example, let's add a reason code to an inventory variance:

1. Open the **Item Transaction Entry** window in Dynamics GP by selecting **Inventory** from the navigation pane and clicking on **Transaction Entry** in the **Transactions** section.

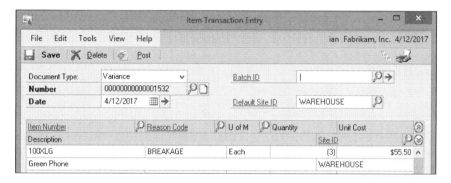

2. In Document Type, select **Variance**.

3. Tab or click away from the **Number** field to accept the default ID.

4. The **Date** of the transaction will default to the User Date, but can be overridden.

5. Enter, or do a lookup, to select the **Default Site ID**.

6. Enter the **Item Number**.

7. Enter or perform a lookup for the reason code (only the reason codes defined for the transaction type being entered).

8. The **Unit of Measure** field will be set to default, but can be altered if required.

9. Enter the **Quantity** of the variance.

10. If the defaults of the **Unit Cost** and **Site ID** fields are acceptable, the transaction can be posted or saved to a batch.

There's more...

Dynamics GP 2013 also maintains the history for bin movement, including reason codes, to allow for reporting and inquiring.

To inquire on bin transfer history, perform the following steps:

1. Open the **Bin Transfer Inquiry** window in Dynamics GP by selecting **Inventory** from the navigation pane and clicking on **Bin Transfer** in the **Inquiry** section.

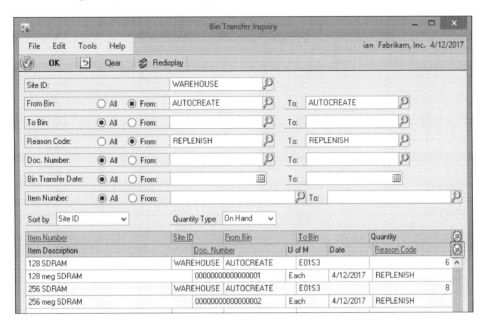

2. Enter, or perform, a lookup for the **Site ID**.

3. Enter any other restrictions needed.

4. Click on **Redisplay** to run the inquiry.

See also

▸ The *Tracking serial and lot numbers on drop ship POs* recipe

▸ The *Tolerance handling* recipe

▸ The *Relating or linking items for suggested sales* recipe

▸ The *Preventing sales of a discontinued inventory* recipe in *Chapter 9, Preventing Errors in Dynamics GP*

▸ The *Selecting multiple serial or lot numbers* recipe

Tolerance handling

Tolerance handling has been introduced to Dynamics GP 2013 to improve accuracy of order quantities in purchase order processing, by automatically closing open purchase orders left in the system from quantity shortages within a defined percentage. It also eliminates the need to correct receiving quantity overages based on a set tolerance.

Quantity tolerances can be defined for both non-inventory and inventory items.

How to do it...

To set a quantity tolerance for a non-inventory item, perform the following steps:

1. Open the **Purchase Order Processing Setup** window in Dynamics GP by selecting **Purchasing** from the navigation pane and clicking on **Purchase Order Processing** in the **Setup** section.

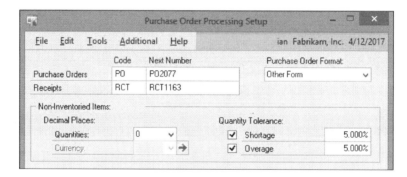

2. To enable quantity tolerance for shortage, perform the following steps:
    1. Mark the **Shortage** checkbox.
    2. Enter the maximum **Shortage** percentage to be allowed.

3. To enable quantity tolerance for overage, perform the following steps:
    1. Mark the **Overage** checkbox.
    2. Enter the maximum overage percentage to be allowed.

To configure quantity tolerance for an inventory item, perform the following steps:

1. Open the **Item Purchasing Options Maintenance** window in Dynamics GP by selecting **Inventory** from the navigation pane and clicking on **Item Purchasing Options** in the **Cards** section.

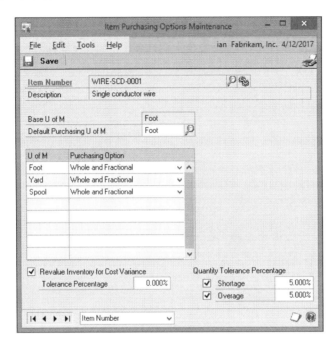

2. Enter, or perform a lookup for, the **Item Number** to have the quantity tolerance defined.

3. To enable quantity tolerance for shortage, perform the following steps:

   1. Check the **Shortage** checkbox.

   2. Enter the maximum shortage percentage to be allowed.

4. To enable quantity tolerance for overage, perform the following steps:

   1. Mark the **Overage** checkbox.

   2. Enter the maximum overage percentage to be allowed.

How it works...

If the quantity received is within the overage tolerance percentage, the receipt can be entered successfully. However, if the quantity entered is out of the set percentage limits, the following message will be displayed and the receiving process cannot be entered.

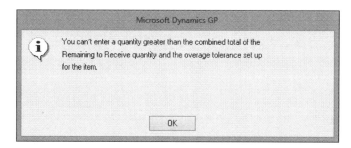

The following table shows some examples of when an overage error would be produced when a five percent overage tolerance has been set and a quantity of 1,000 is ordered:

Quantity received	Error
1,020	No
1,049	No
1,050	Yes
1,075	Yes

If a purchase order is entered with a quantity of 1,000 of an item ordered, and a quantity of 970 is received, the remaining 30 will automatically be flagged as cancelled and the PO will be closed. If, however, 920 items are received, the remaining 80 will remain outstanding on the purchase order as the default assumption of Dynamics GP is that these items will be received in a separate shipment.

The following table, shows some examples of how shortage tolerance works when a 5 percent shortage tolerance has been set and a quantity of 1,000 is ordered:

Quantity received	Quantity cancelled
970	30
951	49
950	50
949	0
925	0

▸ The *Tracking serial and lot numbers on drop ship POs* recipe

▸ The *Relating or linking items for suggested sales* recipe

▸ The *Reason codes for inventory transaction,* recipe

▸ The *Preventing sales of a discontinued inventory* recipe *Chapter 9, Preventing Errors in Dynamics GP*

▸ The *Selecting multiple serial or lot numbers* recipe

Tracking serial and lot numbers on drop ship POs

Microsoft Dynamics GP supports the tracking of serial and lot numbers for sales inventory items that are brought into the inventory system; Microsoft Dynamics GP 2013 introduces the ability to track serial and lot numbers for drop ship purchase orders where the goods will be delivered directly to the customer and never enter the inventory system.

Getting ready

Purchase order processing and inventory control will need to be configured and items need to be created. We also need a drop ship purchase order to receive, but as the sample company does not include one by default we will need to create one:

1. Open the **Purchase Order Entry** window in Dynamics GP by selecting **Purchasing** from the navigation pane and clicking on **Purchase Order Entry** in the **Transactions** section.

2. Change the **Type** to **Drop Ship**.

3. Click away from the **PO Number** field to create a new purchase order.

4. Enter, or do a lookup to select, ADVANCED0001 in **Vendor ID**.

5. Enter, or do a lookup to select, AARONFIT0001 in **Customer ID**.

6. In the scrolling window, in the **Item** field, enter 100XLG.

7. Set the **Quantity Ordered** field to **10**.

8. Enter WAREHOUSE in the **Site ID** field.

9. Click on **Save** in the toolbar to save the purchase order.

How to do it...

The serial or lot numbers can be recorded when receiving the drop ship purchase order:

1. Open the **Purchasing Invoice Entry** window in Dynamics GP by selecting **Purchasing** from the navigation pane and clicking on **Enter/Match Invoices** in the **Transactions** section.

2. Tab or click away from the **Receipt Number** field to create a new invoice.

3. Enter the Vendor's document number in the **Document Number** field.

4. Enter the **Invoice Date**.

5. Enter, or do a lookup to select, ADVANCED0001 in **Vendor ID**.

6. Click on the **Select Purchase Order** button on the toolbar (to the right of the post) to open the **Select Purchase Order Items** window.

7. Locate and click on the purchase order (created in the getting ready section) in the list on the left.

8. In the scrolling window, check the checkbox against the PO line.

9. Check the **S/L** checkbox (next to **Quantity Invoiced**).

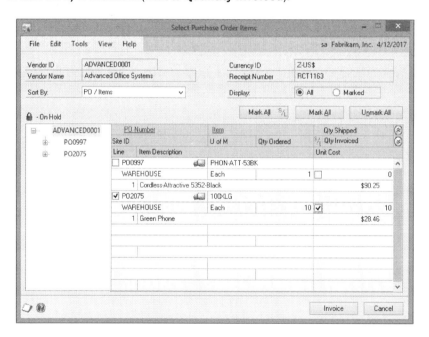

10. Click on **Invoice**, which will open the **Purchasing Serial Number Entry** window.

11. In this case, the `100XLG` item has been set up to allow serial numbers to be auto-generated, so click on the **Auto-Generate** button.

12. Click on **OK** to accept the serial numbers and complete entry of the invoice as normal.

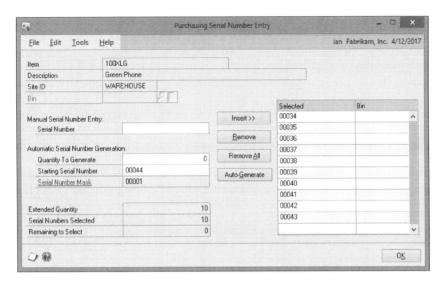

How it works...

With the serial number entered in Microsoft Dynamics GP, the information is available from inquiries and reports, which will improve control and tracking of items dispatched to customers.

There's more...

This new ability to track serial and lot numbers on drop ship purchase orders has been integrated with sales order processing. If the drop ship PO was created from a sales order, when the purchase order is invoiced, the serial/lot number will automatically be assigned to the originating sales order line.

See also

▶ The *Tolerance handling* recipe

▶ The *Relating or linking items for suggested sales* recipe

▶ The *Reason codes for inventory transactions* recipe

▸ The *Preventing sales of a discontinued inventory* recipe in *Chapter 9, Preventing Errors in Dynamics GP*

▸ The *Selecting multiple serial or lot numbers* recipe

Selecting multiple serial or lot numbers

One very welcome addition to Dynamics GP 2013 is the ability to select multiple serial or lot numbers when entering a sales transaction. For each project, the serial number had to be selected and the **Insert** button had to be clicked; now several serial or lot numbers can be selected and the **Insert** can be hit once, saving a great deal of time.

How to do it...

To select multiple serial numbers, perform the following steps:

1. Open the **Item Transfer Entry** window in Dynamics GP by selecting **Inventory** from the navigation pane and clicking on **Transfer Entry** in the **Transactions** section.

2. Enter 100XLG in the **Item Number** field.

3. Tab three times and enter 5 in the **Quantity** field.

4. Enter WAREHOUSE in the **From Site** field.

5. Enter DEPOT in the **To Site** field.

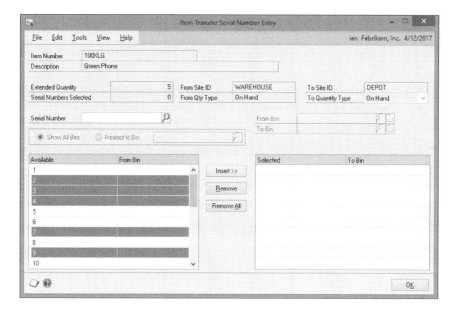

6. The **Item Transfer Serial Number Entry** window will open. Use the Windows standard of *Ctrl* or *Shift* in combination with left-clicking with the mouse to select five serial numbers from the **Available** list and click on **Insert >>**.

There's more...

This multiselect works for both serial numbers and lot numbers throughout Dynamics GP 2013 wherever serial numbers can be selected.

See also

▶ The *Tracking serial and lot numbers on drop ship POs* recipe

▶ The *Tolerance handling* recipe

▶ The *Reason codes for inventory transactions* recipe

▶ The *Preventing sales of a discontinued inventory* recipe in *Chapter 9, Preventing Errors in Dynamics GP*

Relating or linking items for suggested sales

Dynamics GP 2013 brings the ability to relate or link items together, in order to allow for up- or cross-selling within sales order processing. This functionality can also be of benefit when linking together items that are required for the initially entered item to work.

Getting ready

In Dynamics GP, select **Inventory** from the navigation pane. In the **Inventory** area page, select **Item** in the **Cards** area. This will open **Item Maintenance**.

1. Enter, or do a lookup and select, 2-A3284A in **Item Number** to enter the suggested items.

2. Click on the **Suggest Items** button to open the **Suggest Sales Item Maintenance** page.

3. Check the checkboxes in the **Document Type** section to enable the suggested items for quotes, orders, invoices, and fulfillment orders as required.

4. In the scrolling window, enter the **Item Number** and **Suggested Quantity** for each item, which is to be suggested when the sales transaction is entered.

5. In this example, three items have been entered, each with **Suggested Quantity** set to **1**:

   ❑ 256 SDRAM

   ❑ 24X IDE

   ❑ 4-A3539A

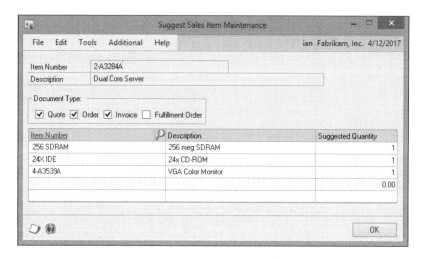

How to do it...

Let's now look at how the related/linked items are used in sales transactions for suggesting items for sale:

1. Open the **Sales Transaction Entry** window in Dynamics GP by selecting **Sales** from the navigation pane and clicking on **Sales Transaction Entry** in the **Transactions** section.

2. Select **Type** and **Type ID** as **Order** and **STDORD**.

3. Enter AARONFIT0001 in the **Customer ID** field.

4. Click on the **Currency ID** field to set the default Z-US$.

5. In the scrolling window, enter 2-A3284A in **Item Number**.

6. Enter 1 in the **Quantity Ordered** field.

7. Select **Override Shortage** and click on **OK**.

8. Enter 000052 in the **Serial Number** field in **Sales Serial Number Entry** when it pops up.

9. Click on **OK** to close **Sales Serial Number Entry**.

10. Tab through the remaining fields and enter the credit limit override password, and click on **OK**.

11. **Suggest Sales Item Entry** will pop up showing the available suggested items.

12. Check the checkboxes next to **256 SDRAM** and **24X IDE**, and accept the **Suggested Quantity** of **1**.

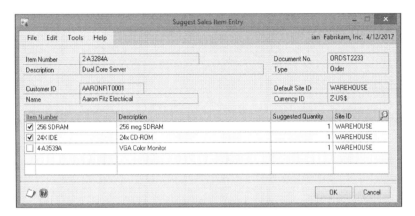

13. Click on **OK** to accept these suggested items.

14. The selected suggested items will be added to the sales transaction for processing as standard transaction lines.

See also

▶ The *Tracking serial and lot numbers on drop ship POs* recipe

▶ The *Tolerance handling* recipe

▶ The *Reason codes for inventory transactions* recipe

▶ The *Preventing sales of a discontinued inventory* recipe in *Chapter 9, Preventing Errors in Dynamics GP*

▶ The *Selecting multiple serial or lot numbers* recipe

Intercompany asset transfer

Dynamics GP has included intercompany processing in some modules for quite some time. With Dynamics GP 2013, intercompany processing has arrived in fixed asset management with the introduction of intercompany asset transfers.

This new functionality can save time in depreciating the asset in the current company and the time needed to create the asset and configure the depreciation in the new company.

How to do it...

To perform an intercompany asset transfer, perform the following steps:

1. Open the **Fixed Asset Intercompany Transfer** window in Dynamics GP by selecting **Financial** from the navigation pane and clicking on **Intercompany Transfer** in the **Transactions** section under **Fixed Assets**.

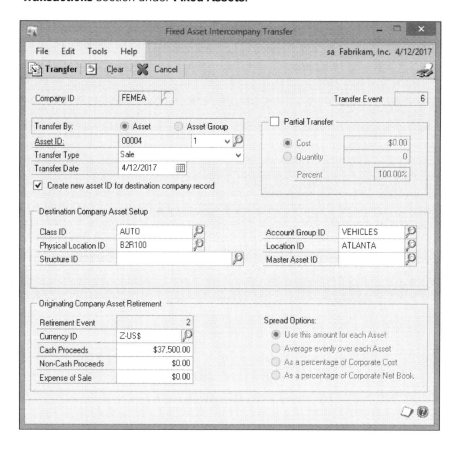

2. Enter, or perform a lookup for, the **Company ID**.
3. Choose Asset to transfer a single asset or Asset Group to transfer multiple assets.
4. If transfering by asset, enter the **Asset ID** and **Suffix**.
5. Select the **Transfer Type**.
6. If a date other than the user date is required, enter or choose the required date.

7. Check the **Create new asset ID for destination company record** checkbox if a new asset ID should be generated. Leaving this checkbox unchecked will use the same asset ID which may cause a conflict.

8. Enter the **Destination Company Asset Setup** information.

9. Enter the **Originating Company Asset Retirement** information.

10. Click on **Transfer** to create the asset in the new company and retire the original.

When the transfer is finished, the **FA Intercompany Transfer Edit List** report will, unless switched off in posting setup, print.

There's more...

As well as transferring a single asset, fixed asset intercompany transfer can transfer groups of assets by selecting to transfer by asset group, or to partially transfer an asset.

See also

▸ The *Historical depreciation report* recipe

▸ The *Fixed assets batches* recipe

Historical depreciation report

One of the regularly and most frequently requested enhancements, fixed asset management, is the ability to generate historical depreciation reports in order to verify depreciation expense for tax purposes.

This feature has arrived with Dynamics GP 2013.

How to do it...

The option to run the historical depreciation report has been added to the standard fixed asset report options. To generate a historic depreciation report, perform the following steps:

1. Open the **Depreciation Reports** window in Dynamics GP by selecting **Financial** from the navigation pane and clicking on **Depreciation** in the **Reports** section under **Fixed Assets**.

2. Select **Depreciation** in the **Reports** field.

3. Click on **New** to open the **Depreciation Report Options** window.

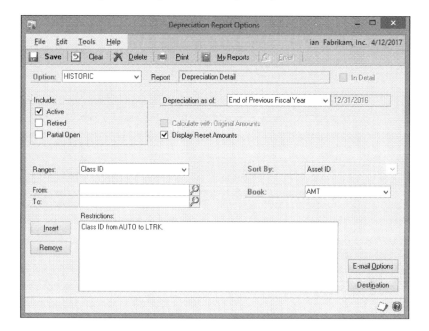

4. Enter HISTORIC in the **Option** field.

5. Choose **End of Previous Fiscal Year**, or **End of Previous Month**, in the **Depreciation as of** field (the default option is **Current Amounts**, which reproduces functionality as it existed in previous versions).

6. Check the **Active** box in the **Include** frame.

7. Add a range of classes from **AUTO** to **LTRK**.

8. Select **INTERNAL** in the **Book** field.

9. Click on **Print** to print the new report option of historic depreciation.

How it works...

In previous versions of Dynamics GP, there was no way to generate historic depreciation reports. In Dynamics GP 2013, choosing a depreciation date, such as **End of Previous Fiscal Year**, allows the user to specify the date for which the depreciation will be calculated.

There's more...

Fixed Asset depreciation has been enhanced in other ways too.

Mass depreciation reversal

In previous versions of Dynamics GP, if depreciation was calculated incorrectly, the reversal had to be done with one asset at a time. In Dynamics GP 2013, the standard **Depreciation Process Information** window has been enhanced with an option to reverse depreciation and this can be run against either an asset group or all assets.

To mass reverse depreciation, perform the following steps:

1. Open the **Depreciation Process Information** window in Dynamics GP by selecting **Financial** from the navigation pane and clicking on **Depreciate** in the **Routines** section under **Fixed Assets**.

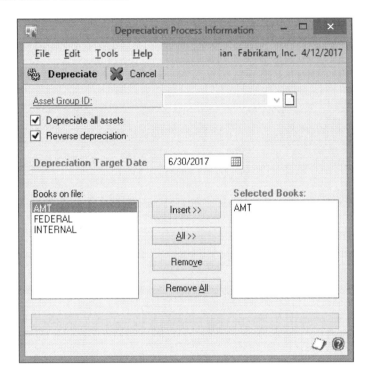

2. Check the **Depreciate all assets** checkbox.
3. Check the **Reverse depreciation** checkbox.
4. Choose the **Depreciation Target Date**.
5. Select the books for which the depreciation is to be reversed.
6. Click on the **Depreciate** button to process the mass reversal.

Reset history in detail

In previous versions of Dynamics GP, if depreciation was reset, the depreciation for closed years used to lump into the last period of the most recent closed year. In Dynamics GP 2013, a new option has been introduced, which will spread the reset transactions across all periods of the asset's life, thereby offsetting the original transactions in the respective periods.

To enable reset history in detail, perform the following steps:

1. Open the **Fixed Assets Company Setup** window in Dynamics GP by selecting **Financial** from the navigation pane and clicking on **Company** in the **Setup** section under **Fixed Assets**.

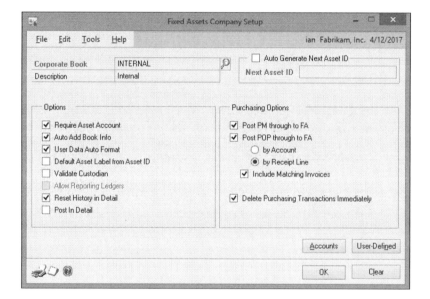

2. In the options frame, check the **Reset History in Detail** checkbox.
3. Click on **OK** to save the changes to the fixed assets company setup.

With this option set, any depreciation reset will have the reset value spread across all periods of the asset's life allowing accurate inquiry and reporting of depreciation.

See also

▶ The *Intercompany asset transfer* recipe
▶ The *Fixed assets batches* recipe

Fixed assets batches

One of the main criticisms of fixed assets integration with the General Ledger has been the lack of transparency for the values being posted. With Dynamics GP 2013, the integration has been enhanced with the introduction of fixed assets batches, which allow users to review batches before they are posted.

How to do it...

To generate a batch of fixed assets transactions for review before posting, perform the following steps:

1. Open the **Fixed Assets General Ledger Posting** window in Dynamics GP by selecting **Financial** from the navigation pane and clicking on **GL Posting** in the **Routines** section under **Fixed Assets**.

2. Tab or click away from the **Batch ID** field to create a new batch.

3. The user date will default into the **Posting Date** field, but can be overridden if required.

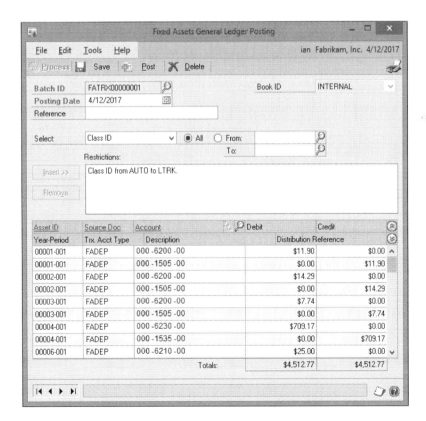

4. If all transactions from fixed assets, which have not yet been posted, need to be, leave the **Restrictions** field blank, otherwise enter the required criteria.

5. Click on **Process** to generate the batch lines, which will then display at the bottom of the window for review.

6. The GL account can be amended if required, although the debit and credit values cannot.

There's more...

Dynamics GP 2013 also includes an **Inquiry** window where fixed asset batches can be viewed after posting.

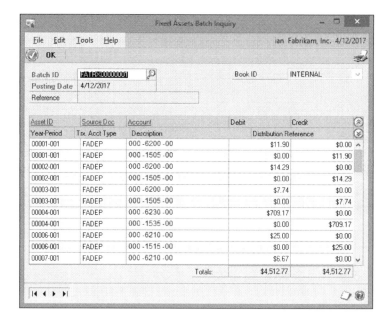

1. Open the **Fixed Assets Batch Inquiry** window in Dynamics GP by selecting **Financial** from the navigation pane and clicking on **Batches** in the **Inquiry** section under **Fixed Assets**.

2. Enter, or perform a lookup for, the **Batch ID** to be viewed.

See also

▶ The *Intercompany asset transfer* recipe

▶ The *Historical depreciation report* recipe

3
Organizing Dynamics GP

In this chapter we will look at:

- ▶ Speeding account entry with account aliases
- ▶ Cleaning account lookups by removing accounts from lookups
- ▶ Gaining visibility by using horizontal scroll arrows
- ▶ Streamlining payables processing by prioritizing vendors
- ▶ Getting clarity with user-defined fields
- ▶ Developing connections with Internet user-defined fields
- ▶ Gaining reporting control with account rollups
- ▶ Remembering processes with an ad hoc workflow
- ▶ Improving financial reporting clarity by splitting purchasing accounts
- ▶ Speeding lookups with advanced lookups
- ▶ Going straight to the site with web links

Introduction

Dynamics GP provides a number of features to better organize the overall system and improve its usefulness for all users; these recipes are designed for the use of administrators rather than typical users. This chapter is designed to demonstrate how to implement and fine-tune these features to provide the most benefit.

Speeding account entry with account aliases

As organizations grow, the chart of accounts tends to grow larger and more complex as well. Companies want to segment their business by departments, locations, or divisions; all of this means that more and more accounts get added to the chart and, as the chart of accounts grows, it becomes more difficult to select the right account. Dynamics GP provides the **account alias** feature as a way to quickly select the right account. Account aliases provide a way to create shortcuts to specific accounts that can dramatically speed up the process of selecting the correct account. We'll look at how that works in this recipe.

Getting ready

Setting up account aliases requires a user with access to the **Account Maintenance** window.

To get to this window, perform the following steps:

1. Select **Financial** from the navigation pane on the left. Click on **Accounts** on the **Financial** area page under **Cards**. This will open the **Account Maintenance** window.

2. Click on the **Lookup** button (magnifying glass) next to the **Account Number** or use the keyboard shortcut *Ctrl + Q*.

3. Find and select account **000-2100-00**.

4. In the middle of the **Account Maintenance** window you can find the **Account Alias** field. Enter AP in the **Alias** field.

This associates the letters AP with the account's selected payable account. This means that the user now only has to enter AP instead of the full account number to use the account's payable account.

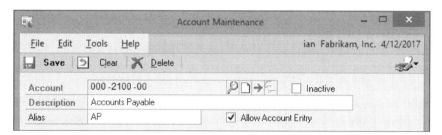

How to do it...

Once aliases have been set up, let's see how the user can quickly select an account using an alias.

1. To demonstrate how this works, click on **Financial** in the navigation pane on the left. Select **Transaction Entry** from the **Financial** area page under **Transactions**.

2. In the **Transaction Entry** window, select the top line in the grid area on the lower half of the window.

3. Click on the expansion button (represented by a blue arrow) next to the **Account** heading to open the **Account Entry** window.

4. In the **Alias** field, type AP and press *Enter*.

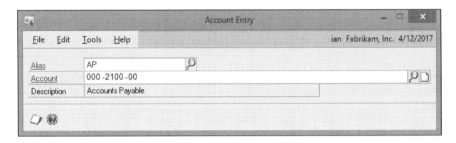

5. The **Account Alias** window will close and the account represented by the alias will appear in the **Transaction Entry** window.

How it works...

Account aliases provide quick shortcuts for account entry. Keeping them short and obvious makes them easy to use. Aliases are less useful if users have to think about them. Limiting them to the most commonly used accounts makes them more useful. Most users don't mind occasionally looking up the odd account, but they shouldn't have to memorize long account strings for regularly used account numbers.

It's counter-productive to put an alias on every account since that would make finding the right alias as difficult as finding the right account number. The setup process should be performed on the most commonly used accounts to provide easy access.

See also

▸ The *Gaining visibility by using horizontal scroll arrows* recipe

Cleaning account lookups by removing accounts from lookups

A consequence of company growth is that the chart of accounts grows and the account lookups can get clogged up by the number of accounts in the system. While the General Ledger will stop showing an account in a lookup when the account is made inactive, other modules will continue to show these inactive codes.

However, Dynamics GP does contain a feature that can be used to remove inactive codes from lookups; this same feature can also be used to remove codes from lookups in series where the code should not be used, such as a sales code in the purchasing or inventory series.

How to do it...

Here we will see how to remove inactive accounts from lookups:

1. Open **Financial** from the navigation pane on the left. In the main area page, under **Cards**, select **Account**.

2. Enter, or do a lookup for, the account to be made inactive and removed from the lookups.

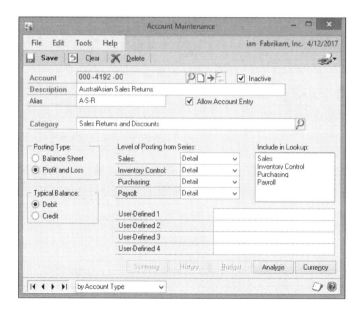

3. Check the **Inactive** checkbox.

4. Press and hold the *Ctrl* key and click on each of the lines in the **Include in Lookup** list.

5. Click on **Save** to commit the changes.

Next time a lookup is done in any of the now deselected modules, the account will not be included in the list.

If the account is to be included in lookups in some modules but not in others, simply leave selected the modules in which the account should be included.

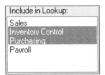

How it works...

Accounts will only be shown in lookups when the series is selected in the **Include in Lookup** list. For series other than General Ledger, simply marking an account inactive is not enough to remove it from the lookup although the code can't be used when the account is inactive.

Gaining visibility by using horizontal scroll arrows

A consequence of company growth is that not only does the chart of accounts grow larger and less intuitive, but also the actual lengths of account numbers tend to grow longer as well. Companies want to be able to report by account, department, location, and so on, which results in a proliferation of segments added to the main account number and can create very long accounts. Dynamics GP can accommodate an account number as long as 66 characters. The longest I've seen used in practice was of 27 characters and even that was unwieldy. Most users only need a portion of that length for their day-to-day work.

This presents a problem because very long account numbers won't fit into the account number field on most screens. For this recipe, we'll look at how Dynamics GP provides a solution to this in the **User Preferences** area.

How to do it...

Here we'll see how to increase the visibility of long account numbers.

1. In the navigation pane on the left, select **Home**.
2. Click on **User Preferences** on the shortcut bar.
3. Check the box for **Horizontal Scroll Arrows**.

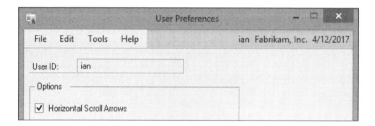

This turns on the functionality that allows users to scroll horizontally within the **Account** field, allowing them to see the full account number.

How it works...

Once horizontal scroll arrows are activated, small arrows appear at the left and right side of the **Account** field, letting users scroll right and left to see the full account number.

There's more...

Horizontal scroll arrows are implemented on a per user basis, meaning each user has to turn this on individually. Administrators can make this active for all users with a SQL script.

Additionally, for companies using alphanumeric characters in their chart of accounts, wide letters such as **M** or **W** are often difficult to see. There is also an option to increase the visible width of a particular segment.

Activating horizontal scroll arrows for all users

Horizontal scroll arrows are activated by the user. However, an administrator can turn this feature on for all users in all companies by running the following SQL script against the Dynamics database:

```
Update
SY01400
Set
HSCRLARW=1
```

Widening segments for better visibility

When companies use alphanumeric characters in their chart of accounts, wide letters, such as M or W, are often cut off. Horizontal scroll arrows don't help because the problem is that the segment field is too narrow, not the entire account field. To resolve this problem, Dynamics GP provides an option to widen the segment fields as well.

In the navigation pane, click on **Administration** and select **Account Format**. For each segment that needs to be wider, select the **Display Width** column and change it from **Standard** to **Expansion 1**, **Expansion 2**, or **Expansion 3** to widen the field; **Expansion 3** represents the widest option.

Companies using only numbers in their chart of accounts won't need to widen the segment field, but firms that include letters as part of their charts will need to increase the width. The following is a list of the expansion options and the letters they are designed to accommodate:

- **Expansion 1**: A, B, E, K, P, S, V, X, Y
- **Expansion 2**: C, D, G, H, M, N, O, Q, R, U
- **Expansion 3**: W

Streamlining payables processing by prioritizing vendors

Management of vendor payments is a critical activity for any firm; it's even more critical in difficult economic times. Companies need to understand and control payments and a key component of this is prioritizing vendors. Every firm has both critical and expendable vendors. Paying critical vendors on time is a key business driver.

For example, a newspaper that doesn't pay its newsprint supplier won't be in business long. However, they can safely delay payments to their janitorial vendor without worrying about going under.

Dynamics GP provides a mechanism to prioritize vendors and apply those priorities when selecting which checks to print. That is the focus of this recipe.

Getting ready

Setting this up first requires that the company figures out who the priority vendors are. That part is beyond the scope of this book. The **Vendor Priority** field in Dynamics GP is a three-character field, but users shouldn't be seduced by the possibilities of three characters. A best practice is to keep the priorities simple by using 1, 2, 3 or A, B, C. Anything more complicated than that tends to confuse users and actually makes it harder to prioritize vendors.

Once the vendor priorities have been determined, the priority needs to be set in Dynamics GP. Attaching a priority to a vendor is the first step. To do that, perform the following steps:

1. Select **Purchasing** from the navigation pane. In the **Purchasing** area page, under **Cards**, click on **Vendor Maintenance**.

2. Once the **Vendor Maintenance** window opens, click on the **Lookup** button (magnifying glass) next to **Vendor ID**.

3. Select a vendor and click on **OK**.

4. Once the vendor information is populated, click on the **Options** button. This opens the **Vendor Maintenance Options** screen.

5. In the center left we find the **Payment Priority** field. Enter 1 in **Payment Priority** and click on **Save**.

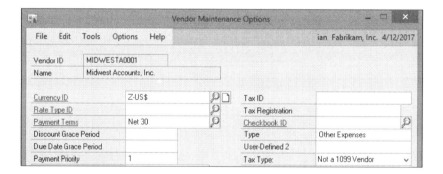

How to do it...

Now that a vendor has been set up with a priority, let's see how to apply that information when selecting checks to print.

1. To use vendor priorities to select invoices for payment, click on **Select Checks** from the **Purchasing** area page.

2. In the **Select Payables Checks** window, enter CHEQUES to name the check batch. Press *Tab* to move off of the **Batch ID** field and click on **Add** to add the batch.

3. Pick a **Checkbook ID** and click on **Save** to save the batch.

4. In the **Select By** field, click on the drop-down box and select **Payment Priority**. Enter 1 in both the **From** and **To** boxes.

5. Click on the **Insert** button to lock in **Payment Priority** as an option.

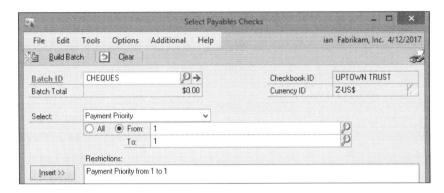

6. Click on **Build Batch** at the top. If there are any transactions where the vendor is set to a priority of **1**, this will populate a batch of checks based on the vendor priority.

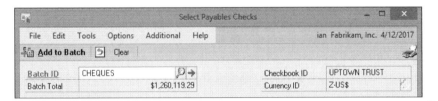

How it works...

Since priority is one of the built-in options for selecting checks, it's easy to ensure that high priority vendors get selected to be paid first. All of this is easily accomplished with basic Dynamics GP functionality that most people miss.

Getting clarity with user-defined fields

Throughout Dynamics GP, maintenance cards typically include at least two user-defined fields. User-defined fields can be renamed in the setup screen for the related module. This provides a great mechanism to add in special information. We'll take a look at a typical use of a user-defined field in this recipe.

How to do it...

For our example, we'll look at using a user-defined field to rename the **User-Defined 1** field to **Region** in **Customer Maintenance**.

1. From the navigation pane, select **Sales**. In the **Sales** page, click on **Setup** and then click on **Receivables** and finally **Options**.

2. In the **User-Defined 1** field, type `Region` and click on **OK** to close each window.

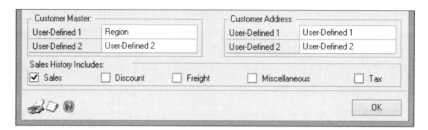

3. Back on the **Sales** page, click on **Customer** under the **Cards** area. On the bottom left above **User-Defined 2** is the newly named **Region** field ready to be filled in.

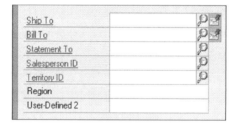

How it works...

Changing the field name only changes the display field; it doesn't change the underlying field name in the database. SmartLists are smart enough to show the new name. In our example, the description for **Region** would appear in a SmartList, not **User-Defined 1**.

User-defined fields like this are present for customers, vendors, accounts, sales orders, fixed assets, inventory items, and purchase receipts among others. Each of these can be renamed in their respective setup screens.

There's more...

All user-defined fields are not the same; some have special features.

Special User-Defined 1 features

User-Defined 1 has special features inside of Dynamics GP. Most of the -n reports inside the Dynamics GP allow sorting and selection by the **User-Defined 1** field. These options aren't provided for **User-Defined 2**. Consequently, administrators should carefully consider what information belongs in **User-Defined 1** before changing its name since the effects of this selection will be felt throughout the system.

Company Setup user-defined fields

In the **Company Setup** window, there are two user-defined fields at the top right and there is no option in Dynamics GP to rename these fields. The **Company Setup** window is accessed by clicking on **Administration** in the navigation pane, and then clicking on **Company** under the **Setup** and **Company** headers.

Expanded user-defined fields

Certain areas such as fixed assets, inventory items, and purchase receipts have more complex types of user-defined fields that can include dates, list selections, and currency.

See also

- The *Developing connections with Internet user-defined fields* recipe
- The *Going straight to the site with web links* recipe
- The *Renaming fields for clarity* recipe in *Chapter 5, Harnessing the Power of SmartLists*

Developing connections with Internet user-defined fields

Dynamics GP provides a built-in set of Internet fields for users to enter information such as web pages, e-mail addresses, and FTP sites. What many people don't know is that these are actually user-defined fields and can be changed by an administrator that allows firms to add a second e-mail address or remove the FTP link if they want to. In this recipe, we'll look at how to customize these fields.

It is important to keep in mind when setting up Internet user-defined fields that these settings affect all the Internet user-defined field names attached to address ID's assigned to a company, customers, employees, items, salespeople, and vendors.

How to do it...

Customizing the Internet user-defined fields is easy, so let's take a look at how to do it. For our example, we'll add the social networking service Twitter as a new label.

1. Select **Administration** from the navigation pane. Under the **Setup** and **Company** headers in the **Administration** area page, pick **Company**.

2. Click on the **Internet User Defined** button and change the **Image** description next to **Label 4** to `Twitter`. Click on **OK**.

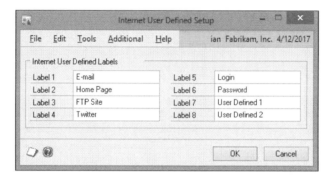

3. Back on the **Company Setup** screen, click on the blue italic letter "I" to the right of the **Address ID** to open the **Internet Information** window. In the **Twitter** field, type `http://www.twitter.com/azurecurve`.

4. Click on the link associated with the **Twitter** field on the left. This opens a web browser and navigates to my Twitter account so that you can follow me. Click on **Save** to update the record.

How it works...

The secret to Internet user-defined fields is how the data is entered. Internet items use a prefix in the field to identify the type of Internet transaction to be used with the link: `http://` is used for web pages, `Mailto://` for e-mail, and `ftp://` for FTP sites. These prefixes tell Dynamics GP what to do when a link is clicked, and if no prefix is entered, Dynamics GP will try to figure out what to do and may or may not succeed.

If `http://www.microsoft.com` is entered in a field, the link to the left will start the default browser and open the Microsoft web page. If `http://` is not included, but www is, GP figures out that it should open a web page. Just putting in `Microsoft.com` isn't enough for GP to understand that the link corresponds to a web page. Similarly, if a user enters `mailto://mpolino@gmail.com` and clicks the link, the default e-mail client opens up and is ready to send an e-mail to me. If no prefix is used with an e-mail address, GP will respond with a "File Not Found" error when the link is clicked. It's not smart enough to know that the @ symbol means that this is an e-mail account.

Using a prefix in the Internet user-defined fields explicitly defines how this link should work and provides the most consistency to users.

There's more...

Some Internet user-defined fields look special but aren't and some really are special.

Login and password

By default, the Internet user-defined **Label 5** field is named **Login** and the **Label 6** field is named **Password**. These fields are supposed to represent the login and password for one of the associated web pages or FTP sites. However, these fields are not encrypted and there is limited security control, so it may not be appropriate to leave these fields named **Login** and **Password** if a company doesn't want users entering that information here.

Label 7 and Label 8

Label 7 and **Label 8** in Internet user defined fields are special fields that allow a user to look up and attach links to files located on the computer or the network. Clicking on the label name on the left opens the associated file. Other fields can accept files and these fields can still accept a prefix and link or free form text, but their special ability to look up file names mean that administrators should consider reserving them for file attachments.

See also

- ▶ The *Going straight to the site with web links* recipe
- ▶ The *Getting clarity with user-defined fields* recipe
- ▶ The *Renaming fields for clarity* recipe in *Chapter 5, Harnessing the Power of SmartLists*

Gaining reporting control with account rollups

Microsoft Dynamics GP provides great functionality for analyzing and reviewing individual accounts and sequential groups of accounts. Many users don't know that it also provides impressive functionality for analyzing non-sequential groups of accounts via a feature known as **account rollup**.

Account rollups are inquiries built to allow users to see different GL accounts rolled up together and to provide drill back capability to the details. Additionally, these queries can include calculations for things such as budget versus actual comparisons and calculations.

FRx Reporter provides similar functionality and an account rollup allows users to access this functionality without the wait time of starting up FRx. Let's see how to mix up some account rollups in this recipe.

Getting ready

Before using account rollups, it's important to understand how to set them up:

1. To set up account rollups, select **Financial** from the navigation pane and then select **Account Rollup** in the **Inquiry** section to open the **Account Rollup Inquiry Options** window.

2. In the **Option ID** field, enter the name `Actual vs. Budget` and click on **Tab**. Select **Yes** to add the option. On the right, set the number of columns to 3.

3. In the first row, type `Actual` in the column heading and set the type to **Actuals**.

4. In the second row, type `Budget` in the column heading and set the type to **Budget**. In the **Selection** column, click on the **Lookup** button (magnifying glass) and select **Budget 4**.

5. In the third row, type `Difference` in the column heading. Set the type to **Calculated**. Click on the blue arrow next to **Selection** to set up the calculation.

6. In the **Column** field, select **Actual** and click on the double arrow (**>>**). Click on the minus (-) button. Back in the **Column** field, select **Budget** and click on the double arrow (**>>**). Click on **OK**.

7. Back in the **Account Rollup Inquiry Options** window, select the **Segment** field and pick **Account**. Use the **Lookup** buttons (magnifying glass) in **From** and **To** to add account 4130 and click on **Insert**. Repeat this process, inserting 4120 and then 4100 into the **Restrictions** box. Click on **Save** and close the window.

Notice when looking up these accounts for selection that these numbers are not sequential; there are numbers of accounts in between.

How to do it...

Now that we've built an account rollup, let's see how to make it work.

1. Select **Account Rollup**, under **Inquiry** in the **Financial** page.

2. In the **Option ID** field, lookup **Actual vs. Budget** with the **Lookup** button (magnifying glass).

3. The screen will show the **Actuals**, **Budget**, and **Difference** values for each period in this year.

   The year can be changed at the top and the display can be changed to show either net change or the period balance for each period in the year, along with a total at the bottom, using the controls next to the year. The value in the **Difference** field is the **Actuals** value minus the **Budget** value calculation that we created when setting up the rollup.

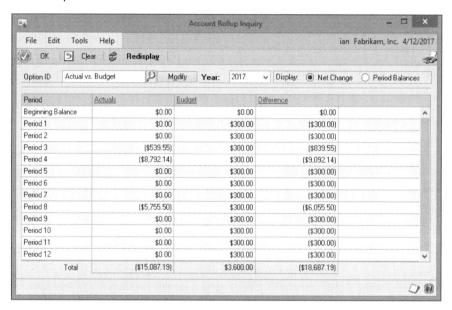

4. Click on a period with an amount in the **Actuals** column and select the blue **Actuals** link at the top. A new window will open with the included accounts and the actual amounts for each account.

5. When drilling down to the **Account Rollup Detail Inquiry Zoom** page, Dynamics GP provides a checkbox option to show accounts even if they have zero balances.

6. Additionally, an option at the top controls the printing of the account rollup information. The rollup can be printed in **Summary** or in **Detail**.

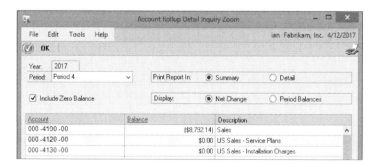

7. Selecting a line and clicking on **Balance** from the **Account Rollup Detail Inquiry Zoom** page drills back to the detail transactions behind the balance.

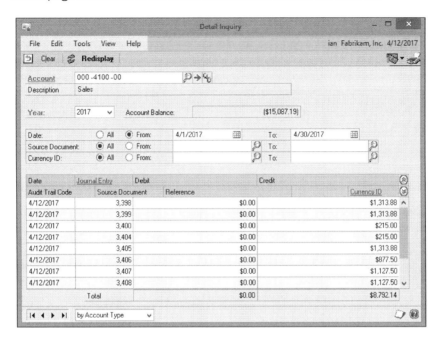

How it works...

Account rollups combine the account totals from disparate accounts for reporting. This is great for tying back multiple accounts that roll up to a single line on the financial statements. Account rollups also work well for analyzing a single segment, such as a department, across multiple accounts. In the past, I've used this for easy comparisons of fixed asset General Ledger accounts to the subledger and for rolling up full-time equivalent unit accounts to get the number of employees across the company with drill back to the employees in each department.

See also

▸ The *Renaming fields for clarity* recipe in *Chapter 5, Harnessing the Power of SmartLists*

Remembering processes with an ad hoc workflow

Dynamics GP provides an option for robust workflow functionality integrated with Microsoft SharePoint technologies. For many users, however, this is more than the functionality they need, and also, many organizations don't feel they are ready for the cost and complexity of Microsoft SharePoint. For users who only need a simple workflow to ensure that they remember the steps for a particular task, a basic workflow can be built using shortcuts and folders.

This process works well for irregular tasks such as month-end or quarter-end processes where tasks are performed infrequently enough to make it easy to forget the steps. For this recipe, we'll look at setting up a basic month-end workflow.

Getting ready

The basic steps of this task are to create a folder to hold the workflow and then to add that folder. For our example, we will assume that a month-end financial closing workflow includes posting a quick journal, processing a clearing entry, and closing the month.

How to do it...

Here are the steps to create a basic, ad hoc workflow:

1. Select **Home** from the navigation pane on the left. This makes the shortcut bar available on the top left.

2. Right-click on the shortcut bar and select **Add | Folder** to add a folder to the shortcut bar that can be used to organize entries. Name the folder Month End and press *Enter*. Now there is a folder to hold month end entries.

3. The next step is to add our three sample entries. Select the **Month End** folder on the shortcut bar. Right-click on the folder and select **Add | Add Window**.

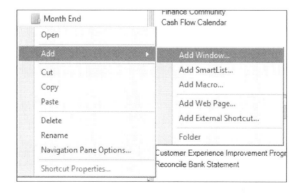

4. Click the plus sign (**+**) next to **Microsoft Dynamics GP**. Click on the plus sign (**+**) next to **Financial** and select the window named **Quick Journal Entry**. Change the name at the top to 1) Quick Journal Entry. Click on **Add**.

    Putting a number in front prevents this shortcut from interfering if the same shortcut appears somewhere else on the shortcut bar.

5. Next, select **Clearing Entry** under **Microsoft Dynamics GP** and **Financial**. Rename it 2) Clearing Entry in the **Name** box and click on **Add**.

6. Finally, select the plus sign (**+**) next to **Company** under **Microsoft Dynamics GP** and select **Fiscal Periods Setup**. Rename this 3) Close Fiscal Period and click on **Add**. Click on **Done** to finish.

7. The items will appear in the shortcut bar on the left under the **Month End** folder. Selecting an item with the mouse click will allow moving items around to adjust the order if necessary.

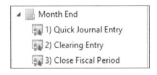

How it works...

Ad hoc workflows provide an option to group a set of steps together and make them all available in one place. Clicking on the arrow to the left of the folder closes it up and keeps the steps out of the way until they are needed. Clicking on the arrow again reopens the folder to run the steps. Some common uses include creating a basic set of steps for new users, month-end and quarter-end processes, and any other process where it is important to ensure that all the steps are followed.

See also

▶ The *Improving consistency with shortcuts and user classes* recipe in *Chapter 4, Automating Dynamics GP*

▶ The *Getting faster access to data with the shortcut bar* recipe in *Chapter 1, Personalizing Dynamics GP*

Improving financial reporting clarity by splitting purchasing accounts

By default in Dynamics GP, when a payables invoice is fully or partially paid, the payment portion of the transaction doesn't flow through the payables account. This can make it more difficult to trace a transaction, since the transaction could skip the payables account all together by crediting cash and debiting an expense.

GP provides an optional setting to force transactions to flow through the payables account and that's what we'll look at in this recipe.

How to do it...

Setting up GP to pass voucher payments through payables is as easy as following these steps:

1. Select **Administration** from the navigation pane on the left. In the **Administration** area page, click on **Company** in the **Company** section.

2. Click on the **Options** button. Scroll down to the setting **Separate Payment Distributions** and check the box next to it.

3. Click on **OK** to close the window and accept the changes.

How it works...

Let's assume a $100 purchase transaction where $20 is paid in cash and the remaining $80 would go to accounts payable. By default, GP will create a transaction distribution that would be as follows:

Account	Debit	Credit
Account A (Purch)	$100.00	
Account B (Cash)		$20.00
Account C (Payable)		$80.00

After the **Separate Payment Distribution** box is checked, GP will create a transaction that would be as follows:

Account	Debit	Credit
Account A (Purch)	$100.00	
Account B (Cash)		$20.00
Account C (Payable)		$100.00
Account D (Payable)	$20.00	

Notice that the full $100 is credited to payables and then the $20 payment is debited to reduce account's payable to the amount due.

Speeding lookups with advanced lookups

Dynamics GP provides very robust functionality in lookup windows for finding data such as accounts, vendors, customers, and items. Various fields can be used for sorting or searching and some additional fields are always provided by default. However, if all of that is not enough, Dynamics GP provides an option for administrators to add additional fields to lookups. This recipe demonstrates how to accomplish that.

Getting ready

Before using advanced lookups, they need to be set up. Up to four custom lookups can be created for each type in the system. We will perform the following steps now:

1. Select **Administration** in the navigation pane under the **Company** heading and then select **Advanced Lookups**.

2. In the **Advanced Lookups** window, use the **Lookup** button (magnifying glass) to select the **Lookup Name**.

3. For our example, select **Customers**. In the first **Sort By** field, scroll down and select **Zip**.

4. Change the **Description** to Zip Code.

5. Click on **Save** to save the lookup and close the window.

These setup steps added a lookup based on zip code to any place where customers are selected in the system.

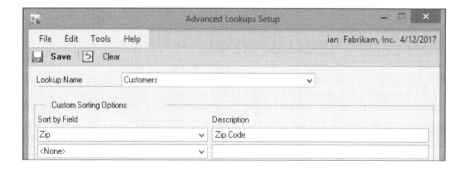

How to do it...

Once an advanced lookup has been set up, let's look at how to use it by completing the following steps:

1. Select **Sales** from the navigation pane on the left. Select **Customer** on the **Sales** area page.

2. In the **Customer ID** field, click on the **Lookup** button (magnifying glass) and click on the arrow next to **Additional Sorts**. A predefined set of lookups is shown at the top of the drop-down box and customer lookups are at the bottom. In the middle is the zip code for lookup created earlier in this chapter.

3. Click on **Zip Code** and the zip codes will appear on the right side of the window. The search box at the top also changes to allow searching by selected lookup, in this case, zip code.

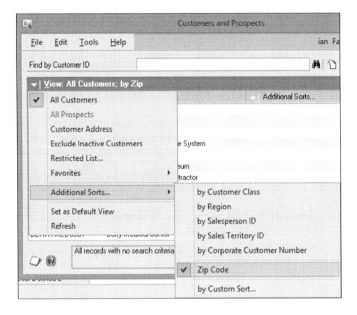

How it works...

Administrators get the chance to set up four extra lookups for each of the lookup options. The following are the lookup options:

- ▶ **Accounts**
- ▶ **Addresses**
- ▶ **Customers**
- ▶ **Employees**
- ▶ **Items**
- ▶ **Open Documents**
- ▶ **Open Payables Documents**
- ▶ **Prospects**
- ▶ **Purchase Orders**

- ▸ **Sales Document Numbers**
- ▸ **Sales Documents**
- ▸ **Vendor Addresses**
- ▸ **Vendors**
- ▸ **Vouchers**

This provides users even more opportunities to ensure that they are selecting the right information with a minimum amount of work.

See also

- ▸ The *Speeding account entry with account aliases* recipe
- ▸ The *Accessing accounts faster with favorites in lookups* recipe in *Chapter 1, Personalizing Dynamics GP*

Going straight to the site with web links

Dynamics GP provides a great feature to tie web page links to specific values in Dynamics GP. For example, when a bank account is selected, a link is made available to that bank's website. The link is contextual, meaning that it is tied to the value in the field. In this recipe, we'll look at setting up and using the **Custom Link** feature.

Getting ready

Before users can benefit from this recipe, an administrator needs to set up the custom links. To setup the links:

1. Select **Administration** from the navigation pane on the left, and then click on **Custom Link** under the **Company** heading.

2. Click on **New** on the bottom left.

3. In the **Prompt** box, select **Checkbook**. In the **Custom Link Label** field, type `Website`.

4. In the **Field Value** box, click on the **Lookup** button (magnifying glass) and check the **First Bank** checkbook.

5. Type `www.firstbank.com` into the **Internet Address** box as the bank's website and then click on **Save** to save the record.

Congratulations, that's all there is to setting up a custom link.

How to do it...

Now, we'll see how to use a custom link by completing the following steps:

1. To demonstrate how the custom link works for users, click on **Financial** in the navigation pane. Select **Bank Deposits** from the **Financial** page under **Transactions**.

2. In the **Checkbook ID** field, use the **Lookup** button (magnifying glass) to select the checkbook used in the setup. Once the checkbook is shown in the **Checkbook ID** field, click on the **Checkbook ID** label.

3. A field will drop down with two options. The first option, **Checkbook Maintenance**, leads back to the **Checkbook Maintenance** window. This is the typical behavior if custom links have not been set up.

4. Select the second link, **Website**, to open a web browser and go to the website set up in the link.

How it works...

This process associates website links with values in specific fields. This allows contextual drill through to web pages for more information. Custom links can be created for checkbooks, credit cards, currency, customers, employees, exchange rates, items, salespeople, tracking numbers, and vendors providing plenty of options to link to more information on the Internet.

There's more...

A single site can be made available for all of the choices or multiple choices can be applied to a single value.

All field values

Checking the **All Field Values** box means that the website entered will be used for all values in this field. For example, if a single currency website is used for all currencies, checking the **All Field Values** box points all currency values to that one website. This option is available for prompts named:

- ▶ Checkbook
- ▶ Credit Card
- ▶ Currency
- ▶ Exchange Rate
- ▶ Tracking Number

Multiple values

For custom links, the **Prompt** box is the key identifier. There can be multiple prompts for a single value creating more than one link for a value. For example, a bank might have a website used to check balances and a completely different one for processing ACH transactions. By creating two links, one named Balances and one named ACH, both links can be available for a single checkbook.

See also

- ▶ The *Developing connections with Internet user-defined fields* recipe
- ▶ The *Getting faster access to data with the Shortcut Bar* recipe in *Chapter 1, Personalizing Dynamics GP*

4
Automating Dynamics GP

In this chapter, we will look at ways to automate Dynamics GP including:

- ▶ Using reminders to remember important events
- ▶ Controlling reporting dates with beginning and ending periods
- ▶ Automating reporting with report groups
- ▶ Speeding entry by copying an inventory item
- ▶ Improving consistency with shortcuts and user classes
- ▶ Speeding month end closing by reconciling bank accounts daily
- ▶ Automating processes with macros
- ▶ Getting early warnings with business alerts
- ▶ Splitting AP across departments automatically with Control Account Management
- ▶ Getting control of accruals and deferrals with recurring GL batches
- ▶ Speeding document delivery with an e-mail

Introduction

Up to this point we've looked at recipes for personalizing Microsoft Dynamics GP for users and ways that Administrators can organize GP for smoother operation. In this chapter, we'll take these themes even further and look at recipes to improve efficiency by automating Dynamics GP, allowing users and administrators to focus on value-adding tasks.

Using reminders to remember important events

It's always nice to be reminded when you're about to forget something important and it's even better to get an automatic reminder triggered by certain events. Well, Microsoft Dynamics GP has prebuilt functionality to remind users when certain thresholds are approaching or met. For example, GP can provide a reminder when invoices are overdue or payables are due.

In this recipe, we'll look at how to set up the built-in reminders.

How to do it...

To set up a reminder, perform the following steps:

1. Click on **Home** in the navigation pane on the left to open the **Home** page. In the **To Do** section, click on **New Reminder**.

2. The **Predefined Reminders** section is at the top and contains a set of commonly-used reminders and the ability to set the number of days around which a reminder is given.

3. For our example, check the **Remind Me** boxes next to **Overdue Invoices** and **Payables Due**. On the **Overdue Invoices** line, enter 5 in the **days after due date** field.

4. Check the **Display as a Cue** box for each of the options selected.

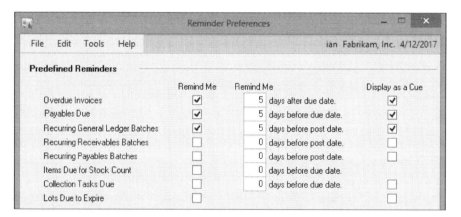

5. On the **Payables Due** line, enter 3 in the **days before due date** field and click on **OK**.

6. Reminders are refreshed when the **Home** page is refreshed. Click on the two swirling arrows in the top-right corner next to the breadcrumbs to refresh the page.

How it works...

After the prebuilt reminders are set up, a reminder will appear in the **Reminders** section of the **Home** page when an invoice is 5 days past the due date; this is great for following up after a 5-day payment grace period.

Similarly, the **Payables Due** option from our example would provide a reminder 3 days before payment is due.

Prebuilt reminders are available for the following:

- ▶ **Overdue Invoices**
- ▶ **Payables Due**
- ▶ **Recurring General Ledger Batches**
- ▶ **Recurring Receivables Batches**
- ▶ **Recurring Payables Batches**
- ▶ **Items Due for Stock Count**
- ▶ **Collection Tasks Due**
- ▶ **Lots due to Expire**

There's more...

Just getting a reminder is nice, being able to drill down into the reminder is even better.

Drilling down into reminders

Clicking on a reminder opens a window that lists each individual reminder. For the prebuilt reminders, each item gets a line of its own. Therefore, each overdue invoice and each upcoming payable in our example gets its own line and clicking on a line drills back into the actual transaction. The reminder's details can be sorted and the **Open** button on the right provides additional drill back options beyond the default drill back available after clicking on a line.

For example, for an overdue payable transaction, such as the one for Business Equipment Centre, the **Open** button includes a link to **Select Checks**, where this voucher can be added to a check batch for payment.

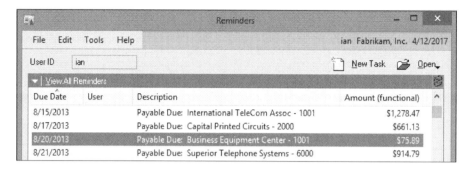

See also

▶ The *Getting early warnings with business alerts* recipe

▶ The *Getting warnings with SmartList alerts* recipe in *Chapter 5, Harnessing the power of SmartLists*

Controlling reporting dates with beginning and ending periods

Dynamics GP provides a number of features to improve and simplify reporting. One of the most overlooked features is the ability to automatically control dates when running reports. That functionality is the juicy goodness covered in this recipe.

Dynamics GP contains a large number of built-in reports, which were created with the included Report Writer tool. They are often referred to as Report Writer reports to distinguish them from other report types, such as SmartLists or SQL Server Reporting Services reports.

Report Writer reports have several common elements, one of which is an option name. A report option is simply a named collection of settings for a particular report. For example, Historical Aged Trial Balance is the name of a report. Prior to running it, a user might name an option for that report as "072009 North" to indicate that the report settings have been limited to information from July 2009 and the North region.

Since many reports are run at regular intervals, the same option can be reused to avoid recreating the report settings each time. This works fine, except for dates as most users set the dates in a report option to a fixed period such as "From: 1/1/2013 To: 1/31/2013". This works until it's necessary to report on February; then users have to manually change the date again. Dynamics GP provides beginning and ending date controls for both fiscal periods and calendar months to eliminate the manual adjustment of dates. Let's see how it works.

Getting ready

Beginning and ending date options can greatly simplify reporting. To set up a report option using the beginning and end of previous periods, perform the following steps:

1. Select **Sales** from the navigation pane on the left.

2. Select **Posting Journals** under the **Reports** section and select **New**.

3. In the **Option** field, type **Last Period**.

4. In **Ranges**, select **Posting Date** from the drop-down box.

5. In the **From** box, use the drop-down selection to select **Beginning of Previous Period**. Repeat this with the **To** box and select **End of Previous Period**, as shown in the following screenshot:

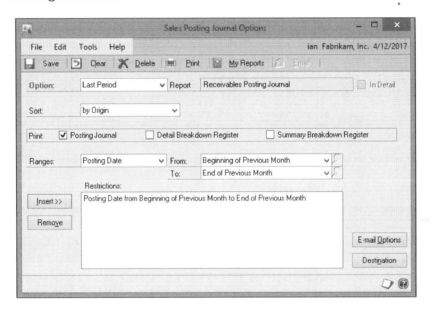

6. Click on **Insert** to update the **Range** and click on **Save** at the top to save this report option.

How to do it...

Once these report options are set up, running a report is incredibly simple.

1. Select **Posting Journals** from the **Sales** area page again.

2. Select the **Last Period** option and click on the **Insert** button in the center.

3. Click on **Print**.

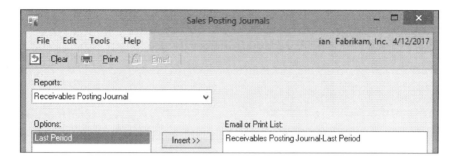

How it works...

Using the beginning and end of previous periods for report dates makes use of the fiscal period setup in Dynamics GP to control report dates. Since much of accounting is backward looking, this provides a fast way to print reports for the last fiscal month right after month end. Dynamics GP also provides an option to use the beginning and ending dates of the current period for in-period reporting.

There's more...

In addition to periods, Dynamics GP provides an option to use beginning and end dates for the previous and current month. Since month means something different than period, this is often confusing to users.

Fiscal period versus month

In Dynamics GP, a **period** is a fiscal period as defined in the fiscal period setup. A **month** is a calendar month. For companies reporting on a calendar basis, the two are interchangeable. For most companies, using period is the better option because it ties reporting to the company's fiscal period in GP. Even for calendar-based firms, using periods instead of months provides some insurance in case the firm decides to change to a different fiscal calendar later.

Beginning and end of previous month settings are often useful for tax-based reporting. Certain taxes, including sales tax, use tax, and payroll taxes are typically calendar based. They require calendar year reporting even if a firm reports financial results based on a fiscal year.

Beyond the period

The focus of this recipe has been on using beginning and ending periods or months to simplify repetitive reporting. In addition to period and month reporting, Dynamics GP offers beginning and ending fiscal year and calendar year choices as well.

Not all reports provide the option of beginning and ending dates, but whenever these two options can be combined, they create a powerful way to reduce the time and effort spent generating reports.

Automating reporting with report groups

Built-in reports in Dynamics GP are also known as Report Writer reports; named after the tool used to modify them. Each report needs a save set of parameters known as an **option**. Options allow reports to be run over and over again with the same group of settings. Even better, multiple report options can be combined into a group of reports. Running a report group runs each report in the group in sequence. Consequently, report groups can significantly reduce the amount of work required to run multiple reports. In this recipe, we'll cover creating and using report groups.

Getting ready

The first step to using report groups is creating them.

1. Before adding reports to groups, users should check the report options to ensure that they don't require user interaction. Report options should not be set to **Ask Each Time** or to print to the screen.
2. Select **Purchasing** from the navigation pane. Select **Groups** under **Reports**.
3. Change **Purchasing Reports** to **Aged Trial Balance** and in **Reports** select **Historical Aged Trial Balance**.
4. Select the first report option and click on **Insert**.
5. Change **Purchasing Reports** to **Analysis** and **Reports** to **Received/Not Invoiced**.
6. Select the first report option and click on **Insert**.
7. Click on **Save**. When prompted, name the group `Last Period` and click on **Save** and close the window.

How to do it...

Once a report group has been set up, running multiple reports is extremely easy:

1. Back on the **Purchasing** area page, select **Groups** under **Reporting**.
2. In the **Purchasing Group** drop-down box, select **Last Period**, the group you set up in the preceding section.

3. Click on **Print**.

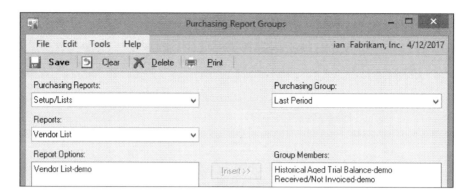

How it works...

Report groups are an absolute life saver for month end and year end. These are times when a consistent set of reports is typically printed for archive purposes. Being able to fire off a report group, go to a meeting, and come back to a pile of completed reports is just really cool.

Another great use for report groups is building a list of reports for fixed assets. Because of limited historical reporting functionally in the fixed asset module pre-Dynamics GP 2013, it was important to print and save year-end fixed asset reports.

Building a list of reports into a report group means that users don't have to remember which reports to run from year to year. They can simply run the appropriate report group.

There's more...

Report groups are provided for each of the module areas in Dynamics GP, but for companies that want to go even farther, report groups can even be combined into groups.

Groups of groups

Reports bundled into groups by module are great. But for even greater efficiency, report groups can be bundled into combined groups allowing cross-module reporting printing in one step. To build combined groups, select **Reports | Combined Groups** from the menu at the top of Dynamics GP.

The **Combined Groups** window works just like the regular report group window except that all of the selections are report groups, not individual report options.

See also

▶   The *Controlling report dates with beginning and ending periods* recipe

Speeding entry by copying an inventory item

When entering master records, it's always a challenge to ensure that records are entered consistently. This is especially true for inventory items since there are a large number of potential settings. Using inventory classes can provide some help, but even classes have their limits.

It's also common for a new inventory item to be very similar to an existing inventory item. Vendors often make small but key changes resulting in the need for a new item to allow proper tracking.

Dynamics GP provides a great feature that allows copying an inventory item when creating a new item. That's the focus of this recipe, so let's take a look how to use it.

How to do it...

To copy an inventory item to a new item number, perform the following steps:

1. From the navigation pane, select **Inventory**. In the **Inventory** area page, click on **Item** under **Cards**.

2. The new item number goes in the **Item Number** field. Enter 1-A3261B for our example and click on the **Copy** button.

3. Use the lookup button (magnifying glass) to select an item to copy from. Select the item **1-A3261A**, if using the Fabrikam sample company. Otherwise any item will do.

4. Notice that there are a number of attributes available to copy to the new item. We'll leave them all checked and click on **Copy** to create the new item.

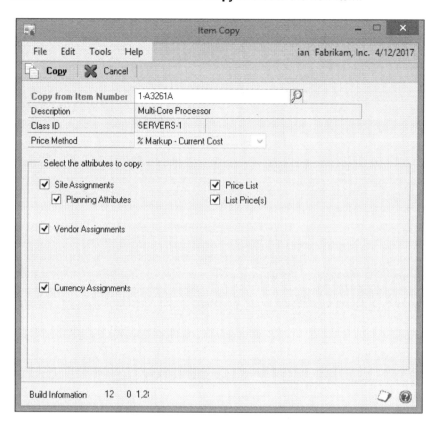

5. When done, there is a new item, with the new item number. Changes can still be made. To illustrate this, change the **Description** field to New Copied Items and click on **Save**.

How it works...

By using an existing inventory item as a base, Dynamics GP provides a mechanism to copy an inventory item to a new item number. The process is extremely flexible, allowing fine-grain control over which settings are copied and changes after the copy is created.

Users need to remember that they can choose not to copy all of the information from one item to another. For example, users might not want to copy vendor assignment if a different vendor will be used for the copied item. Additionally, users may never want to copy price list information from an original item to a copy. The key is to use the copy feature to get only what is required in the new item.

Improving consistency with shortcuts and user classes

Throughout this book, we look at various ways that shortcuts and the shortcut bar can improve the usefulness of Dynamics GP. In this recipe, we take a look at how administrators can control shortcuts by assigning specific shortcuts to specific user classes.

This feature allows an administrator to assign a shortcut to a class of users, so every user in the class gets the shortcut automatically and they can't remove it. For example, this is a great way to ensure that all payables users have a shortcut to the payables transaction entry. It is also useful for attaching a currency website shortcut to a class of senior accountants. The focus of this recipe is to assign shortcuts to user classes.

Getting ready

Assigning shortcuts to user classes requires that the user be logged in as sa. This is the SQL Server system administrator account, otherwise known as the head chef in this cookbook. For this action, other accounts with system administrator access, even those who can create users, won't work. It must be the system administrator account.

User Classes are created in the **Administration** area page. To set up a user class, perform the following steps:

1. Select **Administration** from the navigation pane on the left.
2. On the **Administration** area page, click on **User Classes** under **Setup**.
3. Enter AP USER in the **Class ID** field and AP User in **Description**.
4. Click on **Save**.

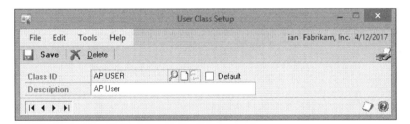

Users also need to be assigned to user classes. If users are not assigned to classes, they can be added with the following steps:

5. Select **Administration** from the navigation pane and select **User**.
6. Enter the system password and click on **OK**, if prompted to do so.

7. Use the lookup button (magnifying glass) next to **User ID** to select a user.

8. Use the lookup button (magnifying glass) next to **Class ID** to select the **AP USER** class and click on **Save** to apply the class.

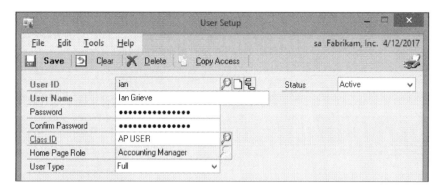

How to do it...

Now that classes are set up and attached to users, we can apply a shortcut to a class of users.

1. Select **Purchasing** from the navigation pane.

2. Click on **Transaction Entry** to open the **Payables Transaction Entry** window.

3. Go to **File | Add to Shortcuts** to add a shortcut to this window in the shortcut bar.

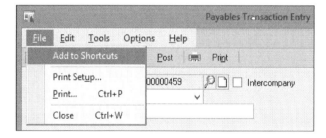

4. Select **Home** in the navigation pane to activate the shortcut bar.

5. Right-click on the **Payables Transaction Entry** shortcut and select **Cut**.

6. Right-click on the **AP User** class, created in the *Getting Ready* section of this recipe, and select **Paste** to move the shortcut to the **AP User** class.

How it works...

Moving a shortcut into a `User Class` folder provides a degree of shortcut control to administrators. It provides a way to ensure that a minimum set of shortcuts is passed down to a set of users. In Dynamics GP 2010, user classes were disconnected from security, making them even more useful for shortcuts. The user classes used for shortcuts don't have to be tied to security at all, which means that classes can be designed to support groups of shortcuts.

As an added bonus, the system administrator can assign keystrokes to those shortcuts, and shortcuts added to a class by an administrator can't be changed or removed.

See also

▶ The *Getting faster access to data with the shortcut bar* recipe in *Chapter 1, Personalizing Dynamics GP*

▶ The Reducing clicks with start-up shortcuts in *Chapter 1, Personalizing Dynamics GP*

Speeding month-end closing by reconciling bank accounts daily

Month-end bank reconciliation is one of the most common time-consuming activities when trying to close the month. With a few process changes, bank reconciliation can be performed daily. Month-end bank reconciliations simply become one more daily activity.

Describing the process to accomplish daily bank reconciliations is the focus of this recipe.

Getting ready

Before a company can perform daily bank reconciliations, bank reconciliations need to be current. If a company's reconciliations are out of balance, the accounts will need to be balanced to the last statement before moving to daily reconciliations.

Additionally, companies will need access to the daily transactions from their bank. In most cases, this information can be easily downloaded from the bank's website for transactions through the previous day.

How to do it...

Daily bank reconciliations do a great job of spreading the work. Let's see how.

1. Download and print the company's bank transactions from the bank's website for the period since the last reconciliation.

2. Select **Financial** from the navigation pane and click on **Reconcile Bank Statement** on the **Financial** area page.

3. Use the lookup button (magnifying glass) to select a bank account to reconcile.

4. In the **Bank Statement Ending Balance** field, enter the ending bank balance for the previous day from the printout from the bank's website. Use yesterday's date for the **Bank Statement Ending Date** and today as the **Cutoff Date**.

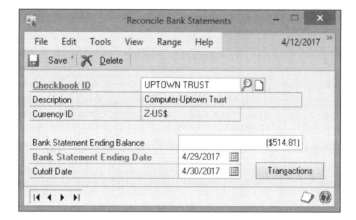

5. Click on **Transactions** to start the reconciliation.

6. Check off completed transactions and complete a typical bank reconciliation but do not click on **Reconcile** once the difference reaches zero. Check off matched transactions on the printout from the website and save that for tomorrow. This helps avoid confusion about what was checked off and what wasn't.

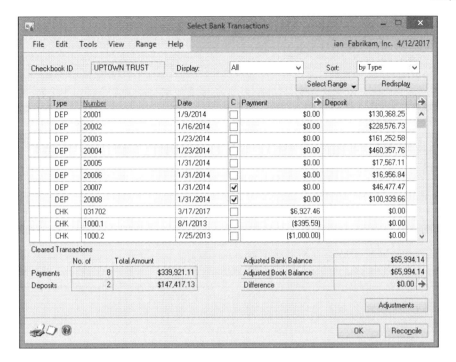

7. Click on **OK** to return to the **Reconcile Bank Statements** window and click on **Save** to save the partial reconciliation.

8. Each day, repeat these steps until the bank statement arrives at month end.

9. When the bank statement arrives, review the statement against the bank reconciliation in Dynamics GP. I have seen a few situations where the website and the paper statement differ. Only then should you click on the **Reconcile** button and reconciliation reports are printed for storage, as shown in the following screenshot:

```
System:     4/18/2013   10:11:33                 Fabrikam, Inc.                        Page:    1
User Date:  4/12/2017                     RECONCILIATION POSTING JOURNAL            User ID: ian
                                               Bank Reconciliation


Audit Trail Code: CMADJ00000001                               Bank Statement Ending Balance: ($514.81)
Checkbook ID:     UPTOWN TRUST                                Bank Statement Ending Date:     4/29/2017
Description:      Computer-Uptown Trust                       Cutoff Date:                    4/30/2017


Statement Ending Balance                          ($514.81)
Outstanding Checks (-)                          $949,058.86
Deposits in Transit (+)                       $1,015,567.81
                                          ------------------
Adjusted Bank Balance                            $65,994.14
                                          ------------------
Checkbook Balance as of Cutoff                   $65,994.14
Adjustments                                           $0.00
                                          ------------------
Adjusted Book Balance                            $65,994.14
                                          ------------------
Difference                                           $0.00
                                          ==================
```

How it works...

Daily bank reconciliation is really just the disciplined application of basic bank reconciliation principles. The easy availability of bank information via the bank's website combined with Dynamics GP's ability to save incomplete bank reconciliations makes this an easy recipe to apply. Additionally, other benefits result, including a better understanding of the company's bank float, faster identification of fraudulent transactions, and an always up-to-date cash position.

There's more...

A common objection is that this is still time consuming for larger organizations and high volume accounts, but this is a hollow excuse as options are available for larger transaction volumes as well. There is, however, one little hiccup when dealing with the bank statement cut off.

High transaction volume accounts

For high transaction volume bank accounts, Microsoft provides an optional electronic bank reconciliation module. This allows companies to take a file from their bank and electronically match it to the bank statement. Where most companies go wrong is that they only get the file on a monthly basis. If there is an error, it's even harder to find in a high volume account at month end.

Companies in this situation should work to get a daily electronic reconciliation file from the bank. Often, firms chafe at the extra costs from their bank, but rarely do they take a hard look at the return provided by not having employees chasing bank transactions during the month end. The stress of month-end closing is also reduced because errors are found earlier in the month, providing time for resolution before a month-end deadline.

Bank statement cut off

Typically, there are a few days mailing delay between the bank statement cutoff and delivery. For this period of a few days, daily bank reconciliation can't be completed. The problem is that reconciliations would go beyond the end of the statement period making it impossible to print bank reconciliation reports that match the statement.

There are a couple of options to deal with this issue. The simplest is just to wait a couple of days and catch up after the statement arrives and the final month-end reconciliation is processed. Another option is to process the reconciliation against only the website data and attach the daily website printout, along with the bank statement and balance reports as evidence for auditors:

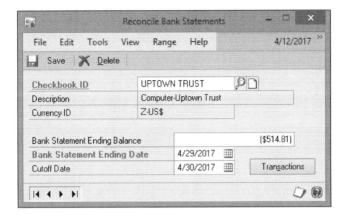

Automating processes with macros

Macros provide a way to automate processes within Dynamics GP. They are actually very easy to create and use. Macros are perfect for moderately complex, but repetitive processes. For example, a cash transfer between bank accounts is a common repetitive task, but there is some complexity to it because the amount is usually different. This example provides a great, practical lesson in macros, so we'll look at it in this recipe.

How to do it...

To create a macro for a bank transfer, follow these steps:

1. From the menu select **Tools** | **Macro** | **Record**.

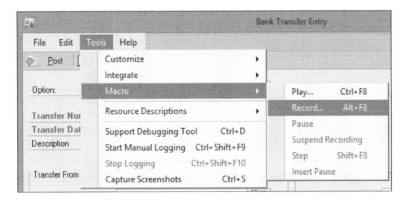

2. Select **Financial** in the navigation pane and select **Bank Transfers** from the **Financial** area page under **Transactions**. Note, where the macro is being saved and name the macro as `Bank Xfer`. Click on **Save**.

3. Tab to the **Description** field and type Bank Transfer.

4. Use the lookup button (magnifying glass) to select a checkbook ID to transfer from. Leave the amount set to zero.

5. Use the lookup button (magnifying glass) to select a checkbook ID to transfer to.

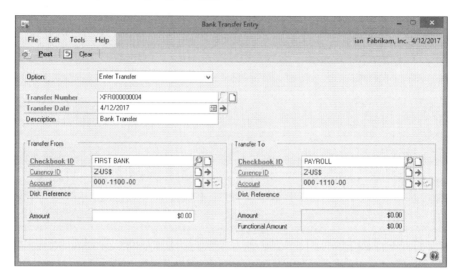

6. From the **Tools** menu, select **Macro | Stop Record**. Click on **Clear** and close the **Bank Transfer Entry** window.

7. Now, select the **Microsoft Dynamics GP** menu item and then select **Tools | Macro | Play**.

8. Find and select the **Bank Xfer** macro saved earlier and click on **Open**.

The macro will run. As the macro runs, the **Bank Transfer Entry** window will open and the description, to and from accounts will fill in automatically. The window will then be left open for a user to add the transfer amount. Click on **Post** when finished, to complete the transfer.

How it works...

Recording a **macro** is easy. **Macros** can be recorded by any user with proper security and because they are stored as a file, they can be shared among users. There are an infinite number of uses for **macros**. They can be reused or built only for a specific scenario. Learning to create and run **macros** provides a terrific opportunity to automate any number of functions in Dynamics GP.

There's more...

Macros can be attached to the shortcut bar and run from there. They can also be run with a keystroke combination. Finally, users can insert pauses in macros or string them together into a set of steps.

Macros and the shortcut bar

Macros can be added to the shortcut bar, making them easy to run with a single click. Adding items such as macros to the shortcut bar is covered in detail in the *Getting faster access to data with the shortcut bar* recipe in *Chapter 1, Personalizing Dynamics GP*.

Macros can be run with a keystroke combination

Once a macro has been added to the Shortcut Bar, a keystroke combination can be added, allowing it to be run from the keyboard. Setting up keystroke combinations for macros is also covered in the the *Getting faster access to data with the shortcut bar* recipe in *Chapter 1, Personalizing Dynamics GP*.

Macro pauses

Pauses can be inserted into macros to allow for data entry in the middle of a macro. To insert a pause, click on **Tools | Macro | Insert Pause** while recording a macro. A box will open allowing the creation of instructions for the user. The problem with pausing macros is that the process to restart a macro is not intuitive. When a user executes a macro, the macro pauses at the selected point and waits for user input. After the user inputs, the user must select **Tools | Macro | Continue** to resume the macro.

That set of steps is not obvious to a user. Also, there is not enough room to reasonably enter instructions and restart steps to the instruction box. Nor is there a keystroke combination to resume a macro after a pause.

Sequential macros

An alternative to pausing macros is to create more than one macro. Create the first macro up to the point where a pause would be inserted. Then, create a second macro for the next portion of the process. Add the macros to the shortcut bar in a folder in the order they should be executed. After the first macro finishes, the user simply needs to insert any data required and click on the second macro to continue the process.

See also

- The *Getting faster access to data with the shortcut bar* recipe in *Chapter 1, Personalizing Dynamics GP*
- The *Remembering processes with an ad hoc workflow* recipe in *Chapter 3, Organizing Dynamics GP*

Getting early warnings with business alerts

It's always nice to find out about problems early because early notification usually means that there is still time to fix the issue. Dynamics GP provides a great mechanism for early warnings in the form of business alerts. Business alerts allow companies to build a criteria for notification and then to get notified via e-mail or within the application. Additionally, a report of information related to the alert can be sent as a part of an e-mail. A wizard-like interface is used to set up alerts, but they can get very complex.

For this recipe, we'll build a basic business alert with all of the foundational pieces for a more complicated alert. For our sample business alert, we'll assume that a company would like to be notified when their bank balance falls below $10,000 to allow them to transfer cash from another account.

Getting ready

Users must be logged in as system administrator (the SQL Server system administrator, otherwise known as the head chef) to create business alerts. Log in as system administrator prior to starting this recipe.

How to do it...

Let's look at how to build a business alert.

1. In the navigation pane, select **Administration**. Select **Business Alerts** under **System**. If the **System Password** box opens, enter the system password and click on **OK**.

2. Leave **Create a New Alert** marked and click on **Next** to start an alert.

3. Select a company database. The company database for the sample company in this example is TWO13.

4. Name this alert as BANK BAL <10k in the **Business Alert ID** field.

5. In the **Description** field, type Bank Bal <10k. Click on **Next** to move on.

6. In **Series**, select **Financial**. Find the **CM Checkbook Master** table in the middle window. Highlight it and click on **Insert** to add this table. Then click on **Next** to continue.

7. After selecting the appropriate tables, it's time to define the alert formula. In the **Define Alert Formula** window, select **CM00100_T1 - CM Checkbook Master** under **Table**. Select **Current Balance** in the **Column Name** field and click on **Add Column**.

8. Click on the less than (**<**) button. Type `10000` in the **Constant** field and click on **Add Constant**. Click on **Next**.

9. After the alert criteria have been established, it's time to set up the alerts. Click on the e-mail selection next to **Send To**. Select **Message and Report** in the **Send** selection. Enter your e-mail address and click on **Insert**. In the **Message Text** area, type **Bank Account Balance is below $10,000** and click on **Next**.

10. Finally, we'll layout the report to accompany the alert. Select the **CM00100_T1 - CM Checkbook Master** table in **Table**. Scroll down to **Checkbook ID** in **Columns**. Select it and click on **Insert**. Scroll down to **Current Balance**. Select it and click on **Insert**. Click on **Next** to move on.

11. Click on **Next** past the **Sorting Options** screen.

12. The **Schedule Alert** window can be used to adjust the timing of alert deliveries. We'll leave the defaults and click on **Finish** to wrap up.

How it works...

This process creates a business alert that checks the bank balance in Dynamics GP every night at midnight and e-mails an alert and detailed report if the balance drops below $10,000. A manager might then get this alert via e-mail on his/her phone and be prepared to move cash even before they leave for the office in the morning. Business alerts are extremely useful for checking items against a threshold. This includes scenarios such as accounts over budget, checkbook balances below a limit, customers over their credit limit, inventory items at their reorder point, purchase orders awaiting approval, and payments past due. This is just a sample of the scenarios that can be created.

There's more...

A great place to start working with business alerts is with the included prebuilt alerts.

Prebuilt alerts

Microsoft Dynamics GP comes with a prebuilt set of common business alerts, including alerts for many of the scenarios described in this recipe and more. Modifying an existing business alert is a great way to learn about the process and move into creating more complex alerts. When creating a business alert, simply select **Modify Existing Alert** instead of **Create New Alert** and walk through the wizard.

There is a *Microsoft Knowledge Base* article that explains how to configure the Microsoft SQL Server for use with business alerts, which can be found at `http://support.microsoft.com/kb/915097`.

See also

▶ The *Using reminders to remember important events* recipe

▶ The *Getting warnings with SmartList alerts* recipe in *Chapter 5, Harnessing the Power of SmartLists*

Splitting AP across departments automatically with Control Account Management

Often companies say that they want to see each division reported as if it was a standalone business. Even though all divisions may be part of a single legal entity, companies frequently need to make decisions based on who is under or over performing. Treating each division as a separate business can provide measurements to consistently compare divisions. Frequently, balance sheet accounts such as fixed assets and accounts payable are included to provide a measure of the capital required to run each division.

However, providing an infrastructure to actually allow each division to function as a business is both expensive and inefficient. Most companies find that using a consolidated payables department for accounts payable is much more effective than providing an AP department for each division. They struggle, however, with reconciling that effectiveness with the benefits of divisional reporting.

Dynamics GP provides a solution for this in a feature known as **Control Account Management**.

In Control Account Management, payables are processed centrally. At month end, a routine is run to allocate open payables from the payables GL account to divisional payable accounts. The allocation is based on a segment of the chart of accounts that corresponds to the company's divisions. This provides a mechanism for financial reporting of payables at the divisional level. At the beginning of the next month, an automatically created reversing entry is processed to repopulate central accounts payable and allow the normal payable's process to continue. In this recipe, we'll see how to make it all work seamlessly.

Getting ready

Before using Control Account Management, the divisional payable accounts need to be associated with the appropriate general ledger segment. For our example, we'll be using the sample company.

1. Select **Financial** in the navigation pane. Under the **Setup** heading, select **Control Account Management**.

2. Ensure that **Activate Control Account Management** is checked at the top. In **Account Segment**, select **Segment 3** to represent the departments. Click on **Account Type** to continue.

3. Set the **Account Type** to **Payables**. Set the **Batch ID** to **AP CONTROL**, and set both **Batch Comment** and **Reference** to **Control Account**.

4. Next to each segment ID, look up or enter the corresponding divisional payable account and click on **Save** when finished. For the sample company, use the control accounts shown in the following screenshot. Click on **Save** when done.

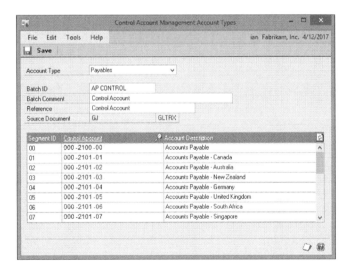

How to do it...

Once the divisional AP accounts have been mapped, it's time to see how this process works each month.

1. Select **Financial** from the navigation pane on the left. Select **Control Account Management** under **Transactions**.

2. Click on **Report** to load the payables distribution data. Review the payable distributions at the bottom of the window.

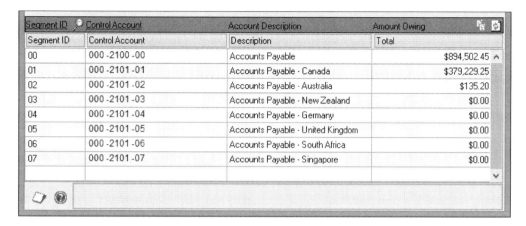

Segment ID	Control Account	Description	Total
00	000 -2100 -00	Accounts Payable	$894,502.45
01	000 -2101 -01	Accounts Payable - Canada	$379,229.25
02	000 -2101 -02	Accounts Payable - Australia	$135.20
03	000 -2101 -03	Accounts Payable - New Zealand	$0.00
04	000 -2101 -04	Accounts Payable - Germany	$0.00
05	000 -2101 -05	Accounts Payable - United Kingdom	$0.00
06	000 -2101 -06	Accounts Payable - South Africa	$0.00
07	000 -2101 -07	Accounts Payable - Singapore	$0.00

3. Select the double arrow on the right, below the printer icon to see more information. From this screen, the batch and date information can be changed. Click on the **Doc Info** and **Dist Info** tabs to see more information about how the payables will be distributed.

4. Click on **Generate** to create the unposted GL transaction and associated reversing transaction.

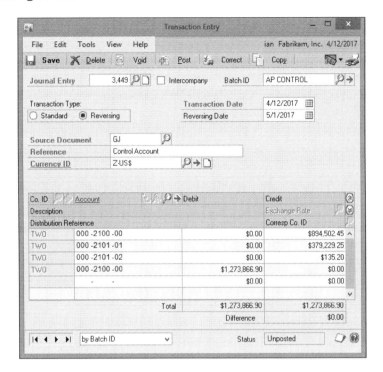

How it works...

The month-end routine examines open accounts' payable transactions and sums the open amounts by the divisional segment of the purchase. GP then uses this information to calculate the outstanding percentage for each division. From there, a reversing transaction is created to move the account's payable balance out to the divisional payable accounts.

By providing a GL segment to identify the division and then mapping it to a corresponding payables account, GP provides a best of both worlds solution. This allows centralized AP management with decentralized reporting at month, quarter, and year end.

The fact that the process resets automatically at the start of the next month makes this a first-class solution to an otherwise difficult process.

There's more...

This process is so exciting that many people want to see if it will meet similar needs for multi-company scenarios.

Multi-company

When people see this process for the first time, it often registers as a potential solution to related multi-company issues. This process will work for splitting centralized AP across multiple companies, if the companies are all stored in a single GP company with an identifying GL segment. If the companies are split across multiple GP databases, this process will not work because it can't post across company databases.

See also

> ▸ The *Improving financial reporting clarity by Splitting Purchasing Accounts* recipe in *Chapter 3, Organizing Dynamics GP*

Getting control of accruals and deferrals with recurring GL batches

Most companies have a need for some minimal level of deferrals and accruals. This could be insurance prepaid for the year that needs to be expensed over 12 months. It could be prepaid revenue that is earned in the first half of the year, but not billable until year end or any number of similar transactions. For straightforward accruals and deferrals, Dynamics GP's recurring batch functionality can be used to manage, track, and post these types of transactions. In this recipe, we'll look at how to set up and process accruals and deferrals using recurring batches.

Getting ready

For our example, assume that corporate insurance is due and paid on January 1 and the payment covers January through December of that year. For simplicity sake, corporate insurance is $12,000 a year and the company is going to recognize $1,000 per month until the full amount is used up.

The key setup piece, is that the payables transaction for $12,000 is debited from prepaid expenses, a balance sheet code, rather than insurance expense.

How to do it...

Now that we understand the background, we'll look at how to set up recognition of the monthly expense.

1. In the navigation pane, select **Financial**. Click on the **Batches** option on the **Financial** area under **Transactions**.

2. Enter Z INSUR DEFER in the **Batch ID** field and set the **Origin** field to **General Entry**.

3. In **Frequency**, select **Monthly**. Enter 12 in the **Recurring Posting** field and click on the **Transactions** button.

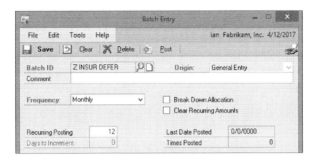

4. Set the **Transaction Date** to **January 15** to process the first month's expense and set up the recurring transaction.

5. Type Recognize Insurance in the **Reference** field.

6. Use the lookup button (magnifying glass) to find the **Prepaid Expense** account and enter a credit for $1,000. On the next line, use the lookup button (magnifying glass) to find the **Insurance Expenses** account and process a debit for $1,000.

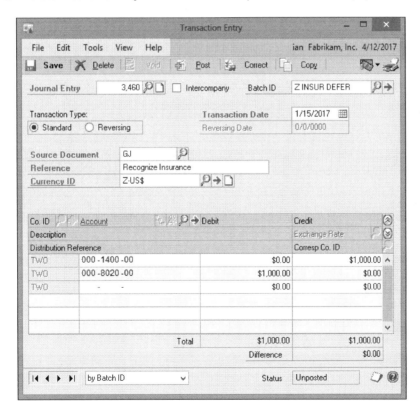

7. Click on **Save** to save the transaction. Close the **Transaction Entry** window and reopen the **Batches** window. Use the lookup button (magnifying glass) to reopen the **Z INSUR DEFER** batch and click on **Post**.

8. Use the lookup button (magnifying glass) to find the **Z INSUR DEFER** batch again. Unlike single use batches, the batch doesn't disappear after posting. The batch now contains the last date posted and the number of times it has been posted. When the number of times posted equals the **Recurring Posting** number, the batch will then disappear.

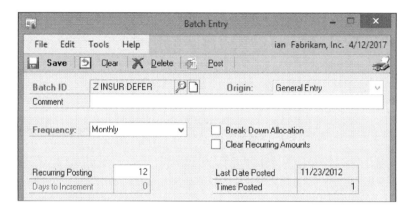

How it works...

Recurring batches provide an opportunity to slowly use up a deferral or build up an accrual amount. Posting these recurring batches is easy. The batches provide information about when they were last posted and this process can be added as a reminder to ensure that posting is completed on time. The ability to date the transaction means that the actual posting process can occur any time during the month and the transaction will post as of the date set in the transaction. This provides another opportunity to reduce month-end work since this month's accruals and deferrals can be posted at the beginning of the month.

There's more...

A few simple best practices can make recurring batches even more effective.

Recurring batch best practices

A couple of simple best practices can provide even more value to recurring batches. Recurring batches are mixed in with other batches in the batch window. Naming recurring batches to start with an underscore (_) will put these batches at the top. Starting the batch name with a z will put them at the bottom.

Since batches will typically be posted multiple times covering several months, it's important to date the batch with a date that will appear in each month. For example, batches dated for the 30th, will cause the posting in February to revert to the last day of the month and never move back to the 30th. This gets even more important when using fiscal months that can end on odd dates. When using a 4-4-5 fiscal period, I've seen months end as early as the 20th. Typically, using the 15th of the month is a great option that will work in all situations.

For those companies that need to manage more than a few accruals or deferrals, Microsoft provides additional options.

Revenue/expense deferral module

For companies with a large number of deferrals to track, Microsoft provides an available revenue/expense deferral module. This module is designed for processing accrual and deferral transactions and is a great option when recurring batches aren't enough.

Field service contracts module

For companies that need to track revenue deferrals related to customer contracts, a better option is the contracts module, part of the Field Service suite, which is also available from Microsoft.

Speeding document delivery with an e-mail

Dynamics GP 2010 added the ability to directly e-mail documents either individually or in bulk. This feature provides a number of options for e-mailing:

- ▶ Sales quotes, orders, fulfillment orders, invoices, returns, back orders, and packing slips
- ▶ Receivable invoices, returns, debit memos, credit memos, finance charges, warranties, and service/repair documents
- ▶ Standard purchase order, blanket purchase order, drop ship purchase orders, and drop ship blanket purchase orders
- ▶ Vendor remittances

Documents can be e-mailed in HTML, DOCX, XPS, or PDF formats. E-mailing HTML- and DOCX-formatted attachments does not require that Word 2010 or higher be installed on the client computer. E-mailing documents in XPS and PDF formats does require Word 2010 or higher on the client, but Adobe Acrobat is not necessary.

In this recipe, we will look at e-mailing documents individually or in bulk, along with some setup items using the sample company.

Getting ready

Before we start, we need to add an e-mail address to a few customers to demonstrate how this feature works.

To add email addresses, perform the following steps:

1. Select **Sales** from the navigation pane. On the **Sales** area page, click on **Customer** under **Cards**.

2. Use the lookup button (magnifying glass) to select the customer CENTRALC0001. Click on the italic letter "i" next to the **Address ID** field.

3. Enter your e-mail address in the **To** field and click on **Save**. Close the window.

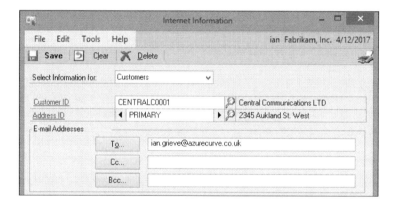

4. In the **Customer Maintenance** window, click on **Save** and close the window.

5. Repeat this process with the customers **AARONFIT0001** and **ASTORSUI001**.

How to do it...

Now that some customers have e-mail addresses, we will look at how to e-mail invoices to them. To e-mail individual invoices, perform the following steps:

1. Select **Sales** from the navigation pane. Click on **Sales Transaction Entry** under **Transactions** on the **Sales** area page.

2. Set the **Type** to **Invoice**. Use the lookup button (magnifying glass) to select the invoice **STDINV2262**.

3. Click on the e-mail icon in the upper-right corner under the company name. Dynamics GP will indicate that an e-mail has been sent.

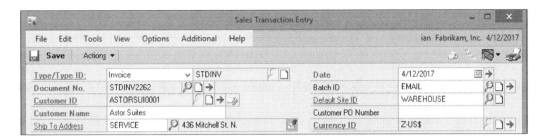

To e-mail multiple invoices at once, perform the following steps:

1. Select **Sales** from the navigation pane. Click on the **Sales Transaction Entry** navigation list at the top of the navigation pane.

2. On the navigation list, click on the **Document Number** header twice to sort by document number in descending order.

3. Check on the boxes next to invoices **STDINV2259**, **STDINV2260**, **STDINV2261**, and **STDINV2262**.

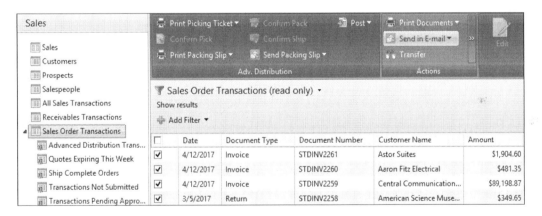

4. Click on **Send in Email** in the navigation menu and then click on **Send**.

5. Dynamics GP will e-mail the selected invoices.

How it works...

E-mailing documents is a fantastic way to speed communication with customers and vendors. Dynamics GP 2010 provides fast, easy, and flexible ways to e-mail documents.

There's more...

Dynamics GP provides a number of setup options to control e-mailing documents.

Setup

The setup of e-mails is controlled primarily by the **Company E-Mail Setup** window. It is reached by selecting **Administration** from the navigation pane and then clicking on the **Email Setup** under **Setup** and **Company**.

The **Company E-Mail Setup** window controls whether or not documents are embedded in the e-mail body and then formats the attachments.

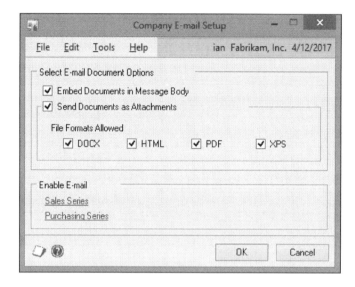

Selecting either **Sales Series** or **Purchasing Series** under **Enable E-Mail** opens the related **E-Mail setup** window, which allows a user to set the message ID that controls the message included in the e-mail. This window also allows a company to set a central return address for these e-mails.

Finally, the content in the **Message ID** field is set up by selecting **Administration** from the navigation pane and then clicking on **Email Setup** under **Setup** and **Company**.

5
Harnessing the Power of SmartLists

In this chapter, we will look at how to leverage the reporting power of SmartLists in Dynamics GP. We will discuss the following:

- ▸ Sorting data to get the information you want
- ▸ Speeding access to information with SmartList favorites
- ▸ Getting warnings with SmartList alerts
- ▸ Improving information returned with SmartList Search
- ▸ Controlling data with SmartList record limits
- ▸ Tailoring SmartLists by adding fields
- ▸ Controlling access by sharing or restricting SmartList favorites
- ▸ Renaming fields for clarity

Introduction

In the previous chapters, we've looked at a number of recipes that touch on SmartLists. This powerful, user-friendly reporting tool has become a foundational feature in Dynamics GP. The underpinnings of most of the lookup windows, reminders, and favorites throughout the system rely on SmartLists. Since SmartLists are so easy to use, many users never delve deeper than the surface. In this collection of recipes, we'll dig deeper into SmartLists to see how to better leverage both their simplicity and their power.

Sorting data to get the information you want

At their core, SmartLists have rows and columns of data, similar to an Excel spreadsheet. They provide a powerful, friendly way to interact with information in Dynamics GP. One of the simplest SmartList features found by most users is the ability to sort a SmartList simply by clicking on a column header. However, SmartLists provide advanced sorting features that are even more powerful, just a little harder to find.

In this recipe, we'll take a look at all of the sorting options for SmartLists, simple and advanced.

How to do it...

To sort a **SmartList, perform the following steps:**

1. Select **Microsoft Dynamics GP Menu** from the top and click on **SmartList**, or click on the SmartList icon on the toolbar.

2. If the SmartList Icon is not shown at the top, right-click on the blue bar next to the menu and select the standard tool bar to turn it on.

3. Select **Financial** in the left pane and then **Account Summary** below it.

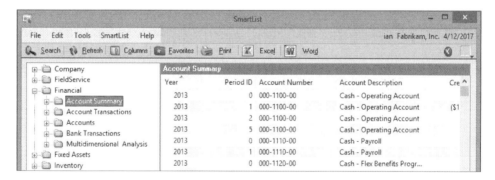

4. Simple sorting is accomplished by clicking on the column name. Select the **Debit Amount** column title to sort by debits. The arrow next to the column name shows whether the sort is ascending or descending.

Account Number	Account Description	Credit Amount	Debit Amount
000-1200-00	Accounts Receivable	($1,314,636.73)	$1,826,936.91
000-1200-00	Accounts Receivable	$1,314,636.73	$1,826,936.91
000-1520-00	Machinery & Equipment	$0.00	$1,409,884.30
000-1520-00	Machinery & Equipment	$0.00	$1,409,884.30
000-1200-00	Accounts Receivable	($206.99)	$1,202,937.06
000-1200-00	Accounts Receivable	$206.99	$1,202,937.06

5. Click on **Debit Amount** again to change the sort order.

6. For more advanced sorting, select **Search** from the SmartList toolbar and click on **Order By**. This window allows sorting by multiple fields, including fields that are included but not displayed on the SmartList.

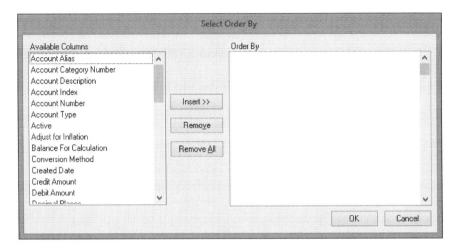

7. Select **Year** and click on **Insert**. Set **Order By** to **Descending**.

8. Select **Period ID** and click on **Insert**. Set **Order By** to **Ascending**.

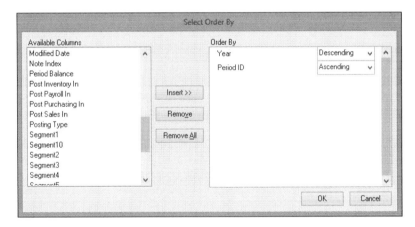

9. Select **Account Number** and click on **Insert**. Set **Order By** to **Ascending**.

10. Select **Debit Amount** and click on **Insert**. Set **Order By** to **Descending**.

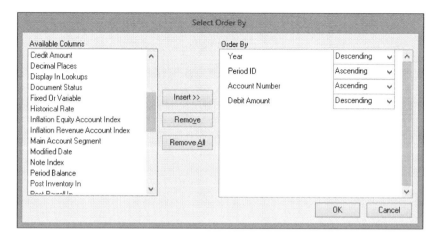

11. Click on **OK** twice to return to the SmartList.

12. Notice, that the SmartList has now been sorted by **Year**, **Period ID**, **Account Number**, and **Debit Amount** following the sorting rules set up in the example.

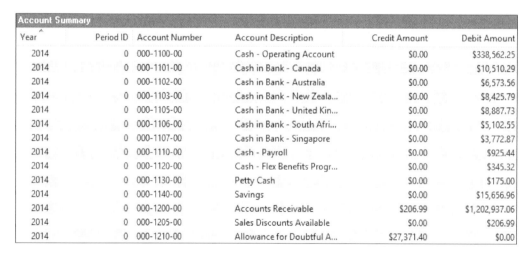

Year	Period ID	Account Number	Account Description	Credit Amount	Debit Amount
2014	0	000-1100-00	Cash - Operating Account	$0.00	$338,562.25
2014	0	000-1101-00	Cash in Bank - Canada	$0.00	$10,510.29
2014	0	000-1102-00	Cash in Bank - Australia	$0.00	$6,573.56
2014	0	000-1103-00	Cash in Bank - New Zeala...	$0.00	$8,425.79
2014	0	000-1105-00	Cash in Bank - United Kin...	$0.00	$8,887.73
2014	0	000-1106-00	Cash in Bank - South Afri...	$0.00	$5,102.55
2014	0	000-1107-00	Cash in Bank - Singapore	$0.00	$3,772.87
2014	0	000-1110-00	Cash - Payroll	$0.00	$925.44
2014	0	000-1120-00	Cash - Flex Benefits Progr...	$0.00	$345.32
2014	0	000-1130-00	Petty Cash	$0.00	$175.00
2014	0	000-1140-00	Savings	$0.00	$15,656.96
2014	0	000-1200-00	Accounts Receivable	$206.99	$1,202,937.06
2014	0	000-1205-00	Sales Discounts Available	$0.00	$206.99
2014	0	000-1210-00	Allowance for Doubtful A...	$27,371.40	$0.00

How it works...

Complex sorting in a SmartList can often bring clarity to information by providing a better arrangement of data. Frequently, users who don't know about this feature take the extra step of exporting the data to Microsoft Excel and then sorting it there. With advanced sorting, this step is unnecessary and it can eliminate the potentially time consuming effort of sending a large amount of data to Excel just for sorting.

Additionally, even when the SmartList is selected with the intention of sending it to Excel, pre-sorting the information can speed up the analysis once the data is exported to a spreadsheet.

See also

▶ The *Building analyses by Exporting SmartLists to Microsoft Excel* recipe in *Chapter 6, Connecting Dynamics GP to Microsoft Office 2013*

▶ The *Getting fine grain control of Excel Exports from SmartLists* in *Chapter 6, Connecting Dynamics GP to Microsoft Office 2013*

Speeding access to information with SmartList favorites

SmartLists are designed for individual users to tailor reporting to their needs. This is important because users have the ability to save their unique SmartLists and make them available to be reused over and over again.

Default SmartLists are represented by an asterisk and can be customized by moving fields around, adding or removing fields, filtering the data to be returned, and sorting data in interesting ways. However, the time and effort required to do all of that is lost if a user can't save and re-use those unique settings. Saved SmartLists are called **favorites** and they are the focus of this recipe.

How to do it...

In this recipe, we'll set up a SmartList and save it as a favorite.

1. Select the SmartList icon from the menu bar at the top, or select the **Microsoft Dynamics GP Menu** from the top, and click on **SmartList**.

2. Select **Financial** and then **Accounts** from the list on the left.

3. Click on the **Account Number** column heading to sort by account numbers.

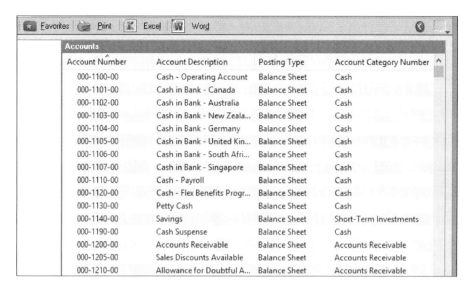

4. Click on **Favorites**. In **Name**, name the favorite account number.

5. Leave **Visible To** set to **System**.

6. Click on **Add** and then click on **Add Favorite** to save the SmartList.

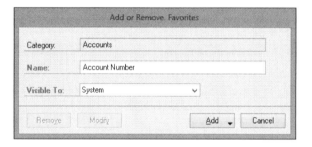

How it works...

SmartList favorites provide a way to save a group of SmartList settings much like options do for built-in reports. This provides a simple way to return to the same SmartList settings over and over. Favorites are saved under the category they are created in on the left. Consequently, our account number favorite is saved under **Financial | Accounts**.

There's more...

SmartList favorites can also be modified and there are even more SmartList recipes to come. Favorites provide fast access to preset SmartLists and GoTo's provide a path back to the source data.

Modifying SmartList favorites

It is possible to change a SmartList favorite by selecting that favorite, making changes and clicking on **Modify** instead of **Add**.

GoTo

Double-clicking on a row in a SmartList drills back to the source data. Sometimes, there is more than one possible source. For example, should a sales row drill back to the sales transaction or to the customer master record? Well, the **GoTo** button in the upper-right corner displays more drill-back options beyond the default double-click selection.

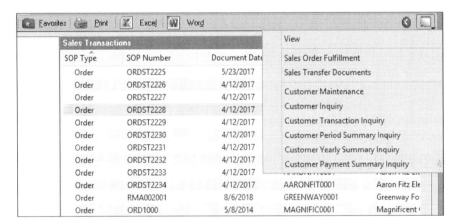

Additionally, the default GoTo can be changed in the **SmartList Options** window. This window is reached by selecting the **Administration** button in the navigation pane and then clicking on **SmartList Options** in the Administration area page.

See also

- ▶ The *Getting warnings with SmartList alerts* recipe
- ▶ The *Controlling access by sharing or restricting SmartList favorites* recipe
- ▶ The *Getting faster access to data with the shortcut bar* recipe in *Chapter 1, Personalizing Dynamics GP*

Getting warnings with SmartList alerts

In the previous recipe, we saw how to save SmartLists as favorites. Now, we can look at how to use a favorite to build a custom reminder. SmartList favorites actually make up the core of the reminder feature in Dynamics GP.

A custom reminder is a warning or alert generated by Dynamics GP and displayed on the **Reminder** window on login. It's used to alert a user about situations that exist in Dynamics GP. For example, reminders can display the number of invoices 60 days or more past due. They can also include the ability to drill back into the transactions that generated the reminder. The basic process takes a SmartList favorite and builds criteria used to drive the reminder.

Built-in reminders were covered previously in the *Using reminders to remember important events* recipe in *Chapter 3, Organizing Dynamics GP*. In this recipe, we'll take a look at creating custom reminders.

Getting ready

The first step in creating a custom reminder is to create a SmartList favorite. That topic was covered in detail in the last recipe, *Speeding access to SmartList favorites*, so this should be easy for everyone. We'll keep this example simple and assume that we simply want to be alerted about debit transactions over $1 million.

How to do it...

Once a SmartList favorite has been created, it can be turned into a custom reminder using the following steps:

1. Select the SmartList icon from the menu bar at the top, or select **Microsoft Dynamics GP Menu** from the top, and click on **SmartList**.

2. Select **Financial** and then **Account Transactions**.

3. Click Search. Set Column Name to Debit Amount. Set **Filter** to **is greater than** and **Value** to **1000000**.

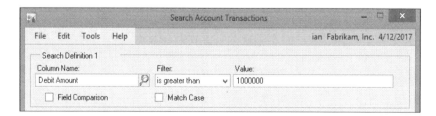

4. Click on **OK**.

5. Click on **Favorite** to save this as a favorite.

6. Name the favorite `Debit > $1m` and leave **Visible To** set to **System**.

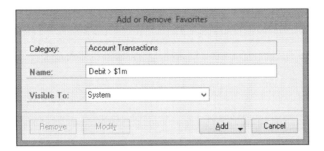

7. Click on **Add | Add Favorite and Reminder**.

8. Click on **Number of records**. Select **is greater than**. Leave the amount equal to zero. Check the **Display as a Cue** box and click on **OK**.

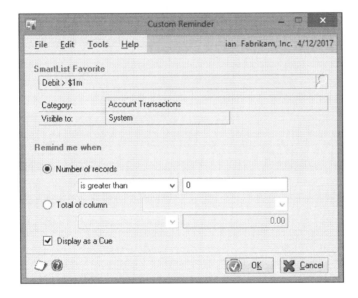

9. On the area page, click on the refresh button. The refresh button is two swirling arrows in the upper-right corner near the **Help** button. This refreshes the current page.

10. In the **Reminders** pane you should see the **Debit > $1m** reminder with the number of debit transactions over a million dollars.

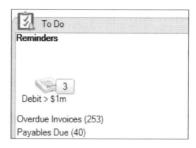

11. Click on the **Debit > $1m** line to drill back into the SmartList favorite:

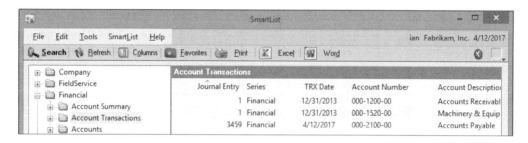

How it works...

Custom reminders start with SmartList favorites as their base and let users build reminders based on those results. This increases the power of reminders because the core SmartList itself can be narrowed to provide very targeted results that can then be used to drive the alert.

Different users will need to be reminded about different things. SmartList favorites provide opportunities to deliver relevant information to the right people in time for them to take action.

There's more...

Custom reminders can also be modified and removed. Users aren't locked in after creating them.

Modifying and removing custom reminders

It is possible to change a custom reminder by selecting **New Reminder** from the homepage, highlighting a reminder to change, and clicking on **Modify** instead of **New**. This reopens the **Custom Reminder** window allowing changes.

Additionally, selecting **Remove** instead of **Modify** will delete that reminder.

See also

▸ The *Improving information returned with SmartList Search* recipe

▸ The *Tailoring SmartLists by adding fields* recipe

Improving information returned with SmartList Search

The basic SmartLists included with Dynamics GP are great, but they really shine once companies figure out how to fine-tune and filter the records that are returned. The Search feature in SmartLists does just that, making it easy to see which invoices were generated on a particular date or which transactions affected a certain general ledger account during the month.

In this recipe, we'll look at how to better control the results that are returned using the Search feature in SmartLists. For our example, assume that auditors want to see any checkbook transactions over 10,000 dollars ($10,000) during the month of April 2017. We'll use the Dynamics GP sample company for this recipe.

How to do it...

To limit the results of a SmartList with the Search feature:

1. Select the SmartList icon from the menu bar at the top, or select **Microsoft Dynamics GP Menu** from the top, and click on **SmartList**.

2. Select **Financial** and then **Bank Transactions**.

3. Select **Search**.

4. In **Search Definition 1**, set **Column Name** to **Checkbook ID**, **Filter** to **is equal to**, and **Value** to **Uptown Trust**.

5. In **Search** just **Definition 2**, set **Column Name** to **GL Posting Date** and **Filter** to **is between**.

6. This opens up two date boxes. Set the dates to **4/1/2017** and **4/30/2017**.

7. In **Search Definition 3**, set **Column Name** to **Checkbook Amount**, **Filter** to **is greater than**, and **Value** to **10000**.

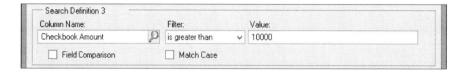

8. Click on **OK**.

9. The resulting SmartList is limited to only first bank transactions in April 2017 with amounts over $10,000.

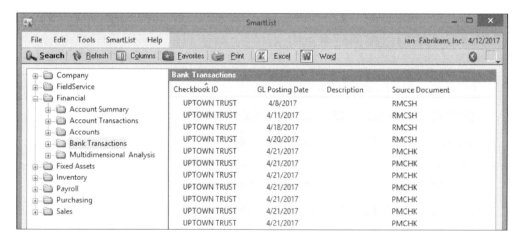

How it works...

By default, there are four available search boxes used to narrow results. However, with the **is between** option just shown in the demonstration, it's possible to effectively have more criteria than just the four boxes. The **is between** option adds two options in a single search box meaning that users don't have to use up to two boxes with the **greater than** and **less than** criteria.

There's more...

The **Field Comparison** and **Match Case** settings provide additional search features and the **Search Type** option changes the way that results are returned.

Field Comparison

The **Field Comparison** checkbox changes the **Value** field to a lookup field allowing the comparison of two values. This is useful for comparing fields in the system. For example, if a user wants to find cases where the subledger posting date is not equal to the GL posting date, **Field Comparison** would be a perfect tool.

Match Case

The **Match Case** checkbox makes a search case sensitive. Sometimes, it is important to find situations where data has been entered in all caps. This is a great way to use the **Match Case** option.

The **Match Case** option can be removed or set as the default via the **SmartList Options** window. This window is available by selecting **Administration** from the navigation pane and selecting **SmartList Options** under **Setup**.

Search Type

SmartLists default to a **Search Type** of **Match All**. This returns results that meet all of the criteria. From a technical standpoint, this is an "and" search. In our example, we found transactions for a specific checkbook between two dates and over a certain amount.

Switching **Search Type** to **Match 1** or **More** changes the search to an "or" type search. Our example would return transactions for a specific checkbook regardless of the date or amount. In short, it would return a mess. However, if I wanted transactions that were orders or invoices, **Match 1** or **More** would be perfect since a document can't be both an order and an invoice.

Wildcard search

In addition to all the SmartList features described in the preceding sections, there is also the ability to search with wildcards, which can be an incredibly powerful enhancement to the search; it is also a feature that is not documented in the SmartList manual or **Help** within Dynamics GP. There are four wildcards available for use:

Wildcard	Explanation
%	Zero or more characters
_	Exactly one character
[charlist]	Single or multiple characters in the list
[^charlist]	Single or multiple characters not in the list

This is an example of using the SmartList wildcard search to search for vendors with a name beginning with A, B, C, or D and where the city they're located in does not begin with a C:

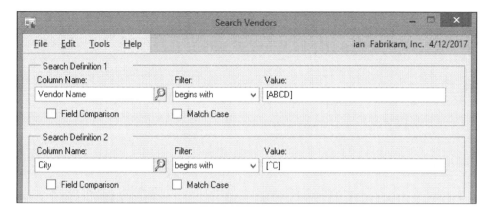

See also

▸ The *Speeding access to information with SmartList favorites* recipe

Controlling data with SmartList record limits

When running a SmartList, the number of records returned by the SmartList is shown in the lower-left corner. By default, SmartLists have a record limit of 1,000 records. The idea behind this default limit is to prevent long running SmartList queries from slowing down the system. However, sometimes it makes sense for queries to return more than a thousand records. For example, if a firm knows that they have more than a thousand fixed assets, it doesn't make sense to limit fixed assets' queries to a thousand, since most of the time this number will need to be adjusted. Similarly, many companies easily have more than a thousand bank transactions in a given month.

There are a few options for increasing or decreasing this record limit including adjusting it on the fly, adjusting the limit for a favorite, and setting a new default limit. We'll take a look at all of these options in this recipe.

How to do it...

To adjust record limits on the fly, complete the following steps:

1. Select the SmartList icon from the menu bar at the top, or select **Microsoft Dynamics GP Menu**, from the top and click on **SmartList**.

2. Select **Financial** and then **Bank Transactions**.

3. Select **Search**.

4. Increase the value in **Maximum Records**, located on the bottom left, to **10,000** and click on **OK**.

Adjusting limits on the fly only works for that session, the changes aren't saved. The easiest way to save new record limits is to save the SmartList as a favorite. To adjust record limits for a favorite, perform the following steps:

1. Select the SmartList icon from the menu bar at the top or select **Microsoft Dynamics GP Menu** from the top and click on **SmartList**.

2. Select **Financial** and then **Accounts**.

3. Select the **Account Number Favorite** setup discussed in the _Speeding access to information with SmartList favorites_ recipe.

4. Select **Search**.

5. Increase the value in **Maximum Records** to **10,000** and click on **OK**.

6. Click on **Favorites** and then click on **Modify** to save the new record limit.

5. The next time the **Account Number Favorite** setup is run, the record limit will be **10,000**.

6. Finally, if the number of records returned is consistently over a thousand, it makes sense to adjust the default record limit for a particular SmartList category. To adjust the default limit, perform the following steps:

   1. Click on **Administrator** in the navigation pane and then select **SmartList Options** under **Setup**.

   2. Select the appropriate **Category**. For our example, select **Accounts**.

   3. Change **Maximum Records** to 10,000 and click on **OK**.

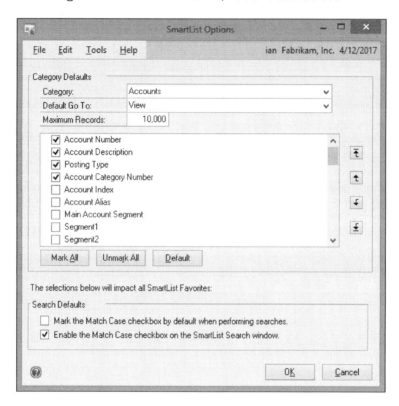

How it works...

By adjusting record limits, users and administrators gain improved productivity. If record limits are consistently too low, users waste time running SmartLists, adjusting record counts, and then running them again. If record limits are consistently set too high, users may create unacceptably long running queries, slowing the system down for all users.

Tailoring SmartLists by adding fields

Default SmartLists contain predefined sets of fields. However, users always want to add additional fields or rearrange existing columns. Fortunately, Dynamics GP provides this functionality out of the box.

Users can add fields to **SmartLists,** remove fields, or rearrange their order, allowing users to fine-tune **SmartLists** to meet their needs. In this recipe, we'll look at adding and rearranging fields in SmartLists.

How to do it...

To add a field to a SmartList, perform the following steps:

1. Select the SmartList icon from the menu bar at the top or select **Microsoft Dynamics GP Menu** from the top and click on **SmartList**.

2. Select **Financial** and then **Account Transactions** in the left pane.

3. Click on **Columns**.

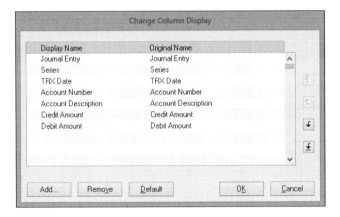

4. Click on **Add**. This exposes all of the available fields for a SmartList, not just the defaults.

5. Select **Account Type** and click on **OK** to add this field to the SmartList.

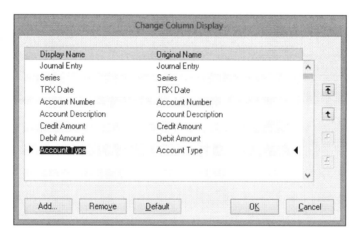

To rearrange fields on a SmartList, perform the following steps:

1. Continue on the current screen and select **Account Type**.

2. Click on the up arrow twice to move **Account Type** above **Credit Amount**.

3. Click on **Debit Amount** and click on the up arrow once to move it ahead of **Credit Amount**.

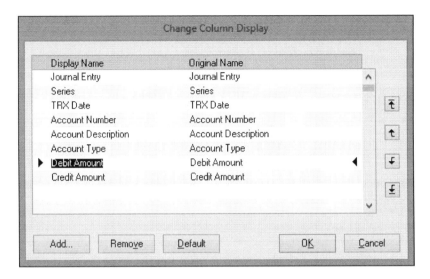

4. Click on **OK** to finish.

The ability to add, remove, and rearrange fields on a SmartList gives users even more control over SmartList reporting. When users can satisfy their own custom reporting needs, it significantly reduces the reporting burden for administrators.

There's more...

Sometimes users need to remove fields from SmartLists as well. Also, field changes are not saved from one session to another, so saving the SmartList as a favorite after the changes are made is important. Finally, it is possible to add, remove, and rearrange fields on the default SmartLists.

Removing fields

Sometimes a SmartList just has more information than needed. To remove fields and clean up a SmartList, click on **Columns**, select the column to delete, and click on **Remove**.

Favorites

Field changes to SmartLists are not saved. Clicking on another SmartList or otherwise moving off from a SmartList will cause field changes to reset. Saving the SmartList as a favorite, after the changes, is the only way to preserve field changes. The recipe *Speeding access to information with SmartLists favorites* has specifics on saving SmartLists.

Default SmartLists

The default SmartLists can also be modified to include or exclude columns and adjust the order as well. This is done by selecting **Administration** from the navigation pane and then selecting **SmartList Options** under **Setup**.

In this window, fields are added or removed by checking or unchecking the box next to a column. They can be reordered using the arrows at the right.

See also

> ▶ The *Renaming fields for clarity* recipe

Controlling access by sharing or restricting SmartList favorites

In the *Speeding access to information with SmartList favorites* recipe discussed earlier in this chapter, we looked at the benefits of saving SmartLists as favorites, along with how to make it happen. A key component of saving a favorite that is often overlooked is setting the visibility of the favorite.

The **Visibility To** field defines who has access to use and modify a particular SmartList favorite. Since there are only a couple of options, it is sometimes more difficult to get the visibility right. For example, consider a user who crafts a SmartList to meet his/her particular need but sets the visibility to **System**, making the SmartList available to everyone. He/she could find that another user has made changes and modified the favorite to save those changes. Now, our original user has to figure out how to put his/her favorite back together.

In this recipe, we'll look at how to set the visibility of a favorite and how to determine the right visibility to set.

How to do it...

The process to set the visibility of a favorite is as follows:

1. Select the SmartList icon from the menu bar at the top, or select **Microsoft Dynamics GP Menu** from the top, and click on **SmartList**.
2. Select **Financial** and then **Account Transactions**.

3. Select **Favorites** and name the favorite as `Account Trans`.

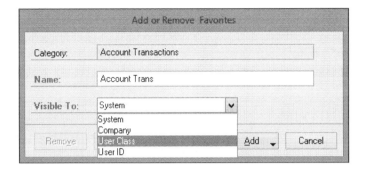

4. Set the **Visible To** property to **User Class** and click on **Add | Add Favorite**.

How it works...

The **Visible To** property of a favorite controls who has access to both run and modify a favorite.

There are four options available for setting visibility:

*   **System**: The favorite is available to all users with access to this SmartList category across all Dynamics GP companies.
*   **Company**: The favorite is available to all users with access to this SmartList category, but only for the company it was created in.
*   **User Class**: The favorite is available to all users in the same user class as the creator. Starting with Dynamics GP 10, user classes are no longer connected to user security, so it's easier for other groupings such as sharing favorites. This works well for limiting access to a small group of users.
*   **User**: The favorite is only available to the user who created the SmartList.

Too many users default to selecting **System** every time, but this exposes the favorite to everyone with access to that SmartList category. In many cases, **User Class** is the best option to select, because it limits access to a much smaller list and that list is most likely to be commonly shared. For critical SmartLists, selecting **User** will ensure that no one else can change it.

There's more...

Visibility isn't the only security control on SmartLists, but it is the most commonly used, and the only user-controllable option. In addition, there are some best practices for naming favorites.

SmartList security

Dynamics GP provides security options for administrators to control access to SmartLists. This only controls who can access a SmartList category, not individual SmartList favorites. For example, this controls which users have access to payroll-related SmartLists, but a user with access to the payroll category would have access to all of the information in that SmartLists category.

Favorite naming best practices

A best practice for naming SmartLists is to include the user's initials at the beginning of the name. This doesn't prevent another user from using or renaming this favorite, but it does remind users that they aren't the creators. It also makes it easy to change the name when modifying a Favorite. Simply change the initials to avoid overwriting the original favorite and click on **Modify**.

Renaming fields for clarity

SmartLists are full of cool features and they are great for throwing together a report quickly. But, sometimes the column names don't mean much to an average user or the way that a company uses a field is different from its original intent.

It's not only possible, but also easy to change the column description that shows up on a **SmartList**. In this recipe, we'll look at how to do that.

How to do it...

To change the name of a SmartList column, perform the following:

1. Select the SmartList icon from the menu bar at the top, or select **Microsoft Dynamics GP Menu** from the top, and click on **SmartList**.

2. Select **Financial** and then **Account Transactions** from the pane on the left.

3. Click on **Columns**.

4. Click on **TRX Date** under the **Display Name** heading. Type `Journal Date` right over the old name and click on **OK**.

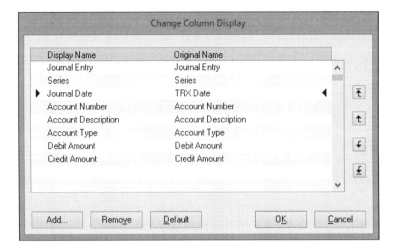

How it works...

Changing the column names in a SmartList doesn't change the name in the database; it uses the new name as an alias to overlay the database name for reporting. Notice that the title in the **Original Name** column doesn't change. This means that there is no way to save the new column name to the default SmartList. However, the new column names can be saved as part of a favorite.

Additionally, when exporting a SmartList to Excel, the new column name is passed to Excel. This means that this recipe can be a great timesaver for users who regularly export SmartLists to Excel and then rename columns.

There's more...

Column names can be changed for default SmartLists.

Default SmartList column names

The column names can be changed for the default SmartLists as well. To demonstrate how to do this, perform the following steps:

1. Click on **Administration** in the navigation pane on the left.

2. In the **Administration** area page, select **SmartList Options** under **Setup | System**.

3. Select **Accounts** for the **Category** field.

4. Select **Account Category Number** and key category description in its place.

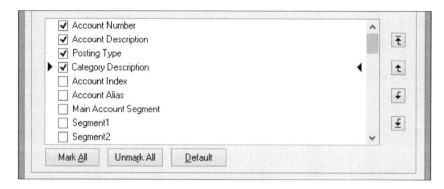

5. Click on **OK** to save the new default description.

This example is quite a relevant one as the **Account Category Number** field actually contains the description of the account category.

See also

▶ The *Tailoring SmartLists by adding fields* recipe

▶ The *Speeding access to information with SmartList favorites* recipe

6
Connecting Dynamics GP to Microsoft Office 2013

Dynamics GP provides tight integration with Microsoft Office 2013 across multiple integration points. This chapter looks at the options for connecting Dynamics GP with Microsoft Office. We will see the following recipes:

- ▶ Building analyses by exporting SmartLists to Microsoft Excel
- ▶ Delivering flexibility by exporting navigation lists to Excel
- ▶ Improving reports by sending SmartLists to Word
- ▶ Communicating with customers using letters from Microsoft Word
- ▶ Skipping the exports by using prebuilt Excel reports
- ▶ Reporting on any Dynamics GP data with direct Excel connections
- ▶ Importing data with Microsoft Word and a Dynamics GP macro
- ▶ Getting fine grain control of Excel exports from SmartList
- ▶ Gaining flexibility by printing documents with Microsoft Word

Introduction

With *Chapter 6, Connecting Dynamics GP to Microsoft Office 2013*, we move out of working only in Dynamics GP and look at connecting Dynamics GP with Microsoft Office 2013. Dynamics GP provides a number of interaction points with Office and we'll look at ways to connect Dynamics GP with Word and Excel. This chapter also covers some ways to use Office applications to improve processes in Dynamics GP.

The connection between Dynamics GP and Office 2013 provides a platform for using all of the great functionality found in Office to leverage the data in GP for analysis, reporting, and communication. Let's go play with Office!

Building analyses by exporting SmartLists to Microsoft Excel

Continuing a simple to complex theme, we move on to another straightforward process, exporting **SmartLists** to Microsoft Excel. Dynamics GP allows users to export any SmartList to Excel with the simple push of a button. In this recipe, we'll look at how to export SmartLists and some of the considerations around exports.

How to do it...

Exporting a SmartList to Excel is easy to do. Here is how:

1. Select the SmartList icon from the menu bar at the top or select **Microsoft Dynamics GP** menu from the top and click on **SmartList**.

2. Select **Financial | Account Summary** from the **SmartList** window.

3. Once the SmartList finishes loading, click on the **Excel** button.

4. Dynamics GP will export the data to Excel in the same order and with the same columns as the SmartList.

5. Once the export is complete, Excel will open with the completed data, as shown in following screenshot:

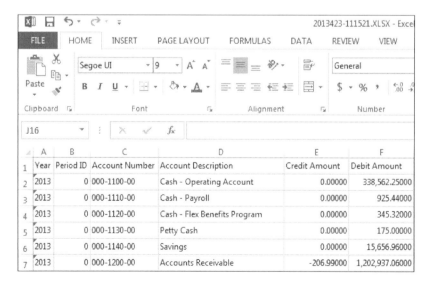

How it works...

The simplicity of the export to Excel process belies the power of this feature. Other applications often require saving the export to a file and then opening that file in Excel. Dynamics GP provides a simple push button connection to Excel. Each time the **Excel** button is pushed, a new Excel file is created to hold the exported data.

One potential drawback to this feature is that once the data is in Excel, it is static data. Changes to the data in Dynamics GP require a new export. The Excel file is not updated automatically.

See also

- ▸ The *Turning on more features with Dex.ini settings* recipe in *Chapter 8, Improving Dynamics GP with Hacks*

- ▸ The *Getting fine grain control of Excel exports from SmartList* recipe

Delivering flexibility by exporting navigation lists to Excel

The big Excel button on the SmartList window provides a visual cue that SmartLists can be exported to Microsoft Excel. That same blinding flash of the obvious is not available for navigation lists. Navigation lists provide another way to interact with information in Dynamics GP and they can be filtered and limited like SmartLists. Navigation lists don't have a big Excel button so in this recipe we will look at how to export navigation list data to Excel.

How to do it...

To export a navigation list to Excel:

1. Select **Financial** from the navigation pane.
2. At the top of the navigation pane, select **Accounts** to open up the accounts list.
3. Mark the checkbox in the header next to **Account Number** to select all accounts.

4. On the ribbon at the top select **Go To** and then **Send to Excel**.

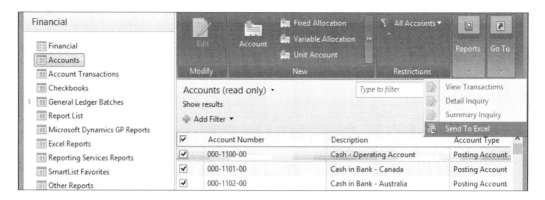

5. Excel will open with the data from the list.

How it works...

Navigation lists provide another way to work inside of Dynamics GP by blending data with a ribbon-like interface. This setup is designed to allow users to perform associated entries, inquiries, and reporting from a single screen for a series in Dynamics GP. The ability to export SmartLists from the navigation list interface means that there is one less reason to leave these consolidated screens.

See also

▸ The *Turning on more features with Dex.ini settings* recipe in *Chapter 8, Improving Dynamics GP with Hacks*

Improving reports by sending SmartLists to Word

Microsoft Excel isn't the only Office product that SmartLists can be exported to. They can also be exported to Microsoft Word. This can be useful for exporting records for inclusion in a report, financial statement footnotes, or any other type of Word document.

Like the export to Excel feature, exporting to Word is very easy to do. In this recipe, we'll take a look at how and why you would want to export SmartLists to Word. For our example, we'll use a very small set of records showing retained earnings beginning balances for several years from the sample company.

This type of data could be useful for inclusion in financial statement footnotes, for example.

How to do it...

To send a SmartList to Microsoft Word:

1. Select the SmartList icon from the icon bar at the top or select **Microsoft Dynamics GP** from the top and click on **SmartList**.

2. Select **Financial | Account Summary** in the left pane of the SmartList window.

3. Click on **Search**. In the **Search Definition 1** panel, set **Column Name** as Period ID, select the **Filter** field value **is equal to**, and enter **Value** as 0.

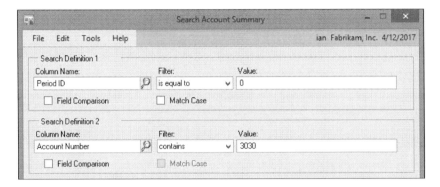

4. In the **Search Definition 2** panel, set the **Column Name** field to Account Number, select the **Filter** field value as **contains**, and enter **Value** as 3030 and click on **OK**.

5. Period 0 contains the beginning balances for each year and account 3030 is the retained earnings account in the sample company.

6. Click on the **Word** button to send this data to Microsoft Word.

7. Microsoft Word will open a new document with the SmartList data included in a Word table format, as shown in the following screenshot:

Year	Period ID	Account Number	Account Description	Credit Amount	Debit Amount
2013	0	000-3030-00	Retained Earnings	($466,119.46)	$36,183.69
2014	0	000-3030-00	Retained Earnings	$460,708.41	$36,183.69

How it works...

The nature of Microsoft Word makes this feature less useful than Excel for processing large amounts of tabular data. However, if users need to insert small amounts of data into a much larger document, then exporting the data to Word is an easy way to get tabular data into a report. Typically, once exported to Word, the data would be cut and pasted into the larger report document, keeping the table intact.

Saving the related SmartList as a favorite makes this process easily repeatable and provides a consistent data set.

See also

▸ The *Improving information returned with SmartList search* recipe in *Chapter 5, Harnessing the Power of SmartLists*

▸ The *Tailoring SmartLists by adding Fields and Renaming Fields for Clarity* recipe in *Chapter 5, Harnessing the Power of SmartLists*

▸ The *Getting fine grain control of Excel exports from SmartList* recipe

Communicating with customers using letters from Microsoft Word

SmartList exports to Word are useful but the **Letter Writing Assistant** feature is where the connection between Dynamics GP and Microsoft Word really shines. The Letter Writing Assistant uses built-in or user developed Word templates to create letters using information in Dynamics GP. Since the letters are based on the mail merge feature in Word, creating and manipulating templates follows the Word mail merge standards. Even better, the Letter Writing Assistant uses a wizard-style interface to build letters.

Dynamics GP comes with a selection of prebuilt letters for collections, customers, vendors, employees, and applicants. In this recipe, we'll look at using the prebuilt letters to create the most common type of mailing, collection letters.

How to do it...

To use the Letter Writing Assistant, perform the following steps:

1. From the menu bar select **Reports | Letter Writing Assistant** to start the wizard and click on **Next** to get started.
2. Select **Prepare the letters using an existing letter** and click on **Next**.
3. Select **Collection**, then click on **Next**.

4. Check the **181 and over** box and click on **Next**. Ranges of customers can also be selected here but we'll limit our example to just clients over 180 days past due for simplicity.

5. Select **Final Notice** and click on **Next**.

6. The next screen provides the ability to unmark certain customers to prevent them from getting collection letters. Click on **Next** to continue.

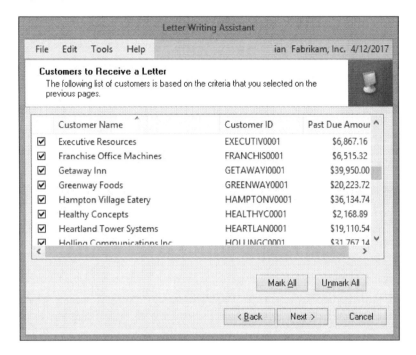

7. Finish the assistant by adding the name and contact info for the company representative and click on **Finish**. Enter your name and contact information for our sample.

8. Microsoft Word will open and each letter will have its own page.

The Dynamics GP Letter Writing Assistant uses a GP wizard and mail merge functionality to insert information from Dynamics GP into letters in Word. The wizard driven nature of this feature makes a complex process extremely simple to complete.

There's more...

In addition to our example, SmartList favorites can be created and used to select information for letters. Additionally, users are not confined to built-in letters but can modify letters or build their own. Finally, there are other starting points for the Letter Writing Assistant, not just the Reports menu.

SmartList favorites

On the **Prepare a Letter** screen of the Letter Writing Assistant, the selection box can be changed to **SmartList Selection**, allowing the use of a SmartList favorite for letter selection and population.

Letter customization

Selecting **Customize the letters** by adding new letters or changing existing letters on the second screen of the wizard changes the wizard path and walks a user through modifying existing letters and creating new letters.

Other starting points

Reports | Letter Writing Assistant is not the only place that the Letter Writing Assistant can be started from. Various windows including **Customer Maintenance**, **Vendor Maintenance**, and **Employee Maintenance** include a **Write Letters** button with the Word logo. Selecting this button drops down a set of options to start the Letter Writing Assistant at the appropriate point in the wizard.

See also

> ▸ The *Speeding access to information with SmartList favorites* recipe in *Chapter 5, Harnessing the Power of SmartLists*

Skipping the exports by using prebuilt Excel reports

The connections we've looked at so far between Dynamics GP and Excel have been one way and static: data moved from Dynamics GP to Excel. Once in Excel, users could analyze and manipulate data but when information in Dynamics GP changed, the user would need to re-export the data and rerun any analyses.

Microsoft Dynamics GP 2010 provided a new set of Excel-based reports to which Dynamics GP 2013 added. These reports use the new **Office Data Connection** (**ODC**) to provide a live connection to Dynamics GP. Unlike exports, when data changes in Dynamics GP, these Excel reports can be easily refreshed to include the new data.

In this recipe, we look at how to deploy and use Excel reports in Microsoft Dynamics GP.

Getting ready

Prior to using Excel reports, they need to be deployed. This can be done to a simple shared file location on the company's network or to **Microsoft SharePoint Server** (**MSS**). We'll look at deploying Excel reports to a shared file location.

1. Create or select a file location. For our example, ensure that the location `C:\xlreports` exists.

2. Select **Administration** from the navigation pane on the left side. On the **Administration** area page, select **Reporting Tools Setup** under **Setup**. Enter the system password if prompted.

3. Select the **Excel Reports** tab, set **Location** to **Network Share** and enter `C:\xlreports` in both **Reports Directory** fields. Check the company the Excel reports should be deployed to and redeploy data connections for all existing companies. Click on **Deploy Reports**.

4. For our example, we are deploying system and user-level Excel reports to the same place for simplicity.

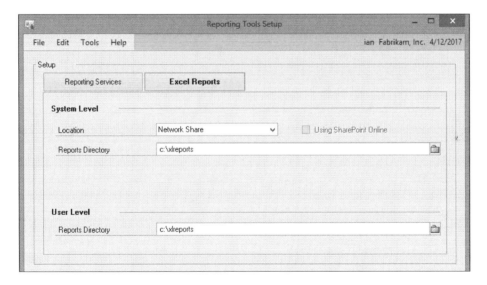

5. Click on **Print Status Report** to view the Deployment report, check **Screen**, and click on **OK**.

6. Validate that the **Deployment Status** field shows **Deployed**.

7. This process has now deployed the Excel reports and the appropriate data connections. Now let's look at how to use them.

How to do it...

There are two options to run Excel reports. They can be run from within Dynamics GP or from Excel. Let's see how to do both.

To start an Excel report from within Dynamics GP, perform the following steps:

1. Select **Financial** from the navigation pane. In the top section of the navigation pane select **Excel Reports**.

2. If Excel reports does not appear after deploying the reports, restart Dynamics GP.

3. Double-click the **Account Summary** report (it will be preceded by the company identifier. For the sample company it's TWO AccountSummary).

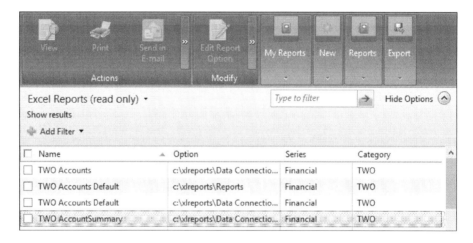

4. Excel will open. Click on **Enable** if a security warning opens in Excel.

5. The Excel report will open with filter handles already in place for filtering columns.

6. Right-click on one of the headings and select **Refresh** to force the report to bring in updated information from Dynamics GP.

To start an Excel report directly:

1. Open up Windows Explorer and navigate to the location where the reports were deployed. Drill into the appropriate company and module. In our example, this was `C:\XLReports\Reports\TWO\Financial`.

2. Double-click on the file named **TWO AccountSummary Default**.

3. Excel will open. If a security warning displays, select **Options | Enable Content** and click on **OK**.

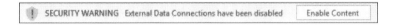

4. The Excel report will open with filter handles already in place for filtering columns.

5. Right-click on one of the headings and select **Refresh** to force the report to bring in updated information from Dynamics GP.

How it works...

Excel reports leverage Microsoft's new Office Data Connection to provide easily accessible, updateable reports. With the older style **Open Database Connectivity** (**ODBC**) connections, users had to have the connections set up on their machines. The portability of the new connectors makes sharing Excel reports based on live data much easier.

Additionally, these reports are much faster than SmartList exports. The data returns almost instantly and is presented with some basic formatting already intact.

For users who want to modify Excel reports or build their own, these reports are still based on Excel at their core. Users can add calculations, move columns, and more, then save the reports with a new name. In most cases, the reports will maintain their connections to Dynamics GP.

There's more...

For users who want to build custom Excel reports, Microsoft offers **Excel Report Builder** as a part of SmartList Builder. Experienced database administrators will find a lot to like in the new Office Data Connectors and there is an easy way to avoid those security prompts.

Excel Report Builder

As part of the SmartList Builder add-on, Microsoft offers an Excel Report Builder that allows the user to select fields, order columns, add calculations, and limit records to create a unique Excel report. The process works just like SmartList Builder and the Excel Report Builder screen is almost identical to SmartList Builder. The end result, however, is a refreshable Excel report.

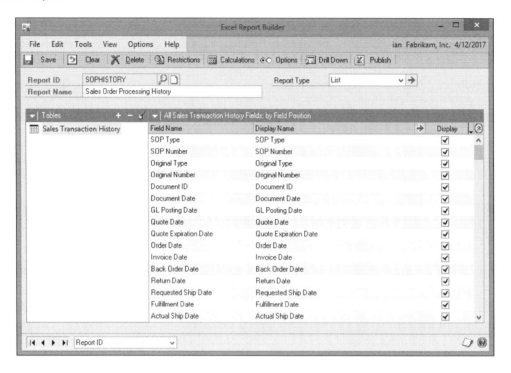

SQL and ODC connections

For experienced administrators, the Excel files can be modified directly by selecting **Data | Connections | Properties** from within Excel and selecting the **Definition** tab. This allows the manipulation of the underlying SQL query letting administrators add, remove, or reorder fields and, in general, manipulate the report in almost any way possible.

Once completed, the changes can be saved to a new Excel file, to the original Excel file, or saved back as part of the ODC file, making the changes available to all reports based on that connector.

This is not for the inexperienced, but knowledgeable database administrators will find tremendous power in the ability to manipulate the underlying SQL code.

Trust and security

When opening Excel reports, Excel will return a security warning because there is a live connection back to a database. To prevent these warnings from showing:

1.   Select the **File** tab in Excel and pick **Options**.

2.   Click on **Trust Center** then **Trust Center Settings**.

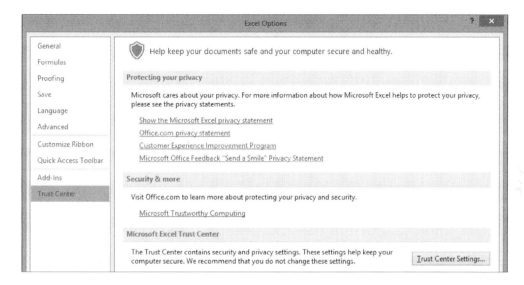

3.   Click on **Trusted Locations** on the left side then **Add New Location** in the center at the bottom.

4.   Add the location of the Excel reports. In our example this was `C:\xlreports`.

5.   Check that subfolders of this location are also trusted and click on **OK**.

6.   Click on **OK** to accept the changes and return to the **Excel Options** window.

See also

▶   The *Reporting on any Dynamics GP data with direct Excel connections recipe*

Reporting on any Dynamics GP data with direct Excel connections

In an earlier recipe, we looked at deploying and using the Excel reports contained in Dynamics GP. For all of the power of those dynamic reports, one thing is missing, the ability to modify the type of data being returned from within Excel. Excel reports allow filtering. However, if a user only needs a subset of data, using filters can make it difficult to work with only the filtered data. Also, Excel reports bring in all of the available rows, creating a much larger data set to work with and possibly overwhelming Excel.

Fortunately there is another option. The Microsoft Query tool included with Excel can work with **ODBC** to connect to live data in Dynamics GP. This process is as fast as Excel reports, allows user changeable parameters from Excel, and can be refreshed just like Excel reports. However, there are no prebuilt reports that use ODBC connections so users have to build these from scratch.

To demonstrate the power of Excel queries we'll build a simple account summary report with user selectable years in this recipe. Our ingredients are Dynamics GP and Microsoft Excel 2013.

How to do it...

To build a direct connection between GP and Excel, perform the followings steps:

1. Open Microsoft Excel 2013 and select **Data | Get External Data | From Other Sources | From Microsoft Query**. This will start the MS Query Wizard.

2. Select the data source used to log in to Dynamics GP. The default data source is named Dynamics GP. Click on **OK**.

3. Enter sa as the username and the sa password. Either sa or another SQL user is required here. A trusted connection can be used if properly set up. Encryption between the GP login and SQL Server prevents a regular GP login from being used for this task.

4. Click on **Options** and select the TWO database. Click on **OK** to start the MS Query Wizard.

5. In the Query Wizard, scroll to the table named GL11110. Click on the plus sign (**+**) to expand the columns available.

6. Find and select the column named **ACTNUMBR_1** and click on the right arrow (**>**) to add it to the **Columns in your query** box, as shown in the following screenshot:

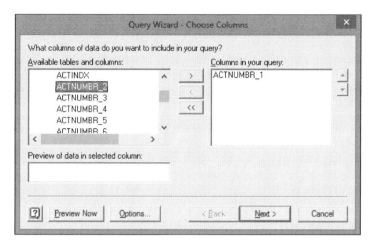

7. Repeat this process for the columns, as shown in the next screenshot.

8. The vertical arrow keys on the right side can be used to reorder columns if necessary. Click on **Next** when finished.

9. In the **Filter Data** window, select **YEAR1**. In the **Only Include rows where** section pick e**quals** and **2017**. Click on **Next** to continue.

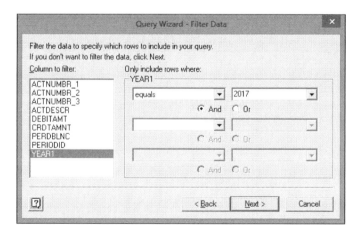

10. Click on **Next** to move past the next screen and select **View data or edit query in Microsoft Query**. Click on **Finish** to open MS Query and review the details.

11. Once MSQuery opens, select **2017** next to **Value**. Change it to **[SumYear]** and press *Tab*.

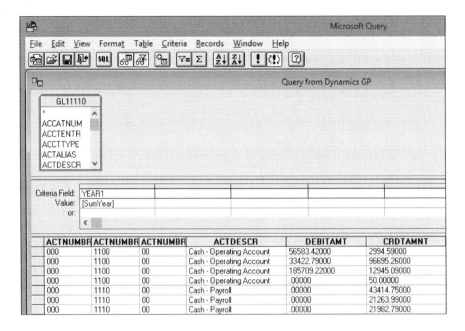

12. Enter 2017 in the box that opens and click on **OK**. This changes 2017 from a value to a variable and then inserts 2017 as the initial value for that variable.

13. Select **File | Return data to Microsoft Office Excel**.

14. In the **Import Data** box, check **Existing worksheet** and enter =A5, then click on **OK**:

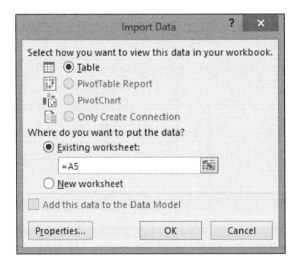

15. The data from Dynamics GP will now show up in Excel, as shown in the following screenshot:

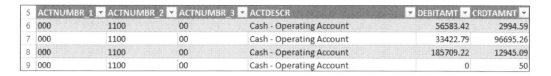

	ACTNUMBR_1	ACTNUMBR_2	ACTNUMBR_3	ACTDESCR	DEBITAMT	CRDTAMNT
5						
6	000	1100	00	Cash - Operating Account	56583.42	2994.59
7	000	1100	00	Cash - Operating Account	33422.79	96695.26
8	000	1100	00	Cash - Operating Account	185709.22	12945.09
9	000	1100	00	Cash - Operating Account	0	50

16. In cell **A1** type `Year`.

17. In cell **A2** type `2017`.

18. Click on the `ACTNUMBR_1` heading from the imported data. Select **Data | Connections | Properties | Definition**, as shown in the following screenshot.

19. Click on **Export Connection File** and save the file to create a portable Office Data Connection file with the embedded parameter.

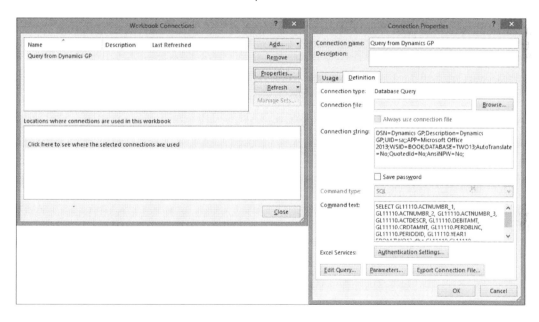

20. Click on **Parameters**.

21. Select **SumYear**. Mark **Get the value from the following cell**. Key in =A2. Mark the checkbox **Refresh automatically when cell value changes**. Click on **OK** and close all of the other open windows.

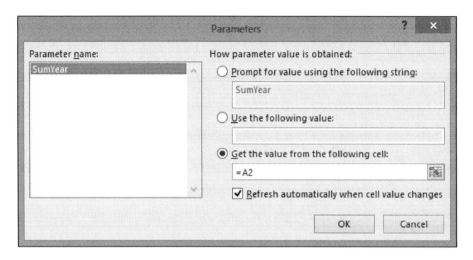

22. Change the cell value in cell **A2** to 2016. Press *Tab* and all the values in the sheet will change to reflect data from 2016:

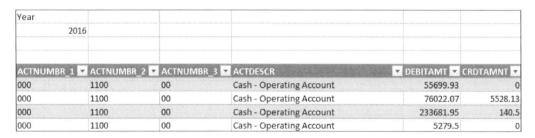

Year						
2016						
ACTNUMBR_1	ACTNUMBR_2	ACTNUMBR_3	ACTDESCR		DEBITAMT	CRDTAMNT
000	1100	00	Cash - Operating Account		55699.93	0
000	1100	00	Cash - Operating Account		76022.07	5528.13
000	1100	00	Cash - Operating Account		233681.95	140.5
000	1100	00	Cash - Operating Account		5279.5	0

23. Save the Excel file. Reopening the file allows the user to simply change the year, press *Tab* and get updated values.

How it works...

This recipe provides a live connection from Excel to Dynamics GP and the data returned is determined by selections made in the Excel spreadsheet. In this case, Excel uses an ODBC connection to return data from Dynamics GP, passing a parameter as part of the query to control the information returned. Any field in the query could be used as the parameter field and multiple parameters can be used as well. This provides incredible control for live reporting of Dynamics GP data.

The key differences between this recipe and the Excel reports covered in the *Skipping the exports by using prebuilt Excel reports* recipe are the type of connection and the need to build ODBC based reports from scratch. GP's Excel-based reports create a portable connection automatically making them easy to share but they don't support user changeable parameters. Excel reports based on an ODBC connection require the user to have the appropriate ODBC connection set up on their PC for initial creation and then save a portable connection. ODBC-based reports also provide greater control over the data returned. Additionally, since there are no prebuilt reports based on ODBC connections, these reports need to be built from scratch, making them harder to get started with.

There's more...

The biggest difficulty that comes up with this recipe is determining which Dynamics GP tables to use. Also, for experienced database administrators even more control is available.

Tables

The part that bedevils users is figuring out what table holds the data they need. Dynamics GP is full of tools to assist with that and some of the more common tools are found under **Tools | Resource Descriptions** in the **Support Debugging Tool**, which is covered in more detail in *Chapter 11, Extending Dynamics GP with the Support Debugging Tool*, and an Excel-based table reference available from DynamicAccounting.net at http://msdynamicsgp.blogspot.com/2008/10/lots-of-dynamics-gp-table-resources.html.

Advanced options

Experienced database administrators will quickly realize that they can use more complex SQL joins, views, and just about anything that they can come up with by using the SQL button in MS Query. There are some limitations, though. Excel may refuse to allow parameters if the SQL query is too complex. The best option in that case is to wrap a complex query into a view or stored procedure, simplifying it for Excel.

Importing data with Microsoft Word and a Dynamics GP macro

Throughout this chapter we've looked at a number of ways to send data from Dynamics GP to Microsoft Word and Excel. With this recipe, we'll look at using Word and Excel to bring data into Dynamics GP.

Microsoft offers a number of import tools for Dynamics GP including **Integration Manager**, **Table Import**, and **eConnect**. In addition there are third-party tools available, such as **Scribe** (`http://www.scribesoft.com/microsoft-dynamics-gp.asp`) or **SmartConnect** (`http://www.eonesolutions.com.au/content.aspx?page=SmartConnect+for+GP`). However, these tools are not included by default and some firms don't purchase them as part of their solution. Additionally, some areas of the system simply don't have reasonable options to import data. In many cases the combination of Microsoft Excel, Microsoft Word, and a Dynamics GP macro can allow importing via the user interface. The basic steps are to create a macro, apply the new data to the macro using Word's mail merge functionality, and then run the macro to import the data. In this recipe we'll take a look at how to do that.

Getting ready

For this example we'll import segment descriptions for the third segment of the chart of accounts in the sample company. This is a common import requirement and somewhat difficult to do since this is normally updating information, not importing from scratch.

To set up the data to be imported:

1. Open Microsoft Excel to a new, blank Excel spreadsheet.

2. In cell **A1** enter Segment3. In cell **B1** enter Description.

3. In cell **A2** enter '01. In **B2** enter Marketing. Be sure to put an apostrophe in front of 01 to force Excel to treat this as text.

4. Repeat this process with the data included until the spreadsheet looks like this screenshot:

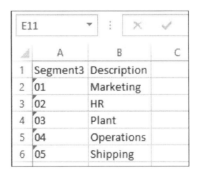

5. Save the sheet to the desktop as Segment3Import.

Now that we have our source data, we can import it into Dynamics GP.

How to do it...

To setup and import data via Microsoft Word and a Macro we first create the macro like this:

1. In Dynamics GP, select **Financial** from the navigation pane and click on **Segment** in the setup area.

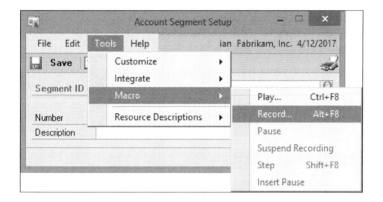

2. Select **Tools | Macro | Record**. Click on **Desktop** on the left to save the macro to the desktop. Name the macro Segment3.mac and click on **OK** to save it.

3. In **Segment ID**, click the lookup button (magnifying glass) and select **Department**. In the **Number** field type 01. Don't use the lookup button.

4. In the **Description** box enter Marketing and click on **Save**.

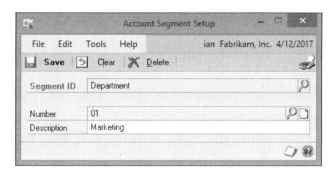

5. Select **Tools | Macro | Stop Record** to end the macro recording.

To use Word's mail merge functionality to add all of the data into the macro:

1. Open Microsoft Word and click on **File | Open**. Select **Desktop** on the left.

2. Change **All Word Documents** to **All Files** in the drop-down box next to the **File Name**.

3. Select the Segment3.mac file created earlier and press **Open**.

4. In Word, select **Mailings**. Then pick **Select Recipients | Use Existing List**.

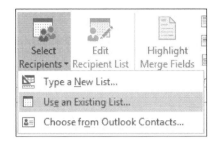

5. Click on **Desktop** on the left side, select the `Segment3Import` file created in *Getting ready* and click on **Open**.

6. Click on **OK** to use `Sheet1$`.

7. Find and select `01` with the left-mouse button. Do not highlight or delete the single quotes around `01`.

```
ActivateWindow dictionary 'default'  form 'GL_Segment_Maintenance' window
'GL_Segment_Maintenance'
  TypeTo field 'Segment ID' , '01'
```

8. Select **Insert Merge Field**, then **Segment3**:

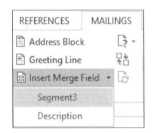

9. This will ultimately replace `01` with the value in `Segment3`.

```
ActivateWindow dictionary 'default'  form 'GL_Segment_Maintenance' window
'GL_Segment_Maintenance'
  TypeTo field 'Segment ID' , '«Segment3»'
```

10. Find and select `Marketing`, but do not highlight or delete the single quotes around `Marketing`.

```
TypeTo field Description , 'Marketing'
MoveTo field 'Save Button'
ClickHit field 'Save Button'
```

11. Select **Insert Merge Field**, then **Description**. This will ultimately replace Marketing with the value in Description.

```
TypeTo field Description , '«Description»'
MoveTo field 'Save Button'
ClickHit field 'Save Button'
```

12. Select **Preview Results** to see what the mail merge will send to GP.

13. Select **Finish & Merge | Edit Individual Documents** then click on **OK** to have Word merge in all of the values from Excel. A new document opens with the macro code duplicated for each value in the source file.

14. Select the new document and select **File | Save As | Other Formats**.

15. Select **Desktop** on the left and change the **Save as** type to **Plain Text**. Name the file Segment3Macro.txt and click on **Save**. Select **OK** when prompted.

16. Close Microsoft Word.

17. Move to the desktop and right-click on Segment3Macro.txt. Select **Rename** and change the file name to Segment3Macro.mac. Click on **OK** when prompted.

So far we've created a base macro and populated it with our data. Next we'll look at running the macro.

1. Back in Dynamics GP select **Financial** from the navigation pane and select **Segment** in the setup area.

2. Select **Tools | Macro | Play** and select **Desktop** on the left side. Click on Segment3Macro.mac and click on **Open**. The macro will run and populate the description. Click on **OK** when the macro finishes.

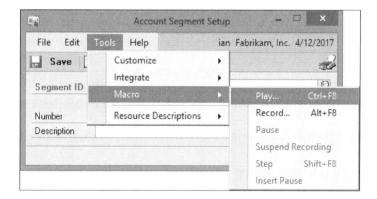

How it works...

Populating Dynamics GP via macros has a long history of use in the product. This process mimics a user's data entry so all of GP's security controls still apply. Additionally, the Dynamics GP business logic is applied as the data is integrated. Macros for import are primarily used when other options are either unavailable or prohibitively expensive in terms of either time or actual costs. Additionally, since the macro simply mimics a user's input, some firms use this process as an accepted way to avoid the paperwork that can be required for updates via SQL.

Though setting up the macro can be a little tedious, imagine how long it would take to correctly enter 200, 2,000, or 20,000 records like this by hand.

There's more...

There are some very important limitations that come with using Microsoft Word and macros to populate Dynamics GP.

Limitations

Because macros mimic screen input, screensavers can interfere with macro entry. I've seen employees sit and jiggle the mouse every five minutes for hours to prevent a group policy controlled screensaver from blanking their screen. This limitation also applies to Terminal Server and Citrix sessions. Leaving a session, even to just check e-mail, terminates the macro.

If a macro is being run overnight the User Date Change message will also interrupt the macro and prevent it running. Adding the following to the [General] section of the Dex.ini file will suppress the following message:

```
SuppressChangeDateDialog=TRUE
```

Additionally, there is no error control in macros. If a macro fails because of data or other issues, users have to delete the macro code up to just before the failure, fix the issue, and continue running the macro from the point it failed. One key point to remember is the macro simply fails; it does not roll back any entered data.

Finally, macros only work with consistent processes. If, for example, GP opens a dialogue box for one set of circumstance but not for another, a macro won't work because it can't process alternative paths.

Getting fine grain control of Excel exports from SmartList

In a previous recipe, we looked at how to export SmartLists to Excel with the push of a button. That method creates a new Excel file each time. In many cases users need to export the same set of data on a regular basis and build it into a formatted report via Excel. There's a way to accomplish this with SmartList exports. The feature is called **Export Solutions** and it's the focus of this recipe.

Getting ready

For our recipe, we'll assume that we have an Account Summary report that we want to format with a title and headers the same way every time. To begin we need to set it up the first time.

1. Select the SmartList icon from the menu bar at the top or select the Microsoft Dynamics GP menu from the top and click on **SmartList**.

2. Select **Financial | Account Summary** on the left to generate a SmartList.

3. Click on the **Excel** button to send the SmartList to Excel.

4. In Excel, select the **File | Options | Customize Ribbon** and ensure that the **Developer** checkbox is marked in the **Main Tabs** list. Click on **OK**.

5. Click on the **Developer** tab and select **Record** macro. Accept the default name of Macro1 and click on **OK**.

6. Highlight Rows 1 to 5, right-click, and select **Insert**.

7. Bold the titles in cells **A6-F6**.

8. In cell **A1**, enter Sample Excel Solution.

9. From the **Developer** tab, select **Stop Recording**.

10. Highlight and delete all the rows.

11. Save the file in C:\SmartLists with the name AccountSummary.xlsm.

How to do it...

To setup an export solution:

1. In Dynamics GP, select **Microsoft Dynamics GP** then click on **SmartList**.

2. Select **Financial | Account Summary** in the left pane to generate a SmartList.

3. Click on **Favorites**. Name the favorite `Export Solution` and click on **Add | Add Favorite**.

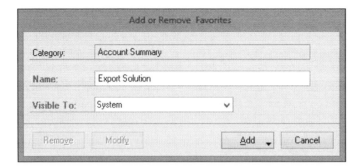

4. Back in the **SmartList** window, select **SmartList | Export Solutions**. Name the solution `ExportSolution`. Set the path to `C:\AccountSummary.xlsm` and the **Completion Macro** to `Macro1`, as shown in the following screenshot:

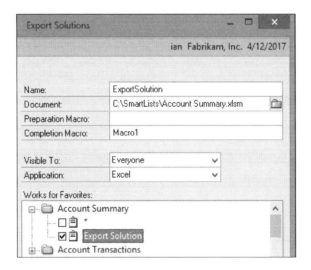

5. Check the box next to the SmartList favorites under **Account Summary** named **Export Solution** and click on **Save**, then close the window.

6. Back in the **SmartList** window, select the **Export Solution** favorite under **Account Summary** and click on the **Excel** button.

7. Instead of opening Excel, there are now two options. The **Quick Export** option performs a typical Excel export. The **Export Solution** option will open the Excel file named `AccountSummary.xlsm`, export the data, and run the macro named `Macro1`.

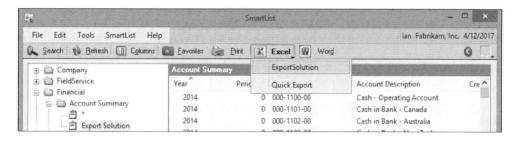

8. Click on the **Export Solution** option and watch the file open and the macro execute.

How it works...

The **Export Solution** feature adds a tremendous amount of power and control to the basic Excel export functionality. The ability to run an Excel macro before and after the export opens up a host of possibilities for reporting. Additionally, once an Export Solution is setup, it's very easy for an average user to run it with just a couple of clicks.

See also

▸ The *Building analyses by exporting SmartLists to Microsoft Excel* recipe

Gaining flexibility by printing documents with Microsoft Word

A feature introduced in Dynamics GP 2010 was the ability to print sales and purchasing documents using Microsoft Word templates instead of Report Writer reports; Dynamics GP 2013 adds a number of additional Microsoft Word templates. The use of Microsoft Word to create documents provides greater flexibility in field placement, logo use, and formatting. Users can now print phenomenal looking documents such as orders, invoices, and purchase orders with Word as the backbone.

For this recipe, we'll look at how to print an invoice using Microsoft Word and the sample company. Then we'll look at some of the setup options around Word templates.

How to do it...

To print an invoice using a Word template in the GP 2013 sample company, perform the following steps:

1. Select **Sales** from the navigation pane on the left.

2. On the Sales area page, click on **Sales Transaction Entry** under **Transactions**.

3. Change **Type ID** to **Invoice**.

4. Use the lookup button (magnifying glass) to select invoice **INVS3014** from the sample company.

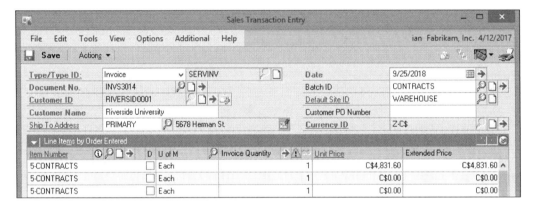

5. Click on the printer icon in the upper-right corner.

6. Check the **Invoices** box on the left side and click on the **Print** button.

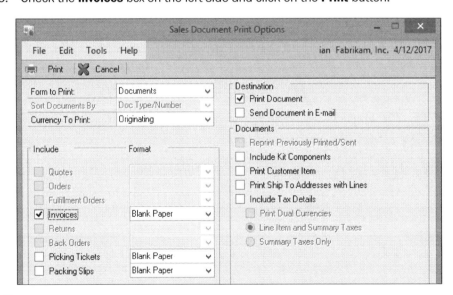

7. Ensure that the **Report Type** in the center is set to **Template** and then check the box next to **Screen**. Click on **OK**.

8. Microsoft Word will open and display the invoice for printing.

How it works...

By using Microsoft Word templates, Dynamics GP opens up a world of formatting possibilities for documents. Currently, Word Templates can be used for statements, invoices, orders, quotes, packing slips, check remittance, and purchase orders.

There's more...

Dynamics GP 2010 and later provides control over what documents use Word templates versus Report Writer documents and users can create their own templates.

Existing Report Writer documents can be converted to Word templates by using the Word Template Generator (available to partners via PartnerSource) after which formatting of the Word template needs to be applied.

Which report to use?

Companies upgrading to Dynamics GP 2010 or later may choose to slowly migrate to Word template documents, meaning that they still need the old style Report Writer documents for a while.

From the main menu, selecting **Reports | Template Configuration** opens the **Template Configuration Manager** window. This window provides control over enabling templates, allowing documents to use Word templates and allowing standard documents when a Word template has been activated. It also holds the images to be sent to Word documents.

All of this is contained in an easy to understand window, as shown in the following screenshot:

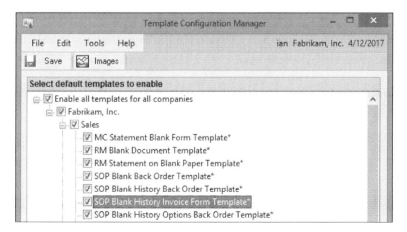

User template creation

Templates can be created by users and specific templates can be assigned to specific companies, vendors, and customers using the **Reports | Template Maintenance** selection from the main menu.

The specifics of creating a new template are beyond the scope of this recipe but templates can be created from scratch or copied from the default templates included with Dynamics GP 2010 and 2013.

Dynamics GP 2013 includes far more original Word templates than did Dynamics GP 2010, making the task of creating modified versions far easier.

7
Exposing Hidden Features in Dynamics GP

Hidden features are the focus of this chapter, which includes the following recipes:

- ▶ Controlling posting dates when not posting by batch
- ▶ Reducing posting steps with better printing control
- ▶ Improving information with tax dates in transactions
- ▶ Gaining the option to process taxes in the general ledger
- ▶ Changing the remit-to address on a payables transaction after posting
- ▶ Understanding all the financial information about an asset with fixed asset details
- ▶ Speeding entry by copying a purchase order
- ▶ Getting control of printing with named printers
- ▶ Speeding month-end processing with Reconcile to GL functionality
- ▶ Improving budget creation with Combine Budgets

Introduction

In this chapter we look at some features in Dynamics GP that many users miss. Some of these features are well known to consultants but somehow users still miss the big benefits that can be gained with these features.

This chapter is really about leveraging features to remove obstacles. It's about those hidden settings that shave seconds off processes, seconds that build up to save hours over the course of a month. Now, it's hidden feature time!

Controlling posting dates when not posting by batch

Transactions in Dynamics GP can be posted individually or as part of a batch. When posting as part of a batch, the batch gets a **posting date** that can be different from the date of the transaction. For individual transaction posting, the posting date can also be different from the transaction but the way to accomplish that is not obvious.

When not posting in a batch, the posting date on a transaction is the date that the transaction will have in the **General Ledger** (**GL**). The document date (order date, invoice date, and so on) is just that, the date of the document, and it is used to calculate aging for sales and purchase transactions. Controlling posting dates is very useful when the timing of a transaction doesn't match the month it needs to be posted in. For example, my auditors once sent a bill in July for audit work done back in January. In this scenario, I didn't want to post the transaction in January because January was closed. I did need the January date in Dynamics GP to ensure that we didn't wait to pay them on thirty day terms. We probably should have made them wait six months since it took them so long to bill us but why irritate the auditors needlessly?

In Dynamics GP, I set the document date to a date in January so that the bill would age and be selected for payment properly but the posting date was a date in July to put the transaction in the current month for the general ledger.

In this recipe, we'll take a look at posting a transaction with a posting date different from the transaction date.

How to do it...

To post a transaction with different posting and transaction dates, proceed with the following steps:

1. In Dynamics GP select **Purchasing** from the navigation pane. Select **Transaction Entry** on the Home page.

2. This opens the **Payables Transaction Entry** window. Go to the **Doc. Date** field and click on the blue arrow, as shown in the following screenshot:

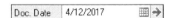

3. The **Payables Date Entry** window will open to display the **Posting Date** field. Add thirty days to the date in the **Posting Date** field and click on **OK**.

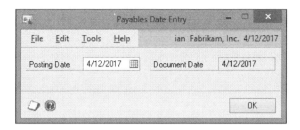

4. Now, when the transaction is completed and posted with the **Post** button, the posting date will be thirty days later than the document date.

How it works...

This is one of those exquisitely simple items that is hidden just enough that users don't find it. The ability to separate the posting date from the transaction date is an important accounting tool that is often not present in lower end systems. The fact that Dynamics GP supports this in both batch and transactional posting is one small difference between an enterprise reporting system and simple accounting software.

Reducing posting steps with better printing control

When posting a transaction in Dynamics GP, a series of posting reports print by default. Typically there is a posting report, with full posting details, a distribution summary report, a distribution detail report and, in many cases, a checkbook report.

Reports are often set to ask for the type of output (printer, screen, or file) each time. If this setting is turned on, each report will open a window allowing the user to change the report destination when the report is run. This significantly increases the amount of time it takes to simply start the printing process because the user has to make a choice each time. Additionally, reports set to print to a printer will open a window allowing users to set the number of copies or limit printing to certain pages.

This means that it's not uncommon to have eight windows open and four reports print every time a user posts. Even worse, the summary and detail distribution reports are subsets of the posting report so some information is duplicated across three reports. With this big a mess, users often click through the prompts without actually reading them or they print reports that they don't really need and cancel reports they should print.

There is a better way. Reports can be turned off, routed only to the screen, or sent to a file. The printer prompt can be turned off since it's rarely used. All of this can save several minutes each time transactions are posted, quickly adding up to a savings of hours in the course of a month along with reduced printed waste. In this recipe we'll see how to control printing during posting. For our example, we'll look at controlling printing when posting a payables transaction entry.

Getting ready

Prior to changing the printing of posting reports, administrators should evaluate what reports really need to be printed or saved at the time of posting. Posting reports can be reprinted at a later date and much of the data is duplicated across reports. Consequently, there is often no need to print any of the reports.

To show the range of options for our example, we will send the posting report to a file, send the summary report to a printer, and turn off the detail report and any other reports.

How to do it...

To get control of posting reports:

1. Select **Administration** from the navigation pane and **Posting** under the **Posting** heading on the **Administration** area page to open the **Posting Setup** window.

2. In **Series**, select **Purchasing**. In **Origin**, select **Payables Trx Entry**.

3. In the lower section, find the report labeled **Trx Entry Posting Journal**. Check the box on the left side under the **Print** heading next to **Trx Entry Posting Journal**. Uncheck all of the four center boxes, then check the one under the file folder icon. Tab to the **Path** field and enter `C:\AP Posting.txt`.

4. This process sets the AP Transaction Entry Posting Journal to default to printing to a file located on the `C:` drive and named `AP Posting.txt`. The folder icon in the top right can also be used to browse and select a file location.

5. Check the box next to **Trx Distribution Summary** under the **Print** heading. Uncheck any boxes in the middle and check the box under the printer icon.

6. This activates the Transaction Distribution Summary report and sends it to the printer by default.

7. Uncheck any other **Print** boxes to turn off the remaining reports and click on **Save** to continue.

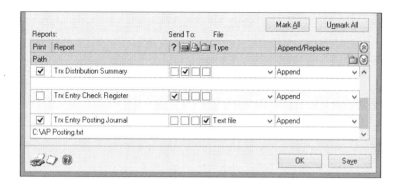

8. Now, when a payables transaction is posted, the posting report will append to a file and the Transaction Distribution Summary report will print to the printer.

How it works...

In most cases, there is no need to print any posting reports. But setting posting reports to ask every time they are printed is the least efficient of all the options. Since posting reports can be reprinted in Dynamics GP, once users are past the initial insecurity of using the system, posting reports should generally be turned off. However, if posting reports are required for control purposes, the number and types of automatic reports should be limited and sent to a file for easy retrieval, e-mailing, and archiving.

There's more...

Printing posting reports makes less sense when users know how to reprint them on demand and there is a way to turn off the rarely used **Print Options** box.

Posting reports

Posting reports are found in the **Reports** section of each module. To continue the theme of a payables transaction, select **Purchasing** from the navigation list. Then pick **Posting Journals** on the **Reports** area page. The first option is the **Transaction Journal** but other posting journals can be selected for printing with the drop-down menu, as shown in the following screenshot:

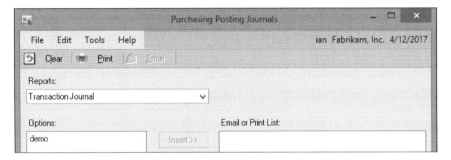

The only exception to this is the posting report for general journal entries. The report exists; it's just called a **Cross-Reference** report instead of a posting journal.

Print Options box

The other box that is frequently skipped during printing is the **Print Options** box. This box displays when printing to a printer. It provides the option to print more than one copy of a report or to print only certain pages of the report. This box is actually controlled via the **named printers** functionality that we'll look at in the recipe *Getting control of printing with named printers* found later in this chapter. For now, we'll just look at turning off this feature.

To turn off the **Print Options** box:

1. Select **Administration** from the navigation pane. Select **Named Printers** from the **Setup** area page. Enter the system password if prompted.

2. Check the box marked **Do Not Display System Print Dialog** and click on **OK** twice.

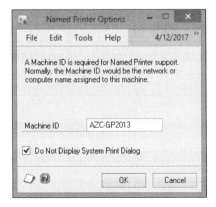

3. Select a default printer for Dynamics GP and click on **OK**.

4. Click on **Save** to assign the default printer to the named printer. Then select **File | Close** to close the window.

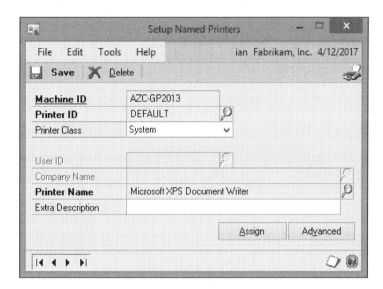

If the named printers feature has already been set up, then steps 3 and 4 won't appear as an option. This process turns off print options for this printer for all users on this workstation.

See also

▸ The *Getting control of printing with named printers* recipe

Improving information with tax dates in transactions

When working with sales tax and use tax it is often useful to set the date of a transaction for tax purposes. For example, assume a February invoice subject to use tax arrives in March. This is after February has been closed and use tax submitted. The invoice still needs to be dated in February to age properly but it needs to appear on tax reports for March to ensure that the taxing authority is paid properly. Dynamics GP includes functionality to support this but it needs to be turned on. The tax date functionality was originally designed to support **value added tax** (**VAT**) popular in Europe and other parts of the world. Firms with this requirement will need to activate tax dates as well. In this recipe, we'll look at how to activate and use tax dates.

Getting ready

Prior to using tax dates, they need to be activated. To activate tax dates functionality proceed with the following steps:

1. Select **Administration** from the navigation pane. On the **Administration** area page, select **Company** under the **Company** heading.

2. Click on **Options** in the **Company Setup** window.

3. Check the box marked **Enable Tax Date** and click on **OK** twice.

The tax date functionality is now set up. Let's look at how to use it in a transaction.

How to do it...

To use tax dates in a transaction, proceed with the following steps:

1. Select **Purchasing** from the navigation pane on the left side, then click on **Transaction Entry** from the **Purchasing** area page.

2. Tab to the **Doc. Date** field, select the blue arrow next to the date, and enter 4/12/2017.

3. A new **Tax Date** field appears in this window. Enter 5/1/2017 in the **Tax Date** field and click on **OK**.

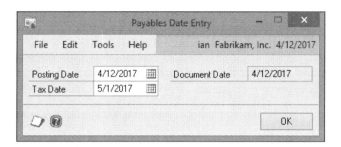

How it works...

The tax date feature is required for processing VAT but it's also very useful for sales tax and use tax reporting. Once the tax date feature has been activated, tax dates on transactions are available to add to SmartLists. This makes reporting on tax dates easy and flexible.

See also

▸ The *Tailoring SmartLists by adding fields* recipe in *Chapter 5, Harnessing the Power of SmartLists*

Gaining the option to process taxes in the general ledger

There are times when companies need to process sales or use tax transactions through the general ledger rather than through a subledger such as sales or purchasing. Perhaps tax was incorrectly calculated or omitted on the original transaction, which is sometimes a requirement for international implementations. It's also possible that a company uses another system to feed the general ledger in Dynamics GP. For example, in one company I worked for, we used a specialized accounts receivable application that was designed for our industry. Data from that application was integrated with Dynamics GP and all other transactions ran through Dynamics GP directly. This can lead to the need to process tax transactions through the GL.

Dynamics GP includes options to calculate and process taxes directly through the general ledger and that is the focus of this recipe.

Getting ready

Prior to processing tax transactions via the general ledger, this feature needs to be turned on. To activate the ability to process taxes through the general ledger:

1. Select **Administration** from the navigation pane. On the **Administration** area page, select **Company** under the **Company** heading.

2. Click on **Options** in the **Company Setup** window.

3. Scroll down in the window and check the box marked **Calculate Taxes in the General Ledger** and click on **OK** twice.

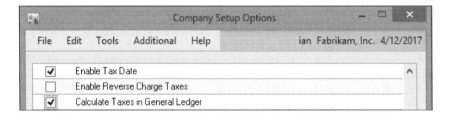

Now that tax calculations in the general ledger have been activated, let's see how they work. We'll use the sample company's tax schedules for our example.

How to do it...

To calculate taxes in the general ledger, perform the following steps:

1. Select **Financial** from the navigation pane. Select **General** under **Transactions** on the area page.

2. Select the new **Tax Entry** button on the bottom left of the **Transaction Entry** window.

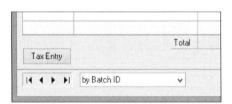

3. On the **Tax Entry** window, set the transaction type to **Credit**. Use the lookup button (magnifying glass) to select or key in the sales account `000-4100-000`. Enter `$1,000.00` in the **Sales/Purchase Amount** field. The following screenshot shows this step:

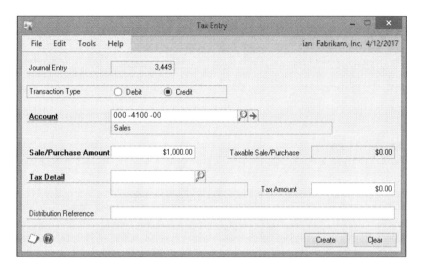

4. Use the lookup button (magnifying glass) to select **USASTE-PS6N0** (state sales tax) in the **Tax Detail** field. Notice that Dynamics GP will fill in the tax amount automatically.

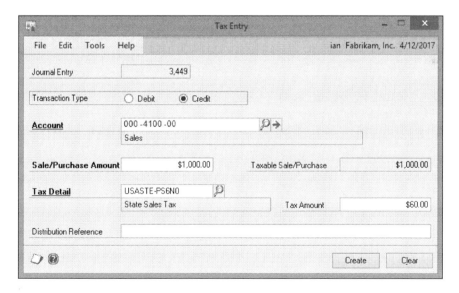

5. Click on **Create** to create the transaction in the general ledger. The created transaction will have the account and amount entered along with the appropriate tax. Since this is only one side of the entry, enter 000-1200-00 (other receivables) in the next open line to make the transaction balance.

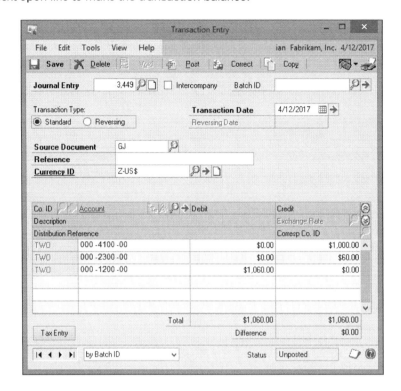

The ability to calculate taxes as part of a general journal entry provides the ability to accommodate tax adjustments and changes in tax law. It also provides flexibility to work with other systems connected to Dynamics GP.

See also

▸   The *Improving Information with Tax Dates in transactions* recipe

Changing the remit-to address on a payables transaction after posting

One of the long standing issues with Microsoft Dynamics GP was how it handled remit-to addresses on payables transactions when the vendors default remit-to address was changed.

The remit-to address on the vendor card was used as the default on payables transactions when they were created. If the transaction was posted and the vendor card updated, the remit-to address on the transaction was left unchanged and, until the release of Dynamics GP 2013, there was no way to update it.

How to do it...

To change the remit-to address on a posted payables transaction, proceed with the following steps:

1. Select **Purchasing** from the navigation pane, then select **Edit Transaction Information** under **Transactions**.

2. In the sample company, use the lookup button (magnifying glass) to select vendor **ASSOCIAT0001**.

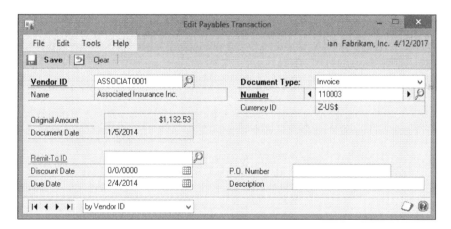

3. Enter `110003` in the **Number** field, which will load the transaction details that can be amended.

4. In the **Remit-To ID** field enter or perform a lookup for the address ID to be used as the remit-to address for this invoice. Invoices entered prior to Dynamics GP 2013 will show a blank **Remit-To ID** field; those entered in Dynamics GP 2013 will display the remit-to ID from the payables transaction.

See also

See *Chapter 2, New in Microsoft GP 2013*, for details of other new Dynamics GP 2013 features.

Understanding all the financial information about an asset with fixed asset details

Dynamics GP has a nice module for tracking and maintaining **fixed assets**. However, many users have trouble figuring out the history of a specific asset. Often users find that while reviewing fixed asset general ledger postings something looks wrong, but they can't figure out where to go in the fixed asset module to validate how transactions posted.

Dynamics GP provides the ability to see every transaction for a fixed asset and its link back to the general ledger. This functionality can be hard to find. In this recipe we'll look at how to trace fixed asset transactions.

How to do it...

To get the specifics of fixed asset transactions, perform the following steps:

1. In Dynamics GP, select **Financial** from the navigation pane. Then select **Financial Detail** under the **Inquiry | Fixed Assets** area.

2. Use the lookup Button (magnifying glass) to select asset **00001** with suffix **1**. Set the **Book ID** to **INTERNAL**.

3. The **Financial Detail Inquiry** window will open and display all of the transactions for this asset.

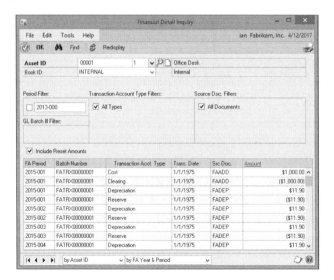

4. The grid at the bottom displays the fixed asset period, GL batch number, account type, date, source document, and amount. The key fields are **Transaction Acct. Type** and **Src Doc**. These fields provide details about the type of transaction. For example, the first two lines demonstrate the cost and clearing entry for the initial purchase of the asset.

5. The **Batch Number** column is the batch sent to the GL. It can be reviewed using a SmartList.

6. Below that is the first depreciation entry transaction. It affects the depreciation and reserve accounts.

7. Select the first depreciation line and click on the blue **Amount** hyperlink to get more information about this transaction line. Dynamics GP shows full details of the line including GL batch, posting date, account, and user information. Click on **OK** to close this window.

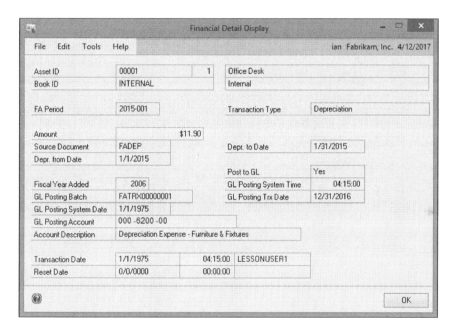

8. Back on the **Financial Detail Inquiry** screen, scroll down to the end of the transactions. Notice that there are two transaction lines without GL batches. Typically this indicates that there is a fixed asset transaction waiting to be processed to the GL. If, however, a batch is missing for a transaction that is not at the end of the list, it can indicate a problem transaction that was not sent to the GL.

FA Period	Batch Number	Transaction Acct. Type	Trans. Date	Src Doc.	Amount
2016-011	FATRX00000001	Reserve	1/1/1975	FAXFR-C	($273.76)
2016-011	FATRX00000001	Cost	1/1/1975	FAXFR-C	($1,000.00)
2016-011	FATRX00000001	Cost	1/1/1975	FAXFR-C	$1,000.00
2016-012	FATRX00000001	Depreciation	1/1/1975	FADEP	$11.96
2016-012	FATRX00000001	Reserve	1/1/1975	FADEP	($11.96)
2017-001	FATRX00000002	Depreciation	1/1/1975	FADEP	$11.90
2017-001	FATRX00000002	Reserve	1/1/1975	FADEP	($11.90)
2017-002		Depreciation	1/1/1975	FADEP	$11.90
2017-002		Reserve	1/1/1975	FADEP	($11.90)

How it works...

The **Fixed Asset Financial Detail Inquiry** window provides all the information necessary to trace all of the transactions related to a fixed asset. This is extremely useful for understanding what actually occurred. Any number of items can affect fixed assets including incorrect depreciation settings, wrong asset lives, and problems with the fixed asset calendar. Being able to understand all the transactions that affect an asset is an important troubleshooting tool that is often overlooked.

Speeding entry by copying a purchase order

Creating purchase orders can be a time consuming process. It's not uncommon to have a large number of line items being ordered. Validating part numbers and prices can also take time. Dynamics GP provides a mechanism to create a new purchase order by copying information from an existing purchase order. Unlike copying an inventory item, where the copy icon is in the main window, the process to copy a purchase order is not obvious. Copying a purchase order is the focus of this recipe.

How to do it...

To copy a purchase order, perform the following steps:

1. Select **Purchasing** on the navigation pane, then click **Purchase Order Entry** on the **Transactions** section of the area page.

2. Click on **Actions**, then select **Create and Copy New PO**.

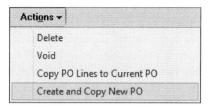

3. Use the lookup button (magnifying glass) to select a **Source PO Number** to copy from. In the sample company, select purchase order **PO0997**. Dynamics GP will fill in the rest of the information.

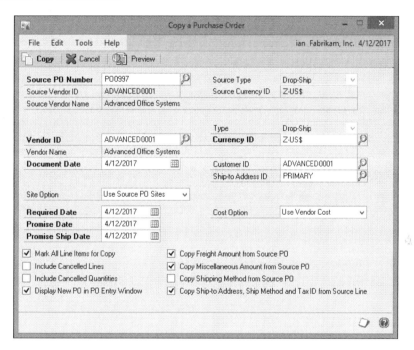

4. Users can change various settings to fine tune the copy. To demonstrate this, uncheck **Copy Freight Amount from Source PO**. Also change the **Required Date** to 5/31/2017.

Required Date	5/31/2017			Cost Option	Use Vendor Cost
Promise Date	4/12/2017				
Promise Ship Date	4/12/2017				
✓ Mark All Line Items for Copy				☐ Copy Freight Amount from Source PO	

5. Click on **Copy** to create a new purchase order. The new purchase order can be changed or adjusted just like one that has been entered from scratch.

How it works...

It's unclear why Microsoft chose to hide the copy functionality for purchase orders, but it's great that this feature exists. The ability to selectively copy a purchase order and then adjust the end result is a huge time saver. This is a feature that definitely needs to move out of hiding.

There's more...

Creating a sales order can be just as time consuming as creating a purchase order. Fortunately, sales order processing also provides a mechanism that allows a transaction to be created by copying an existing one.

Copying a sales order

Unlike when copying a purchase order, the header of the sales order needs to be created before copying can be done. To copy a sales order, perform the following steps:

1. Select **Sales** on the navigation pane, then click on **Sales Transaction Entry** on the **Transactions** section of the area page.

2. Select a **Type/Type ID of Order/STDORD**.

3. Click in the **Document No.** field so a number is defaulted.

4. Enter, or do a lookup for, **Customer ID** AARONFIT0001.

5. Set value in **Currency ID** field to Z-US$.

6. Click on **Actions**, then pick **Copy**.

7. Use the lookup button (magnifying glass) to select a document number to copy from. In the sample company, select sales order **ORDST2222**.

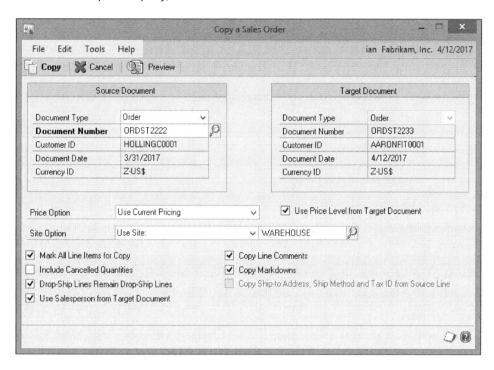

8. Users can change various settings to fine tune the copy. For example, the **Price Option** field can be changed to **Use Source Document Pricing** or **Zero Pricing**.

9. Click on **Preview** to see the lines on the document that will be copied.

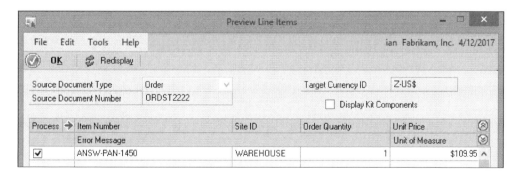

10. If dealing with a multiline order, unmark the checkbox in the **Process** column to remove lines that should not be copied.

11. Click on **OK** to return to the **Copy a Sales Order** window and then click on **Copy** to complete the copy process.

Getting control of printing with named printers

In the *Reducing posting steps with better printing control* recipe we touched on the edge of named printers functionality by turning off the system print dialog. However, there is much more than that to named printers. The idea behind named printers is to allow the assignment of different printers to different functions in Dynamics GP. For example, check printing could be directed to a dedicated check printer or invoices could be automatically sent to a high speed printer. Even better, these settings are by workstation so there is a geographic component to the setup. Users in one building can point checks to a check printer in their building without interfering with a different set of users in another building. In this recipe, we'll look at setting up named printers.

Getting ready

Prior to creating named printers, there is some setup required. Perform the following steps:

1. Select **Administration** from the navigation pane. Select **Named Printers** from the **Setup** area page. Enter the system password if prompted.

2. Click on **OK** twice.

3. Select a default printer for Dynamics GP and click on **OK**.

4. Click on **Save** to assign the default printer to named printers.

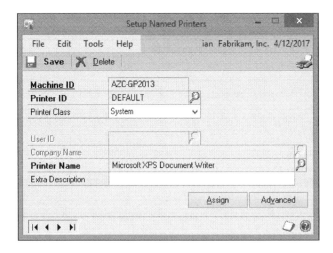

5. Create a new **Printer ID** named CHECKS. Use the lookup button (magnifying glass) to select a printer for checks. Click on **Save** and close the window.

How to do it...

To set named printers, perform the following steps:

1. Select **Administration** from the navigation pane. Select **Named Printers** from the **Setup** area page.

2. Notice that printers for this machine ID can be set for a specific user and company. For now, we'll leave these alone. Change the **Task Series** to **Purchasing** as shown in the following screenshot:

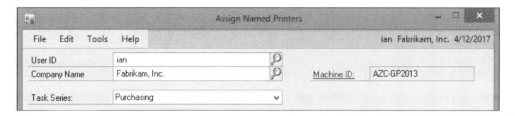

3. Click on the blue **Printer** hyperlink to add another printer.

4. In **Task Description** find **Payables – Computer Checks/Cheques Printer**. Change **Printer Class** to **System**.

5. Pick the printer named **CHECKS** in the **Named Printers** window that opens.

6. Click on **OK** to complete the assignment of a check printer to the check printing function.

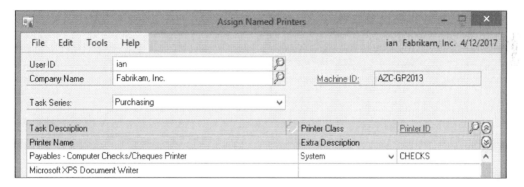

7. Now when checks are printed via the **Computer Checks** function in **Purchasing**, from this computer and by this user, the checks will print to the designated check printer. Any other printer request combination will be sent to the default printer.

How it works...

Named printers provides fine grain control over printing functions in Dynamics GP. It provides the ability to control printing by user, computer, and printer. This ability to control printing provides additional security as well since it can be used to control which reports print to shared printers in the organization. The named printers feature can provide huge time saving and cost benefits by preventing printing to less efficient or erroneous printers.

There's more...

Even more control is available via printer classes.

Printer classes

When setting up printers in named printers, the option exists to select a printer class. Printer classes are preset options controlling what users can select to print to a printer. For example, an expensive color printer might be limited to only certain users to prevent accidental printing to that printer. The available printer classes are:

▸ **System**: These Printer ID's are available to all users and companies

▸ **User**: Printer ID is only available to a single user for all companies

▸ **Company**: All users of this company can access this Printer ID

▸ **User & Company**: Printer ID use is restricted a single user and company

▸ **Any Printer ID**: Any printer available on the workstation can be used

▸ **Manual Selection**: Printer is selected by the user at the time of printing

▸ **None**: Default printer is used

See also

▸ The *Reducing posting steps with better printing control* recipe

Speeding month-end processing with Reconcile to GL functionality

One process that can be extremely time consuming is balancing subledgers to the general ledger to ensure that everything in the system is in balance. An out of balance situation can occur if users change the GL account on a subledger transaction. For example, if a user changes the payables account on an AP subledger transaction, the AP subledger no longer matches the AP GL account.

Another common occurrence is that users post general ledger transactions to an AP or AR control account without going through the appropriate subledger. This means that the general ledger is updated but not the subledger, resulting in an out of balance situation.

Dynamics GP provides a feature to facilitate reconciling accounts payable and accounts receivable to the general ledger. The **Reconcile to GL** feature uses Microsoft Excel to provide an analysis of matched and unmatched transactions. In this recipe, we'll look at how to use the Reconcile to GL feature to balance subledger accounts to the general ledger. For our example we'll look at balancing accounts payable.

How to do it...

To use the Reconcile to GL feature:

1. In Dynamics GP, select **Financial** from the navigation pane and click on **Reconcile to GL** in the **Routines** area.

2. In the **Reconcile to GL** window set the Module to Payables Management.

3. Use the lookup button (magnifying glass) next to **Accounts** to select account **000-2100-00**.

4. Repeat this process for account **000-2105-00** on the next line. Since the sample company tracks discounts we need both accounts.

5. For the sample company, don't change the dates.

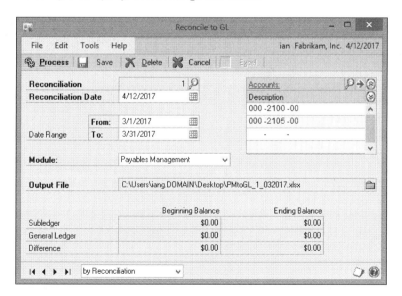

6. Set the **Output File** path for where the Excel spreadsheet will be created.

7. Click on **Process** to start the reconciliation. Microsoft Excel will open with a reconciliation sheet.

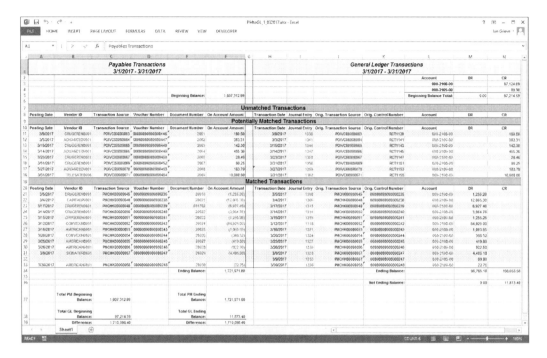

8. Subledger transactions are on the left and general ledger transactions on the right side. Unmatched transactions are at the top followed by potentially matched transactions and matched transactions. At the bottom is a reconciliation of the differences.

9. Finally, users would use the unmatched and potentially matched information to make adjusting entries in the GL or subledger to correct out of balance transactions.

How it works...

The reconcile feature for accounts payable, accounts receivable, bank reconciliation, and inventory control fills an important role during month-end close. Balancing subledgers to the general ledger is an important step in ensuring the correctness of financial statements. The Reconcile to GL feature in Dynamics GP makes this easier than ever. The use of Microsoft Excel as the balancing mechanism provides a familiar, easy to use interface for users.

There's more...

The Reconcile to GL routine has been in Dynamics GP for a while but has seen significant improvements in Dynamics GP 2013. Each reconciliation is numbered and can be saved for later recall; the created spreadsheet is saved to a user-specified file and can be recalled by clicking on the Excel button on the toolbar.

Balancing the year

Whether through inexperience or a lack of oversight, it is not unusual to find firms where the subledger and general ledger have been out of balance for most of the year. The best way to approach this problem is to start with the oldest out of balance month and work forward one month at a time. Trying to balance the entire year at once requires an overwhelming amount of data and can actually make balancing more difficult.

When standard functionality isn't enough

While the Reconcile to GL feature of Dynamics GP works well, it is limited to the accounts payable, accounts receivable, bank reconciliation, and inventory subledgers. There is a third-party option named **The Closer** from Reporting Central. The Closer offers similar reconciliation functionality for accounts payable, accounts receivable, and inventory control as well as cash, sales order processing, cost of goods sold, and accrued purchases. For companies that require more than simple accounts receivable and accounts payable reconciliation this is a great option. More information about The Closer is available at `http://www.Reporting-Central.com`.

Improving budget creation with Combine Budgets

When training new users of Dynamics GP, one of the regular issues raised is the creation of budgets and how they want to be able to send separate files out to each of the budget holders and have an easy way of combining them together. Prior to Dynamics GP 2010 this wasn't possible; however, Dynamics GP 2010 introduced **Combine Budgets**, which provides this functionality.

How to do it...

This example assumes you have two budgets created on the system; `MASTER2017` and `SALES2017` where the latter needs to be combined into the former. Perform the following steps for the same:

1. In Dynamics GP, select **Financial** from the navigation pane and click on **Budgets** in the **Cards** area.

2. In the list of available budgets, click on **MASTER2017**.

3. Click on the **Open** button and then select **using Microsoft Dynamics GP**.

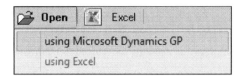

4. This will open the **Budget Maintenance** window and populate it with the MASTER2017 budget.

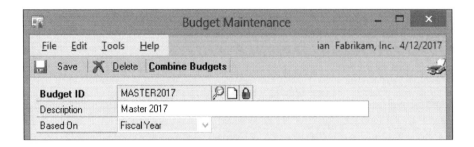

5. Click on the **Combine Budgets** button on the toolbar.

6. The **Master Budget ID** field will repopulate with **MASTER2017** from the previous window.

7. Enter SALES2017 in the **Combine with Budget ID** field.

8. If the budget being combined with the master budget is no longer needed, mark the **Delete Budget After It Is Combined** checkbox.

9. Click on **Process** to combine the budgets.

How it works...

Combine Budgets performs a merge of all the figures in the second budget with those in the master budget; for example, if account 000-2100-00 has $20,000 in the master budget and $12,500 on the combined budget, the resulting figure after combination on the master budget will be $32,500.

By combining budgets in this way, a separate budget can be created for each budget holder and then combined together into a single master budget for use in reporting tools such as management reporter or for commitment accounting.

8
Improving Dynamics GP with Hacks

In this chapter we'll look at the following recipes:

- ▸ Building custom help with window notes
- ▸ Using comments without needing a comment name
- ▸ Keeping the chart of accounts clean by reactivating Account Segment warnings
- ▸ Reducing licensing needs by preventing multiple company logins
- ▸ Using a CNAME alias to prevent resetting all passwords in migrations or DR failovers
- ▸ Turning on more features with the Dex.ini settings
- ▸ Entering and tracking use tax with credit card functionality
- ▸ Correcting a lost password by resetting the system password
- ▸ Warning the user if Caps Lock is on during login
- ▸ Getting greater journal entry control by clearing recurring batch amounts

Introduction

Hacking computer systems is a time-honored tradition and by hacking I mean finding ways to make a system do more and go further than its creators ever intended, not using a system in an inappropriate way.

Microsoft Dynamics GP is incredibly flexible. Over the years, users have found that there are ways to use Dynamics GP to solve business problems by applying conventional features in unconventional ways. This can include using a different feature to supply missing functionality, applying best practices to improve clarity, exposing hidden settings, or applying some simple code to add functionality to the system.

In this chapter, we'll look at ways to improve the usability of Dynamics GP by hacking the system with a few changes, some unconventional uses of features and a little free code.

Building custom help with window notes

Each master record and transaction in Dynamics GP includes the ability to add **notes**. These notes are attached to the associated record and can be accessed whenever that record is open. Dynamics GP also contains another set of notes. These notes are attached to each window in Dynamics GP and are available whenever that window is open, regardless of the record being used. Window notes are stored at the company level so different Dynamics GP companies can have different notes. In addition, notes assigned to a window are available to all users who can access that window, making them an ideal candidate for alternative uses.

The most common hack for window notes is to provide additional help or specific data entry instructions to users. For example, a note on the **Inventory Maintenance** window could be used to inform users that the new nut and bolt inventory items belong in the FASTENERS Class ID, not FIXTURES. Another example would be to use a note on the **Customer Maintenance** window to remind users that new customers from Texas belong in the West region, not in the South. In this recipe, we'll look at setting up custom help using **window notes**.

How to do it...

The following steps will help you use window notes to set up custom help:

1. In Dynamics GP select **Sales** from the navigation pane. Select **Customer** in the area page under **Cards**.

2. Click on the small, white note in the lower-right hand corner of the window:

3. In the note enter the following:
    - ❑   Common States and Regions:
    - ❑   Texas – West
    - ❑   Virginia – South
    - ❑   Tennessee – South
    - ❑   Ohio – Midwest
    - ❑   Pennsylvania – East

4. Click on **Attach** to save the note.

5. Notice, that the icon changes from an empty white note to a yellow one with writing on it designed to indicate the presence of information:

How it works...

While Dynamics GP is extremely flexible and customizable, there are times when customizing any system to control user behavior provides diminishing returns. Using window notes to provide customized help is one of those in-between measures that makes it easier for users to do their job correctly but requires minimal effort to implement.

The drawbacks to using window notes in this way are that they are difficult to lock down with security. Most users will have access to change notes, and will not just view them. Additionally, users need to actually click on the icon to view additional help. I have seen cases where custom programming was used to open the note each time the window opens but this has its own drawback in that it quickly becomes annoying for users who don't need the extra help.

Window notes don't eliminate the need for training and monitoring but they can make it easier for users to get data entry right.

Using comments without needing a comment name

Many of the transaction documents in Dynamics GP provide a place for **comments** that can be printed on the document. Some common examples of these types of documents include quotes, sales orders, invoices, and purchase orders. Comments were originally intended to be recurring messages and were typically used to thank clients for their business, remind clients of holiday hours, or provide similar standardized messages. Consequently, each comment had a **Comment ID** allowing users to add a consistent comment to a document with a minimum amount of work. This worked great for standard, recurring comments. Unfortunately, the world in which we live is not standard and it's only occasionally recurring. Users really wanted to provide ad hoc comments to clarify the specifics of a transaction.

Ad hoc comments can include clarifications to a vendor similar to "ship the Hex head version not the Phillips head." They can provide information to customers such as "we've shipped 6 of the 10 items requested. The others will ship on Tuesday." In short, almost anything a user could come up with can end up in a comment that needs to appear on the document. The problem with this is that if each comment gets an ID, the system is soon overwhelmed with Comment IDs and it becomes easier to contribute to the problem by creating a new ID for each comment than to figure which comment could be reused.

There is an option to create and use comments without assigning a Comment ID. These comments appear on a document as if an ID had been used and users have the option to modify the comment. By creating a comment without an ID this process doesn't pollute the list of actual, recurring comments that a business wants to use. Creating comments without a Comment ID is the focus of this recipe.

How to do it...

The following steps will help you create comments without using a Comment ID:

1. Select **Sales** from the navigation pane then select **Sales Transaction Entry** under **Transactions**.

2. Click on the right arrow in the lower-left side to select the first available **Sales Transaction**:

3. Leave the **Comment ID** field blank and click on the blue arrow next to the **Comment ID** field:

4. In the **Comment** box type This is a comment without an ID and click on **OK**.

5. Notice, that a new indicator appears between the **Comment ID** prompt and the **Comment ID** field to show that there is a comment without an ID:

6. Any document that already shows comments will include comments entered without an ID. The documents don't have to be changed at all.

How it works...

This recipe is the perfect solution for ad hoc comments without polluting comment IDs. As a plus it continues to allow the use of traditional comments with an ID. The biggest problem with this process is that it is hidden so deeply that most users don't find it.

There's more...

This works for all Comment ID boxes including line item comments.

Line item comments

Our example showed a transaction-level comment that would appear at the bottom of a document. However, each line in a document like a purchase order or invoice can also use comments without an ID the same way.

Clicking on a line item in a document and selecting the blue arrow key opens up additional details about that line and exposes another **Comment ID** field. This works exactly like transaction-level comments except that the comments appear below each line item on the document by default.

Keeping the chart of accounts clean by reactivating the Account Segment warnings

Dynamics GP includes functionality to automatically name new accounts based on the account segments selected. For example, if a user creates account number 01-4000-000 and the three segments correspond to Company A, Revenue Account, and South Region, Dynamics GP can automatically name the account Company A-Revenue-South. This is a huge time saver, reducing data entry for new accounts. The specifics of this feature are covered in the *Preventing account selection errors with chart segment names* recipe of *Chapter 9, Preventing Errors in Dynamics GP*.

If, however, a user keys a segment without an associated description, they get an informational message providing the opportunity to add a description. Included in that informational message is the option to turn off the message.

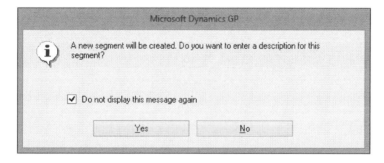

The actual wording of the checkbox is **Do not display this message again** and it really means it. Once this box is checked for a user, the feature that allows the entry of a segment description on the fly is completely disabled for that user. Additionally, there is no option within Dynamics GP to turn it back on. This can be a real nightmare if the user designated to create accounts accidentally turns this off.

Since Microsoft has forgotten to include a switch to turn this feature back on, administrators will need to hack their way through some simple SQL code to make this available again. Turning Account Segment warnings back on is the focus of this recipe.

How to do it...

The following steps will enable you to re-enable the Account Segment warnings:

1. Open Microsoft SQL Server Management Studio and connect to the SQL Server used for Dynamics GP. Use either a username and password or windows authentication to connect.

2. Because of the way that security is implemented between Dynamics GP and the SQL Server, a Dynamics GP user login will not work here. The exception is the sa user which is also the SQL Server system administrator login.

3. Click on **New Query** and select the appropriate company from the drop-down box on the top-left side. The sample company is named TWO. In the query area on the right enter the following script:

```
Delete from SY01401
where coDefaultType = 13
```

4. This will enable Account Segment warnings for all users.

5. To turn on Account Segments for a single user, add this third line and change myUserID to the appropriate user ID:

```
and USERID = 'myUserID'
```

6. Click on **Execute** to run the script.

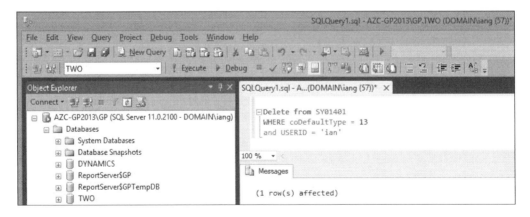

How it works...

Fixing features that the developer left out is what hacking is all about. In this case, Microsoft simply missed the option to turn this feature back on for a user and it can be very painful if the primary account entry user accidently turns it off. Fortunately, an administrator can re-enable the Account Segment warning with just a few lines of SQL code.

Reducing licensing needs by preventing multiple company logins

Microsoft Dynamics GP is licensed on the basis of concurrent users. This means that if a company has ten user licenses, any ten users can log in at once but the eleventh user is prevented from logging in. Many firms also manage multiple companies in Dynamics GP and users have a tendency to log in to more than one company at a time to make switching between companies faster. However, each company login uses up a concurrent license. In our previous example with ten licenses, if each user logs into two companies simultaneously, only five individuals will actually get to log in.

For companies where the number of actual users is very close to the number of licenses this presents a real problem. I've seen cases where an AP clerk can't log in to print checks and a controller couldn't log in to review accounts because users were logged in to multiple companies. An obvious solution to this problem is to purchase additional licenses. However, that is also an expensive solution. A better option is to prevent users from logging in to multiple companies.

Unfortunately, there is no built-in functionality to prevent users from logging in multiple times so in this recipe we'll turn to a hack from a surprising place, Microsoft.

How to do it...

The following steps will help prevent users from logging in to multiple Dynamics GP companies simultaneously:

1. Open Internet Explorer and navigate to: `http://blogs.msdn.com/ developingfordynamicsgp/archive/2008/08/25/preventing-users- from-logging-into-multiple-companies-example.aspx`.

2. Download and save the `Prevent User Logging In To Multiple Companies.zip` file to your desktop.

3. Right-click on the downloaded file and select **Extract**. Then click on the **Extract** button.

4. After the files are extracted, repeat this process with the new file named `v10.00 Prevent User Logging In To Multiple Companies.zip`. Despite the v10.00 designation in the filename, this file works just fine in version 2013.

5. Back in Dynamics GP, select **Microsoft Dynamics GP | Tools | Customize | Customization Maintenance**.

6. Click on **Import** then **Browse**. Navigate to the location where you extracted `v10.00 Prevent User Logging In To Multiple Companies` on the desktop and pick the `MicrosoftActiveXDataObjects 2.8 Reference.package` file. Click on **OK** to install.

7. Repeat steps 5 and 6 using the `SwitchCompany.Package` file.

8. Apply this customization to each user's workstation using steps 5, 6, and 7.

9. Once applied, users will be prevented from logging in to multiple companies simultaneously. If they try, users will get a message and an indication of what company they are already logged in to.

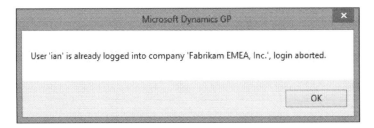

How it works...

This hack uses a free, unsupported **Visual Basic for Applications (VBA)** file created by David Musgrave, a developer at Microsoft. David was kind enough to release this code as a free benefit to the Dynamics GP community.

If there are any issues with installation, there are additional troubleshooting steps in the included `Installation Instructions.txt` file.

Using a CNAME alias to prevent resetting all passwords in migrations or DR failovers

Microsoft Dynamics GP uses an ODBC connection for database access and the server name from this connection is used in the password encryption algorithm. This means if you need to migrate Dynamics GP to another server for any reason, such as a migration or SQL Server failover for disaster recovery, every single user will need their password to be reset. For implementations of Dynamics GP with a low user count this isn't too much of a burden, but I've dealt with clients who have over 250 users in Dynamics GP which makes resetting all passwords, even when using a GP macro, a chore not to be undertaken lightly.

It is possible, however, to avoid resetting all passwords by creating and using a DNS CNAME alias in place of the server in the ODBC connection.

Passwords still need to be reset when the CNAME alias is introduced to the system, but it removes the requirement to reset them in future when GP is moved between servers.

Getting ready

Before the ODBC connection can be changed, the CNAME alias needs to be created:

1. Log on to the DNS server.

2. Open **DNS Manager** under **Administrative Tools** in the Windows **start** menu.

3. Expand **Forward Lookup Zone** and right-click on the relevant zone which in this example is **DOMAIN.azurecurve.co.uk** and select **New Alias (CNAME)....**

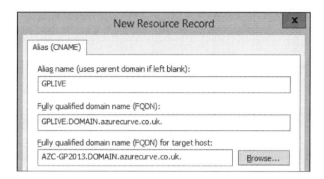

4. In the **Alias** field enter GPLIVE.

5. Then enter your fully qualified machine name (which in this example is AZC-GP2013. DOMAIN.azurecurve.co.uk.) in the **Fully qualified domain name (FQDN) for target host** field.

6. Click on **OK** to save the new alias.

How to do it...

With the CNAME alias created on the DNS Server, we can now update the ODBC connection to use the alias rather than the actual server:

1. Open **ODBC Data Source Administrator (32-bit)** by opening a **Run** window and typing %windir%\SysWOW64\odbcad32.exe and click on **OK** (on an x86 system you can open **ODBC Data Source Administrator (32-bit)** from the Control Panel).

2. Click on **System DSN**.

3. Select **Dynamics GP 2013** and click on **Configure**.

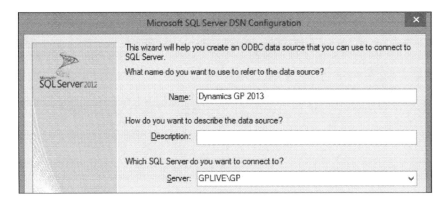

4. Amend the **Server** field to replace the server name with the DNS CNAME alias; in this example, the **Server** now reads **GPLIVE\GP** as the alias is set up as **GPLIVE** and the **SQL Instance** is called **GP**.

5. Click on **Next**.

6. Enter the password for the supplied **Login ID** and click on **Next**.

7. Click on **Next**.

8. Click on **Finish**.

9. Click on **OK**.

10. Repeat these steps on every machine that has Dynamics GP installed.

How it works...

Now that the DNS CNAME alias has been created and configured on each machine, it is simply a case of changing the target host of the CNAME alias if the server hosting the Dynamics GP databases is changed either for a migration or because the original host needs to be replaced with a backup server for disaster recovery purposes.

If users have already been created when the CNAME alias is introduced, all user passwords will need to be reset; but the CNAME removes any need for this in future when Dynamics GP is migrated to a new server or a failover to a SQL Server with a different name.

Turning on more features with Dex.ini settings

Microsoft Dynamics GP contains a number of features that can't be controlled via the interface; the controls for these features reside in an initialization file known as the Dex.ini file which Dynamics GP loads settings from as it starts. The Dex.ini settings affect only the computer on which the file is installed. This means that the system can behave differently for different users if their Dex.ini files are different.

As an example, Dex.ini settings can be used to control the date warning that appears when midnight passes, allow the installation of update files without a warning, and dramatically speed up the export of SmartLists to Excel. If a particular setting is not present in the Dex.ini file a user can simply add it to the end of the file.

If there are errors in the Dex.ini file, it can prevent Dynamics GP from opening so users should make a copy of the Dex.ini file before making changes. In this recipe, we'll look at how to apply some of the most common and useful Dex.ini settings.

Getting ready

Before we can change Dex.ini settings, we need to open up the file. To open and modify the Dex.ini file perform the following steps:

1. Open the **Notepad** utility provided with all copies of Microsoft Windows.

2. In **Notepad**, select **File | Open**. Navigate to the **GP** install folder which is typically found in **%ProgramFiles(x86)%\Microsoft Dynamics\GP2013** (or **%ProgramFiles%\ Microsoft Dynamics\GP2013** on an x86 machine).

3. Open the **Data** folder and select Dex.ini to open the file. If the Dex.ini file is not visible, type *.ini in the **File name** field to show files without a .txt extension.

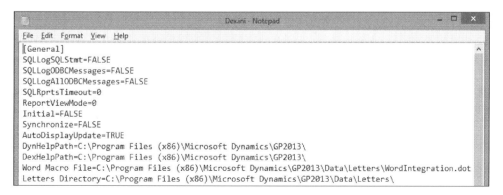

How to do it...

To demonstrate how to change the settings in the Dex.ini file we'll start by turning on an alternative setting to dramatically speed up exporting SmartLists to Excel and then we'll look at other common settings.

1. To force Dynamics GP to export SmartLists to Excel using the much faster `recordset` method instead of the default line-by-line process, go to the `Dex.ini` file and add the line `SmartlistEnhancedExcelExport=TRUE` to the bottom of the `Dex.ini` file.

2. To force Dynamics GP to always open in a full screen, go to the `Dex.ini` file, find the setting named **WindowMax**, and set it to `WindowMax=True`.

3. To suppress sounds in Dynamics GP but not other applications, find the setting **SupressSound** and set it to `SupressSound=True`.

4. Prevent the warning that appears when adding new code or modules to Dynamics GP by finding **AutoInstallChunks** and setting it to `AutoInstallChunks=True`.

5. One of the problems that occurs when exporting Report Writer based reports is that long sets of data wrap to the next line in the export. This makes opening and analyzing exported data in Excel difficult. To prevent text report lines from wrapping when exporting, find the `Dex.ini` setting named **ExportOneLineBody** and set it to `ExportOneLineBody=True`.

6. In the *Reducing posting steps with better printing control* recipe in *Chapter 7, Exposing Hidden Features in Dynamics GP*, we looked at how to turn off the print dialog box via the interface. The same result can be accomplished by finding the **NoPrintDialogs** setting and changing it to `NoPrintDialogs=True`.

7. Finally, when the computer time passes midnight, Dynamics GP displays a message indicating that the date has changed and asks the users if they want to change the date in Dynamics GP. This message can be turned off by setting `SuppressChangeDateDialog=True`. The date in the open Dynamics GP session won't automatically change to the next day, the warning is simply suppressed.

8. When finished, select **File | Save** to save the `Dex.ini` file and restart Dynamics GP to see the changes.

There's more...

These settings are just a sample of common changes that can be made via the `Dex.ini` file. There are a lot more settings available.

Additional Dex.ini settings

Some of the other additional `Dex.ini` settings are as follows:

▶ **OLEPath=\\server\folder\ole**: This sets the path for linked and embedded files and should be the same for all users. When using a **Universal Naming Convention** (**UNC**) path like `\\server\` the complete folder structure must exist. Dynamics GP will not create it with the first note. If a mapped drive is used such as `f:\` the folder structure does not have to be created beforehand.

It is recommended that UNC paths rather than mapped drives is used, as UNC paths will work on all machines on the domain, whereas mapped drives need to be configured on each machine (either manually or via a logon script).

▶ **ShowAdvancedMacroMenu=True**: This setting turns on an additional menu for working with macros.

▶ **DPSInstance=1**: This setting allows the use of multiple process servers on a single physical machine. Process servers can be used to move the load of certain functions, such as posting off a user's machine and on to a central process server.

See also

The *Troubleshooting issues with a DexSQL log* recipe in *Chapter 10, Maintaining Dynamics GP.*

Entering and tracking use tax with credit card functionality

Use tax is a form of self-reported sales tax. Companies in the United States who purchase items not intended for resale are typically required to pay sales tax. If they are not charged sales tax at the time of purchase, they are required to report and remit use tax on these items.

Dynamics GP is well equipped to deal with sales tax but use tax presents more of a challenge. Essentially, use tax needs to be applied to an account's payable transaction but the payment of use tax is sent to a taxing authority, not to the transaction vendor. A common way to accomplish this in Dynamics GP is to use the built-in credit card functionality to shift the use tax liability from the vendor to the taxing authority.

In this recipe, we'll use the sample company and look at hacking credit card functionality to enter and track use tax.

Getting ready

Before we start, we need to set up a use tax detail and a credit card for a taxing authority. The following steps will help you set up a use tax detail:

1. Select **Administration** from the navigation pane. Select **Tax Details** from the area page under **Setup | Company**.

2. Type IL USE TAX in the **Tax Detail ID** field and set **Type** to **Purchases**.

3. Set the **Account** field to 000-6630-00 and the **Percentage** field to 7%. Click on **Save** to continue.

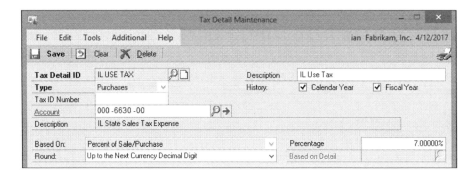

Part two of the setup is creating a credit card to "pay" the use tax amount and transfer the liability for payment from the vendor to the taxing authority. To set up a use tax credit card perform the following steps:

1. Select **Administration** from the navigation pane. Select **Credit Cards** from the area page under **Setup | Company**.

2. Name the credit card IL Use Tax and select the **Used by Company** box.

3. Click on **Credit Card** and set the **Vendor ID** field to ILSTATE0001.

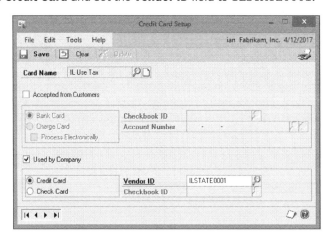

4. Click on **Save** to finish the setup.

How to do it...

Now that we've completed the use tax setup, let's see how to apply use tax to a transaction.

1. Select **Purchasing** from the navigation pane. Select **Transaction Entry** from the area page under **Transactions**.

2. Use the lookup button (magnifying glass) next to **Vendor ID** to select ACETRAVE001.

3. Press *Tab* until you get to the **Document Number** field and type 1234.

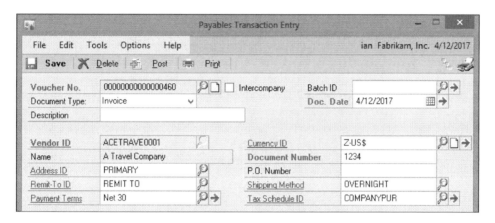

4. Move to the **Purchases** field and enter 1,000.00. Press *Tab* until you get to **Tax** and click on the blue arrow next to **Tax** to open the **Payables Tax Entry** window.

5. In the **Payables Tax Entry** window, use the lookup button (magnifying glass) to select the tax detail **IL USE TAX** replacing the existing tax detail named USEXMT+PSONO that defaults from the vendor. Click on **OK** to return to the payables transaction.

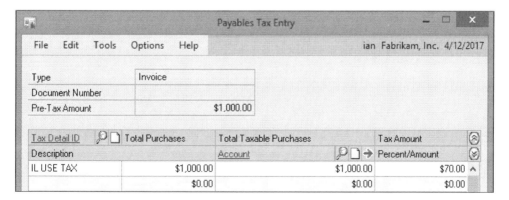

6. Now that tax has been applied to the transaction, if we leave it like this, the vendor will get paid $1,070. That won't work since we actually owe the vendor $1,000 and we owe the Illinois taxing authority $70. To fix this, press *Tab* to get to the **Credit Card** field and enter 70.00.

Purchases	$1,000.00	1099 Amount	$0.00
Trade Discount	$0.00	Cash	$0.00 →
Freight	$0.00	Check	$0.00 →
Miscellaneous	$0.00	Credit Card	$70.00 →
Tax	$70.00 →	Terms Disc Taken	$0.00
Total	$1,070.00	On Account	$1,000.00

7. Tab off the **Credit Card** field and the **Payables Credit Card Entry** window will open. Use the lookup button (magnifying glass) to select **IL Use Tax** as the **Card Name**. Click on **OK** to continue.

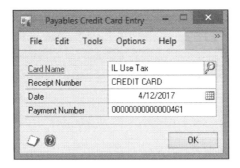

Notice, that the **On Account** field is now **$1,000**. This is the amount due to the vendor. When this transaction is posted, two AP vouchers will actually be created, one to Ace Travel for $1,000 and one to the Illinois taxing authority for $70. At month end when a check is generated to the Illinois taxing authority, each use tax voucher is included in the check, providing an effective audit trail for use tax transactions.

How it works...

Combining sales tax and credit card functionality to solve a use tax need is a perfect example of a useful hack. The vendor ends up being paid the right amount and so does the taxing authority. In addition, the expense side of the tax doesn't have to go to a tax expense account. The account can be changed to apply to the same account as the purchase to reflect the true cost of the transaction.

Because this is a hack, it's not perfect. Payments to the vendor are overstated by the tax amount because the tax wasn't actually paid to the vendor. This could result in an incorrect 1099 for vendors due one at tax time. The 1099 amounts can be adjusted on each transaction, but this is often missed. Generally though, these issues are minor compared to the benefits of applying use tax to transactions.

Correcting a lost password by resetting the system password

Part of the security matrix of Dynamics GP is the **system password** which provides another layer of protection after users have already logged in to Dynamics GP. Certain processes like changing security settings or setup options may require an additional password known as the system password. Even if a user has appropriate rights to set up options, they can't change those options without the system password.

While the use of a system password is technically optional, it is typically used in Dynamics GP implementations. In many environments it is also entered very infrequently and typically by administrators. Consequently, the system password can be lost or forgotten as people leave the company or change roles. Imagine how painful it could be to explain that security can't be changed because the system password has been lost!

Fortunately, there is a process available for administrators with access to the SQL Server to reset the administrator password. In this recipe, we'll look at how to do that.

How to do it...

To reset the system password perform the following steps:

1. Open Microsoft SQL Server Management Studio and connect to the SQL Server used for Dynamics GP. Enter a username and password or use Windows authentication to connect.

2. Because of the way that Dynamics GP maintains security with the SQL Server, a Dynamics GP username can't be used here. The only exception is the SQL system administrator (sa) user.

3. Click on the **New Query** button. Select the **Dynamics** database from the drop-down box on the top-left side. Enter the following script in the code area on the right:

```
Use Dynamics
Go
Update SY02400 Set Password = 0X0020202020202020202020202020202020
Go
```

4. Click on **Execute** to run the script. This resets the system password.

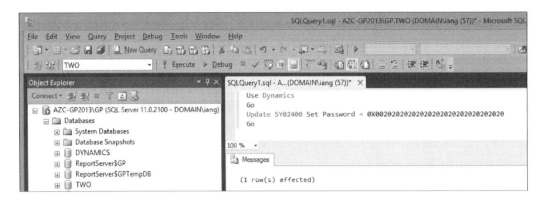

Open Microsoft Dynamics GP and select **Administration** from the navigation pane.

1. Select **System Password** from the area page under **System**.

2. Enter a new system password. Re-enter the new system password as confirmation and click on **OK** to save.

How it works...

The long line of strange numbers after **Set Password** simply sets the password back to blank. The password isn't encrypted, it's simply masked. With enough time, energy, and access to a company's SQL Server it would be possible to decode the masking. Then again, if a troublemaker has access to a firm's SQL Server, they don't need the system password to make a mess. This tip belongs with a company's database administrator. Ordinary users should be prevented from running queries that update information via SQL.

There's more...

In addition to resetting the system password, a similar script can be used to reset a lost budget password:

1. Click on the **New Query** button and select the **Company** database, containing the budget which needs its password to be reset, from the drop-down box on the top-left side. Enter the following script in the code area on the right, replacing `myBudgetID` with the **Budget ID** to be reset:

```
Update GL00200 Set BUDPWRD = 0X00202020202020202020202020202020202020
Where BUDGETID = 'myBudgetID'
Go
```

2. Click on **Execute** to run the script to reset the budget's password.

Warning the user if Caps Lock is on during login

Login passwords for Dynamics GP are case sensitive and limited to three tries. This means that the words `password` and `Password` are viewed as completely different when logging in because of the capital `P` in `Password`. After three failed login attempts, Dynamics GP closes and the user has to restart before trying to log in again. When a user unknowingly has the *Caps Lock* button on it almost always leads to failed logins and user frustration.

In recognition of this, Ian Grieve, a Senior Consultant with Perfect Image Limited and one of the authors of this book, has produced a, freely available, VBA utility which checks for *Caps Lock* activation and warns the user, in a non-intrusive manner, if it is on during login. This method uses the desktop alert code produced by Aaron Berquist of High Dynamics Range in association with David Musgrave.

In this recipe, we'll look at deploying and using this utility to warn users if *Caps Lock* is on.

How to do it...

To warn users if *Caps Lock* is on during login perform the following steps:

1. Open Internet Explorer and navigate to: `http://www.azurecurve.co.uk/2012/10/vba-customisation-to-microsoft-dynamics-gp-2013-login-window-to-display-login-alert-if-caps-lock-on/`.

2. Download and save the `LoginCapsLockWarning.7z` file (7-zip from `http://www.7-zip.org` required to extract the solution) to your desktop.

3. Right-click on the downloaded file and pick **7-zip** then click on **Extract here**.

4. In Dynamics GP, select **Microsoft Dynamics GP | Tools | Customize | Customization Maintenance**.

5. Click on **Import** then **Browse**. Navigate to the location where you extracted `LoginCapsLockWarning` on the desktop and pick the `LoginCapsLockWarning.package` file. Click on **OK** to install.

6. This customization will need to be applied to each user's workstation by repeating steps 4 and 5.

7. Once applied, a user will be warned with a non-invasive desktop alert in the bottom-right corner of the Windows desktop if the *Caps Lock* button is on when logging in.

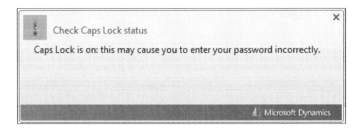

There's more...

There are two alternative methods available to the one created by Ian Grieve.

Patrick Roth's solution

Patrick Roth, a Senior Escalation Engineer in Developer Support at Microsoft, wrote a VBA utility that checks for *Caps Lock* activation and warns the user with a message box pop up if *Caps Lock* is on during log in. He made the utility, which installs in the same way as Ian Grieve's, freely available to the community via the Developing for Dynamics GP blog: `http://blogs.msdn.com/developingfordynamicsgp/archive/2009/07/22/determine-if-the-caps-lock-button-is-enabled-on-password-entry.aspx`.

Vaidhyanathan Mohan's solution

Vaidy Mohan, Microsoft Dynamics GP and CRM Consultant with Elcome International LLC, has produced a Visual Studio Tools add-in that checks for *Caps Lock* activation and warns the user with a message box pop up which does not use VBA and is, therefore, fully compatible with the new GP 2013 web client and which is freely available via his Dynamics GP – Learn and Discuss blog: `http://vaidymohan.com/2013/02/26/caps-lock-reminder-for-microsoft-dynamics-gp-2013`.

This solution is deployed by copying the downloaded `.dll` into the `Addins` folder on the client machine.

Similar to the *Reducing licensing needs by preventing multiple company logins* recipe discussed earlier in this chapter, these hacks, with the exception of Vaidy's, use a free, unsupported Visual Basic for Applications file. The selected package file will need to be applied to each user's computer for the *Caps Lock* warning to appear but that is a small price to pay for a recipe that significantly reduces user frustration.

Getting greater journal entry control by clearing recurring batch amounts

For years, Dynamics GP has provided a feature called a Quick Journal. Quick Journals allow users to set up a journal entry shell where the accounts remain the same but users can change the amounts each time they create an entry.

The Quick Journals feature is great, in principal, for transactions where only the amounts change regularly but it has a number of flaws. Specifically, the transactions can't be placed in batches and they can't be controlled with batch approval which has led many companies to choose not to use Quick Journals.

The recurring batch functionality in Dynamics GP provides the batch and approval functionality that many companies need, but until version 2010 the only option to change the amounts was to overwrite each line. This process left a lot of room for user error making it an imperfect solution as well.

Dynamics GP 2010 introduced the ability to clear the amounts from a recurring batch after it is posted. This allows a user to build a journal entry but not be locked into the same amounts each time. It also allows the use of batch approval.

Let's see how to clear recurring batches in this recipe.

How to do it...

To set up recurring batches to clear after posting perform the following steps:

1. Select **Financial** from the navigation pane, and then **Batches** under **Transactions**.
2. In **Batch ID** enter Test.
3. Set **Origin** to **General Entry**.
4. Change **Frequency** to **Monthly** to set up a recurring batch.

5. Select the **Clear Recurring Amounts** checkbox.

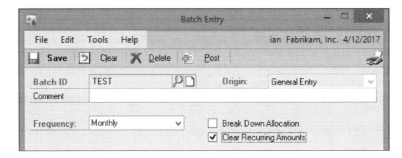

6. Click on **Transactions** to add recurring journal entries.

After the recurring batch is posted, the amounts will clear allowing users to enter new amounts the next time.

See also

The *Getting control of accruals and deferrals with recurring GL batches* recipe in *Chapter 4, Automating Dynamics GP*.

9
Preventing Errors in Dynamics GP

In this chapter we'll look at some ways to prevent errors in Dynamics GP by:

- ▶ Preventing posting errors by managing batch dates
- ▶ Reducing out of balance problems with Allow Account Entry
- ▶ Ensuring entry in the correct company by warning about test companies
- ▶ Protecting Dynamics GP with key security settings
- ▶ Providing clean vendor information by properly closing purchase orders
- ▶ Preventing account selection errors with chart segment names
- ▶ Ensuring proper year-end closing by checking posting types
- ▶ Preventing sales of a discontinued inventory item
- ▶ Correcting errors by backing out, correcting, and copying GL entries

Introduction

The longevity and popularity of Microsoft's Dynamics GP Enterprise Resource Planning software is a testament to the system's robustness, but any system is vulnerable to errors. There are times when users make entry mistakes, network outages occur and computer hardware fails, any of these events can cause errors in Dynamics GP. For a Dynamics GP administrator, some of the most common and most controllable errors are those related to user activities. For example, an administrator can't control when a network switch is going to fail, but they can ensure that proper security is in place to prevent users from deleting tables.

Preventing errors frees up administrator and user time to focus on more important items. In this chapter, we'll look at some common setup and procedural changes that administrators and users can make to help prevent errors in Dynamics GP. Additionally, we'll take a look at how to fix erroneous transactions that managed to make it to the general ledger.

Preventing posting errors by managing batch dates

In most modules, Microsoft Dynamics GP provides the option to post transactions individually or to collectively post a group of transactions in a batch. The common best practice when implementing Dynamics GP is to use **batch posting**, not individual transaction posting.

The reason behind this preference is that batches and batch posting provide a number of benefits over transactional posting. These benefits include the ability to save transactions without posting them, improved error handling, and the ability to post multiple transactions or multiple batches at once. Additionally, batches can be used to control the date that transactions are posted on, thereby making it easy to ensure that transactions are posted in the right period.

In this recipe, we will look at batch naming and posting techniques along with error handling options designed to minimize posting errors.

Getting ready

To set up the process to post transactions by batch perform the following steps:

1. In Dynamics GP, select **Administration** from the navigation pane. Select **Posting** under the **Posting** section on the **Administration** area page.
2. Select the **Series** to change settings for. For our example, select **Purchasing**.
3. Select a posting **Origin**. In this example, select **Payables Trx Entry** to control posting settings for accounts payable voucher entry.

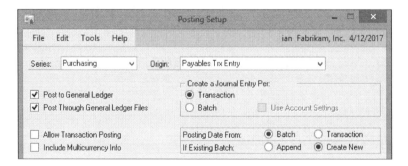

4. Uncheck **Allow Transaction Posting** to force posting to the general ledger by batch.

5. Select **Transaction** under **Create a Journal Entry Per** to avoid rolling up transactions in the general ledger.

6. Sending batches of subledger transactions to the general ledger as a single transaction has its roots in ledger paper accounting. This practice moved to software when disk space was at a premium. It is almost never needed now and complicates tracing subledger transactions through the general ledger.

7. Click on **Save**, and then **OK** to finish.

How to do it...

To set up a batch using best practices perform the following steps:

1. Select **Purchasing** from the navigation pane. Select **Batches** under the **Transactions** section on the **Purchasing** area page.

2. Name the batch with your initials and today's date. My example batch is named `IG-2017-04-17`.

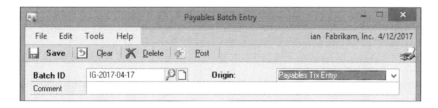

- By naming batches this way, users searching for a batch will see the available batches sorted in order by user initials and then date.

- Typically, firms either let users post their own batches, or they use a designated individual/group to post batches from multiple users.

- If users post their own batches, start the batch name with the initials followed by the date like `IG-2017-04-17`. This will cluster a user's batches together when posting, making it easier to post multiple batches for a single user.

- If a different individual will post transactions for multiple users, start the batches with the date followed by the initials like `2017-04-17-IG`. This clusters batches together by date making it easier to select the right batches across multiple users.

      ❑   Dates in batch names should start with the year and then the period like `2017-04`. This naming convention clusters batches together when approaching year end or period end. For example, it's typical at period end to have some left over transactions from the previous period and new transactions for the current period. Starting dates with the year and period helps ensure that users pick the correct batch to post.

      ❑   Single digit periods and days should use a zero in front since Dynamics GP sees batch names as text. Not using a leading zero will cause a batch for period 10 to come before a batch for period 9.

3. Select **Payables Trx Entry** in the **Origin** field.

4. Set **Frequency** to **Single Use** for our example. **Recurring batches** have a **Frequency** other than **single use** (monthly, weekly, and so on). They are designed to be posted multiple times. For recurring batches, the following recommendations apply:

      ❑   Start recurring batches with the letter `z` to cluster them at the bottom of lookup windows. It may make sense to date recurring batches with their end date instead of creation date to make it easy to identify when this batch will stop recurring.

      ❑   Provide a complete description and notes for recurring batches since the rational for the recurring batch may fade from memory over time.

      ❑   If there are multiple transactions in a recurring batch, ensure that they are all designed to stop repeating at the same time.

5. Enter today's date as the **Posting Date** for the batch following these recommendations:

      ❑   **One period per batch**: Users shouldn't mix transactions from multiple periods in a single batch as this makes it impossible to post the transactions in the proper period since the entire batch will post in one period.

         The only exception to this is **general ledger** (**GL**) batches which always use the date on the transaction for posting; there is no option to post GL batches by date.

      ❑   **Post using the batch date**: Posting using the batch date ensures that all the transactions in the batch post using the same date and the date is visible with a glance at the batch. This contrasts with individual posting where the posting data could be different on each transaction.

         For transaction posting, the true posting date is hidden behind an expansion arrow on the date field making it difficult to validate the posting date on multiple transactions.

6. Click on the **Transactions** button to add transactions to a batch.

7. Once transactions are entered, batches can be posted from the same window. When posting batches:

   ❑ Non-recurring batches should disappear when posted. In the event that this doesn't happen, users need to select the printer icon in the upper-right corner to print the batch edit list either to paper or to the screen. Printing the batch edit list prior to posting is a best practice but this process can be impractical for batches with large numbers of transactions.

   ❑ The **Transaction Edit List** will show batch-level errors at the top and transaction-level errors below any problematic transactions. The most common batch-level error is a closed fiscal period preventing batches from posting. For transaction-level errors, missing accounts or account-related problems are seen most often.

   ❑ Batches that contain errors may fail posting and end up in **Batch Recovery**. **Batch Recovery** is found in the **Administration** area page under **Routines**. Batch recovery will either resolve minor errors and continue the posting, or return the batch to a state where a Transaction Edit List can be printed and reviewed for corrections.

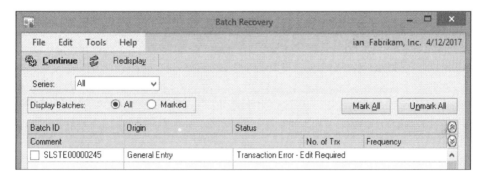

How it works...

Following these batch-level posting techniques simplifies batch management by providing a standard process and naming convention for all users. Posting errors are reduced by managing posting dates at the batch level and ensuring that batches only cover a single period.

Transactions posted in a batch have a better chance of recovery in the event of a catastrophic posting error like a network outage during posting. While this isn't acknowledged explicitly in any of the software documentation, there is a wealth of painful stories illustrating that transactions posted by batch recover from errors better than individually posted transactions.

See also

- ▸ The *Getting control of accruals and deferrals with Recurring GL Batches* recipe in Chapter 4, *Automating Dynamics GP*

- ▸ The *Controlling Posting Dates when not posting by batch* recipe in *Chapter 7, Exposing Hidden Features in Dynamics GP*

- ▸ The *Preventing entry of wrong dates by Closing Periods* recipe in *Chapter 10, Maintaining Dynamics GP*

Reducing out-of-balance problems with Allow Account Entry

Balancing subledgers like accounts payable or accounts receivable to the general ledger can be a time consuming process at period end. A common reason that a subledger doesn't match the corresponding account in the general ledger is that a user has made an entry directly to the general ledger.

Transactions in Dynamics GP generally flow down from subledgers into the general ledger. With rare exceptions, transactions made in the general ledger do not flow back upstream to a subledger. This means that when users make an entry directly to a general ledger account, the information doesn't flow back up to a related subledger, resulting in an out-of-balance situation.

A scenario like this is easily prevented by disabling an often overlooked feature known as **Allow Account Entry**. Disabling the Allow Account Entry setting prevents making entries directly to the general ledger for certain accounts. When this feature is deactivated for an account, transactions must flow from a subledger; direct entries to that account from the general ledger are blocked by the system.

In this recipe, we will look at how to deactivate the Allow Account Entry feature and we'll see how it works in practice.

How to do it...

To require transactions to flow through a subledger for a particular account perform the following steps:

1. Select **Financial** from the navigation pane then select **Accounts** under the **Cards** section.

2. Use the lookup button (magnifying glass) to select account **000-2100-000**, the Accounts Payable account in the sample company.

3. Uncheck the box marked **Allow Account Entry** and click on **Save** to finish.

To illustrate what happens when this feature is deactivated for an account perform the following steps:

1. Back on the **Financial** area page, select **General** under **Transactions**.

2. Use the lookup button (magnifying glass) in the **Account** field at the bottom of the window to select account **000-2100-000**.

3. Dynamics GP responds with a message that **Account 000-2100-000 does not allow account entry**.

How it works...

This feature is simple to implement but extremely powerful. A simple checkbox can dramatically improve the process of balancing transactions at period end. There are a number of accounts that can benefit from turning off Allow Account Entry; common accounts that are prime candidates for preventing direct general ledger entry include cash, accounts payable, accounts receivable, inventory, payroll accounts, fixed assets, accumulated depreciation, and depreciation expense.

There's more...

There can be valid reasons for adjusting some of these accounts in the general ledger so administrators need to understand the process to accomplish this.

Adjustments

There are times when an adjustment to one of these accounts is needed in the general ledger. Perhaps a network outage happened during posting that resulted in a transaction properly posting to the subledger but not moving to the general ledger. In a scenario like this, an administrator can temporarily check the box to allow account entry and uncheck the box as soon as the correction is posted. This is an occasional inconvenience when compared to the benefits of smoother monthly balancing. Because of the potential effects on balancing, the ability to adjust this setting should be limited to select users.

See also

> ▶ The *Speeding month-end processing with Reconcile to GL functionality* recipe in *Chapter 7, Exposing Hidden Features in Dynamics GP*

Ensuring entry in the correct company by warning about test companies

Most companies using Dynamics GP set up a **test company**. This is normally a copy of the live, production, GP database and may reside on its own server. A test company may be used for testing things like new processes, modules, or even, if it resides on a separate server, test upgrades.

A test company is used in addition to the sample company because it contains a copy of the firm's actual data. Consequently, they have different uses. For instance, the sample company is great for learning about new modules that a firm is not yet licensed for, since unlicensed modules aren't available in a test company. A test company is great for trying out the process to close a year or provide training to new users.

A common problem occurs when a user mistakenly logs into the test company and enters a transaction. When they find their mistake they have to enter it again in the production database and even more problems can occur if a user mistakenly enters a test transaction in the production company.

Dynamics GP provides a feature to help prevent these scenarios from occurring. There is a small trick that can be used to warn users when they log into a test company; this is similar to the message that users get when they open the sample company. Warning users when entering a test company is the focus of this recipe.

How to do it...

To warn users that they are opening a test company perform the following steps:

1. Sign in to a test company in Microsoft Dynamics GP. This recipe will not work with the sample company because of the way it is set up.

2. In Dynamics GP select **Administration** from the navigation pane. Select **Company** under the **Company** section on the Home page.

3. Next to the company name in the **Company Name** textbox type <TEST>.

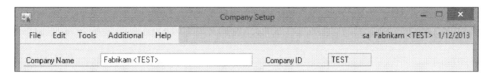

4. Click on **Save** to save the setting.

5. Restart Microsoft Dynamics GP and log into the same test company.

6. A warning message will appear alerting the user that this is a test company.

How it works...

Warning users about test companies is a great way to prevent errors. I've seen it be a real life saver when a user realized that they didn't see the warning and were entering test data in the production company. This recipe is so simple to implement that everyone should use it.

There's more...

If you have a company for historical data, you can get a similar message to the test company message covered in this chapter by adding <HISTORICAL> to the company name.

See also

▶   The *Coloring windows by company* recipe in *Chapter 11, Extending Dynamics GP with the Support Debugging Tool*

Protecting Dynamics GP with key security settings

Security is an important part of any ERP system and Dynamics GP provides a robust security model which rolls up individual item access into tasks and tasks into roles. Roles can then be applied to individual users, providing fine-grain control of security with minimal work after the initial setup.

While the setup and maintenance of security in Dynamics GP could fill a book by itself, there are a couple of critical settings that every administrator needs to be aware of.

Dynamics GP security contains a master switch that turns all security on or off. The original purpose of this switch was to allow set up and testing of the system while security was still being configured. Then, like Chevy Chase's Christmas lights in the movie National Lampoon's Christmas Vacation, a master switch could be flipped and security would be active. As Dynamics GP has matured, it has become easy to add users to a Power User role, giving them access to everything in the system during setup and testing while leaving security active. The master security switch still remains and administrators need to ensure that it is on.

Located below the security master switch is an account security switch. Often users think that if security is on, turning on account security must mean more security. What account security does is limit access to accounts based on an organizational structure that needs to be set up first. If an organizational structure is not set up, all users are denied access to the chart of accounts and it appears that the chart of accounts has been deleted. Few checkboxes in Dynamics GP can induce the stomach-dropping fear that comes with inadvertently checking the account security box. This is easily one of the most panicky support calls I see and certainly it is the one with the easiest fix.

Setting up security and account security aren't recipes, they are more like Thanksgiving dinners. For this recipe, we'll trim it down to a snack and show how to ensure that security is on and account security is off.

How to do it...

To activate security and deactivate account security in Dynamics GP perform the following steps:

1. Select **Administration** from the navigation pane. Select **Company** under the **Company** section on the **Administration** area page.

2. Check the **Security** box on the lower-right side to activate security. If it is already marked, security is on, congratulations!

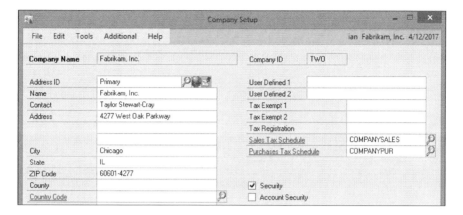

3. Below that is the **Account Security** box. Simply uncheck the box to ensure that account security is off.

How it works...

These are two very basic settings that often trip up administrators. It's maddening to see a very detailed security model with a lot of work put into it and then find the security box unchecked. Don't even think about the effect on an administrator's career if an auditor finds this box unchecked. It's also career limiting to have the CFO asking where the chart of accounts has disappeared to because someone accidently turned on account security. Don't misunderstand, account security is a great feature, it's just not one that should be turned on lightly.

There's more...

Given the power of these checkboxes, access to them should be secured as well. For complicated security setups and additional security features consider third-party solutions.

Security for security

The **Security** and **Account Security** checkboxes are powerful. Once they are set correctly it is important that security be restricted to the Company setup window to prevent a user from disabling security entirely by simply unchecking a box.

Security solutions

There are several third-party solutions that build on Dynamics GP security making security management easier and adding additional features. For example, FastPath's Configurator AD product synchronizes user passwords with Windows Active Directory passwords, allowing multiple single sign-on options. Additionally, Configurator AD provides an interface outside of Dynamics GP to assign security roles to users. This allows a central security manager to assign Dynamics GP security to users without using up a Dynamics GP license or providing excessive access to the security manager. More information is available at `http://www.gofastpath.com`.

Providing clean vendor information by properly closing purchase orders

It's not unusual for a purchase order to be left open in Dynamics GP due to a vendor's inability to deliver goods. However, when the time comes to close an incomplete purchase order, too many users simply change the P.O. line quantity to match the quantity delivered and close the P.O. The problem with this process is that it reduces visibility of the performance of a vendor. By changing the quantity ordered there is no way to track the fact that the vendor didn't deliver goods.

A better way to close a purchase order is to put any undelivered amounts in the quantity cancelled line. This makes performance information available to SmartLists and Excel reports, making it possible to analyze the performance of a vendor over time. As an example, an analysis may show that it may make sense for a firm to pay a little more to a reliable supplier instead of dealing with the frustration of product outages.

In this recipe, we'll look at the right way to close a partially received purchase order using the sample company.

How to do it...

To properly close a partially received purchase order perform the following steps:

1. Select **Purchasing** from the navigation pane. Select **Purchase Order Entry** under the **Transaction** section on the **Purchasing** area page.

2. Use the lookup button (magnifying glass) to select purchase order **PO1016**. Change the **Quantity Cancelled** value to 5 to zero out this P.O.

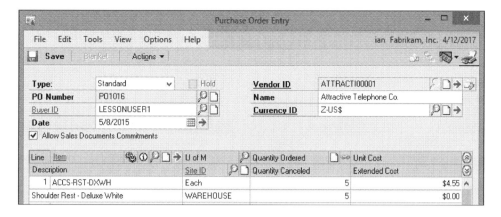

3. Click on **Save** to save the changes. The P.O. closes automatically when the last line is cancelled.

How it works...

Properly closing purchase orders in Dynamics GP allows a company to make intelligent sourcing decisions about which vendors are able to meet the firm's needs. Companies gain the data necessary to analyze vendor performance and make decisions based on factors beyond just price. After all, having a cheaper product to sell isn't very helpful if it never arrives.

Preventing account selection errors with chart segment names

Given the typical meticulous tendencies of most accountants, it's a little bit of a surprise that the descriptions in an average chart of accounts are a complete mess. Most charts of accounts are initially very pristine but as accounts are added by various people over time, their descriptions become inconsistent. This makes it very difficult to ensure that users select the right account.

As an example, assume that the first segment in the chart of accounts represents the company, the second is the natural account, and the third is a department. An account description would ideally be something like "ABC Co.-Cash-Marketing" or "ABC Co.-Accounts Payable-Operations". In reality, accounts tend to look like "Marking Cash, ABC" or "AP Ops". This makes it hard for users to find and select the right account.

Dynamics GP provides a mechanism to ensure that new accounts follow a set naming pattern. Rather than adding a description to the chart of accounts, every unique option in each segment is given a name in a setup screen. When that item is selected, Dynamics GP provides the name of that segment from the setup. This builds the name of the resulting account on the fly and creates a consistent naming convention for the chart.

We'll use the sample company to set up and use Account Segment descriptions to cook this recipe.

Getting ready

To set up account segment descriptions perform the following steps:

1. Select **Financial** from the navigation pane. Select **Segment** under the **Setup** section.

2. Set **Segment ID** to **Division**. Use the lookup button (magnifying glass) in the **Number** field to find number **100**. Add or change the description to Sales.

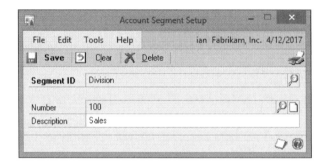

3. Set **Segment ID** to **Account**. Use the lookup button (magnifying glass) in the **Number** field to find number **1100**. Add or change the description to Accounts Receivable.

4. Set **Segment ID** to **Department**. Use the lookup button (magnifying glass) in the **Number** field to find number **02**. Add or change the description to Marketing.

How to do it...

To create an account description using account segments perform the following steps:

1. Select **Financial** from the navigation pane. Select **Account** under the **Cards** section.

2. In the **Account** field, enter 100-1100-02 and press *Tab*.

3. The name will be automatically built in the **Description** field from the descriptions of the three segments in the account number.

How it works...

Having consistent account descriptions prevents errors by providing clear and consistent account naming, making it easy for users to select the right account. This recipe also makes it easy for users who create accounts. They no longer have to wrestle with the right naming order. Unfortunately, it does not provide a mechanism to fix existing accounts. Users will have to cook up that recipe on their own.

See also

▸ *Keeping the chart of accounts clean by reactivating Account Segment warnings* recipe in *Chapter 8, Improving Dynamics GP with Hacks*

▸ The *Importing data with Microsoft Word and a Dynamics GP macro* recipe in *Chapter 6, Connecting Dynamics GP with Microsoft Office 2010*

Ensuring proper year-end closing by checking posting types

When setting up accounts in the chart of accounts, users are required to select a posting type of either balance sheet or profit and loss. These selections correspond to their respective financial statements, the balance sheet and the profit and loss statement, also known as the income statement. Asset, liability, and equity accounts should have a posting type of balance sheet. Revenue and expense accounts need the profit and loss posting type. This is important because the posting type controls the behavior of year-end closing for these accounts.

The year-end closing routine in Dynamics GP zeros out the accounts with a posting type of profit and loss and updates the selected retained earnings account. This process resets the profit and loss accounts to prepare for a new year and uses the ending balance in the balance sheet accounts to create the beginning balance in the new year.

If accounts are incorrectly set up as profit and loss accounts, their year-end balance will be erroneously cleared to retained earnings. Similarly, accounts incorrectly set up as balance sheet accounts will not get cleared to retained earnings to reflect the previous year's net income. In short, if the posting type is not correct during the year-end closing, companies end up with a mess that can be difficult to fix. Correcting entries can possibly be made if the number of accounts is very small, but even this can be time consuming and difficult to get right. There is no way to roll back a year-end closing without reverting to a pre-closing backup or an expensive consulting engagement with Microsoft.

Because of this, validating that the posting type is set correctly is an important step prior to closing the year. There are two typical processes to validate posting types, using a SmartList to view exceptions and using a report to review all accounts. In this recipe, we will cook up both options.

How to do it...

The two main options for validating posting types are an exception-based SmartList and a built-in dynamics GP report. Many firms use a standard, generalized numbering system for their chart of accounts based on the first digit of the natural account. When a schema like this is followed, it makes it possible to double check that the accounts have the correct posting types. A typical scenario uses accounts starting with one, two, or three as balance sheet accounts representing assets, liabilities, and equity respectively. Those starting with four or higher are used for the profit and loss statement.

The benefit of this type of set up is that users can create a SmartList that only shows the exceptions. This makes it very easy to find and correct errors. If there is no pattern or identifier designed into the account structure a report built into Dynamics GP can still be used to review account posting types.

For our example, we use the sample company which is set up with the last balance sheet account as 3999 and the first profit and loss account as 4000.

To review account posting types with a SmartList perform the following steps:

1. Click on the **SmartList** icon to open the SmartList window.
2. Select the **Accounts** SmartList under the **Financial** section.
3. Click on the **Search** button.
4. In the **Search Definition 1** section set **Column Name** to **Account Number**, **Filter** to **is less than**, and **Value** to 000-4000-00.

5. In the **Search Definition 2** section set **Column Name** to **Posting Type**, **Filter** to **is equal to**, and **Value** to **Profit and Loss**.

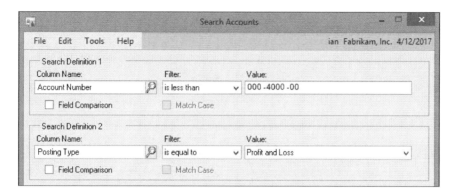

6. Click on **OK** to display low numbered accounts that are improperly listed as profit and loss accounts.

7. Click on the **Print** button to print this report to make the appropriate corrections in the **Account Maintenance** window later.

8. Click on **Favorites** and save this SmartList as a favorite named `YE BS Errors`.

9. Click on **Search** again.

10. Change the **Search Definition 1** values to **Account Number**, **is greater than**, and `999-3999-99`.

11. Change the **Search Definition 2** values to **Posting Type**, **is equal to**, and **Balance Sheet**.

12. Click on **OK** to display high-numbered accounts that are improperly listed as Balance Sheet accounts.

13. Click on the **Print** button to print this report and allow a user to make the appropriate corrections in the **Account Maintenance** window later.

14. Click on **Favorites** and save this SmartList as a favorite named `YE PL Errors`.

If a firm's chart of accounts is not set up in a way that makes identifying exceptions possible, a user still needs to print the chart of accounts and review the posting types' accounts individually prior to year end.

To print and review the chart perform the following steps:

1. Select **Financial** from the navigation pane. Select **Account** from the **Financial** area page under the **Reports** and **Financial** sections.

2. Under the **Reports** header, select **Posting**. Click on the **New** button.

3. In the **Option** box type `Posting Type`.

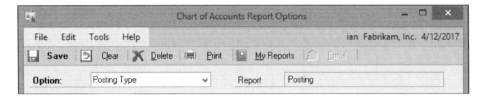

4. Click on **OK** to finish.

5. Select the **Print** button and review the report for posting type corrections.

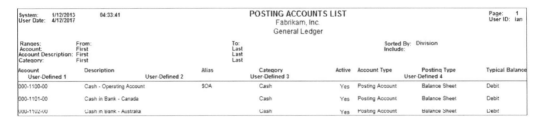

Once incorrect posting types have been identified, they can be corrected using the **Account** window on the **Financial** area page under **Cards**.

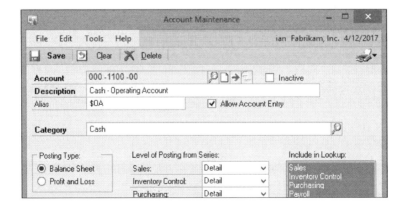

How it works...

Reviewing posting types prior to running year-end close is a simple solution to preventing an embarrassing situation. Firms that are able to use exception-based reporting get a fast, easy validation that posting types are correct. Even when exception reporting is not available, reviewing posting types is an important procedure to prevent a year-end disaster.

See also

▶   *Chapter 5, Harnessing the Power of SmartLists*

Preventing sales of a discontinued inventory item

Companies frequently discontinue inventory items. Perhaps an item's sales volume is too low, or it has been replaced with a new model, or the item is no longer available from a supplier. By default in Dynamics GP, discontinued inventory items can still be sold. The reason is that companies would still want to sell these items and clear out the inventory if the opportunity arose but they don't want to purchase more of a discontinued item.

The problem comes when companies need to prevent the sale of discontinued items. There could be a safety or health issue contributing to the importance of not selling a particular item. The typical advice in cases like this is to write off the discontinued inventory to prevent the sale. But, that removes visibility to the inventory that might be returnable for credit in the case of a safety recall. Additionally, in the event of a health issue, the inventory may need to be retained for inspection or proof of proper disposal. Writing the items off or moving them to a different item number may not be appropriate in these cases

There is a mechanism to reduce errors by preventing the sale of a discontinued inventory. In this recipe, we'll look at how to do just that.

How to do it...

To prevent Dynamics GP from allowing sales of a discontinued inventory:

1.   Select **Sales** from the navigation pane. Select **Sales Order Processing** under the **Setup** section on the **Sales** area page.

2.   Click on the **Options** button.

3. In the scrolling window at the bottom of the form, scroll down and uncheck **Allow Sale of Discontinued Items**. Click on **OK** to finish.

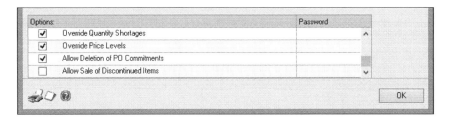

When a user enters a discontinued item in sales order processing, the system presents an error message and requires the user to select an active item as a replacement.

How it works...

Preventing the sale of discontinued inventory items is easy but since the setting is buried in sales, not inventory, most administrators never find it. One important point about this setting is that it is universal for a company; if the sale of discontinued items is prevented then it's prevented for all discontinued items.

There's more...

Prior to Dynamics GP 2013, there was no individual control; it either blocked the sale of all discontinued items, or allowed the sale of all. Dynamics GP 2013 has seen the introduction of the Inactive flag on individual items.

When an item is inactive it can be neither purchased nor sold; existing transactions for the inactive item can still be processed, although the quantity cannot be changed. This means an order which has been shipped can be transferred to an invoice even if the item is now inactive.

To discontinue an item and set it as inactive perform the following steps:

1. Select **Inventory** from the navigation pane. Select **Item** under the **Cards** section on the **Inventory** area page.

2. Type 24XIDE to load the item **24x CD-ROM**.

3. Set the **Item Type** drop-down box to **Discontinued**.

4. Select the **Inactive** checkbox.

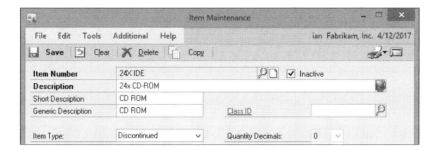

5. Click on **Save**.

Once the item has been deactivated, the only transaction types that can be entered for an inactive item are:

- Returns from sales or for purchases
- Inventory transfers between sites or bins
- Increase or decrease variances
- Decrease adjustments

See also...

- *Chapter 2, New in Dynamics GP 2013*

Correcting errors by backing out, correcting, and copying GL entries

This chapter is dedicated to preventing errors but for this recipe we want to look at fixing errors; specifically, the **Correct Journal Entry** functionality in Dynamics GP. The occurrence of errors is inevitable. The recipes in this chapter are designed to help users and administrators minimize errors, but once an error occurs, fixing it quickly is the next priority.

A common problem happens when users post journal entries to an incorrect period. They create a transaction using the current date and forget to change it to post the entry in the previous period.

Dynamics GP includes functionality to fix journal entry errors by backing out a journal entry and optionally presenting a duplicate journal entry for the user to change and repost. This same functionality allows copying a journal entry for users who forgot to use a recurring batch.

In this recipe, we'll use the sample company to look at fixing errors by backing out, correcting, and copying journal entries.

How to do it...

To back out and correct a journal entry perform the following steps:

1. Select **Financial** from the navigation pane. Select **General** under the **Transactions** section.

2. Select **Correct** from the top-right corner.

3. In the **Action** field, pick **Back Out a Journal Entry and Create a Correcting Entry**. Set the year to **2013** and enter 802 as the **Original Journal Entry**. Click on **OK** to continue.

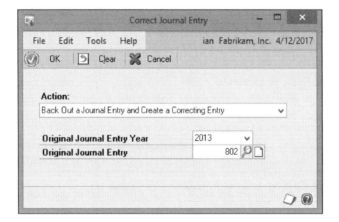

4. Click on **OK** to acknowledge that this is a recurring entry and click on **Select** to choose the only option. The sample company has a very limited number of journal entries that didn't originate in a subledger and this is the best example.

5. The backout transaction will open in the **Transaction Entry** window with the debit and credit amounts switched. This reverses the effect of the original entry.

6. Dynamics GP also provides a connection to the original entry in the **Reference** field.

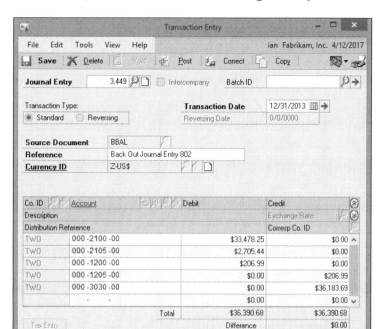

7. In the **Batch ID** field enter CORR and click on *Tab*. Select **Add** to add the batch and **Save** to save the batch. Click on **Save** in the transaction to save it. Dynamics GP will create the correcting entry once the backout entry is saved.

8. Change the **Transaction Date** on the correction transaction to 11/30/2017 to simulate correcting a transaction posted in the wrong period. At this point, transaction lines could be added or deleted and amounts can be changed. Users can adjust any part of the transaction to correct the entry.

9. Click on **Save** to save the transaction. Both the backout transaction and the correction are now in the CORR batch waiting to be posted.

   Because this is a general journal entry, the entry is posted based on the transaction date so mixing different dates in a single batch is OK.

The process for copying a journal entry is similar and works like this:

1. On the **Transaction Entry** window, select **Copy**.

2. Set the **Year** field to 2014 and enter 27 as the **Original Journal Entry**. Click on **OK** to continue.

3. The user now has a copy of the original journal entry which can be changed or adjusted as necessary.

How it works...

Backing out and correcting journal entries provides an easy mechanism to fix errors. Because the original transaction is retained and a reversing transaction is used, it's easy to audit the process and address questions about these corrections. Since copying a journal entry starts with a posted entry, these transactions are also less likely to contain errors.

There's more...

For our example we used an entry that originated in the general ledger. There is also a setting that allows the correction of entries that originated in subledgers.

Subledger corrections

Generally, corrections to a subledger transaction should be made in the originating module. For example, AP transactions should typically be voided and re-entered in purchasing, and not just corrected in the general ledger. However, if a transaction needs to have only the general ledger portion corrected, subledger transactions can be backed out, corrected, and copied via this method as well. In order to make this work, there is a setting that must be activated. To activate the ability to back out, correct, and copy transactions that originated in a subledger perform the following steps:

1. Select **Financial** from the navigation pane. Select **General Ledger** under the **Setup** section.

2. Select the **Voiding/Correcting of Subsidiary Transactions** checkbox and
    click on **Save**.

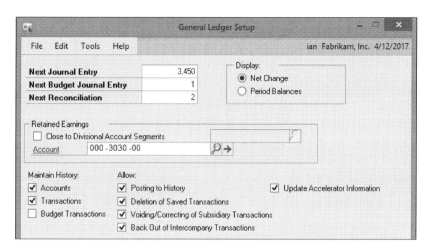

10
Maintaining Dynamics GP

In this chapter we will look at some common maintenance items:

- Speeding up navigation lists by disabling Business Analyzer
- Preventing entry of wrong dates by closing periods.
- Improving performance by adjusting the AutoComplete settings
- Cleaning up Accounts Receivable with Paid Transaction Removal
- Providing correct tax information by updating 1099 information
- Maintaining updated code by rolling out service packs with Client Updates
- Improving stability by managing dictionaries
- Safeguarding data by backing everything up
- Resolving errors with the Check Links utility
- Speeding login by clearing the Menu Master table
- Validating balances with the Reconcile utility
- Troubleshooting issues with a DexSQL log
- Speeding security setup with user copy

Introduction

Basic maintenance is important in order to keep Dynamics GP healthy and secure; no complex system runs well without regular maintenance to prevent errors and improve system performance. A significant amount of maintenance isn't normally required for a Dynamics GP implementation, but there are some areas where regular maintenance can provide significant benefits in terms of safety and performance. In this chapter, we will look at recipes designed to help maintain a healthy Dynamics GP system. Most of these recipes will typically be performed by an administrator or power user, since some recipes can have adverse consequences when not properly performed.

Speeding up navigation lists by disabling Business Analyzer

Reporting services' reports can be of great benefit to users of Dynamics GP by presenting relevant information to them on the Home page and also in the navigation lists. However, loading Business Analyzer in the navigation pane FactBox can cause the lists to load slowly so some customers may want to disable the FactBox.

Unfortunately, Dynamics GP only allows the FactBox to be hidden manually by individual users and needs to be hidden on each of the navigation lists separately. Fortunately, Dynamics GP databases are stored in SQL Server and can be updated with a simple SQL Trigger that runs each time a user opens a navigation list for the first time; this recipe will show you how to add this SQL Trigger.

How to do it...

To hide Business Analyzer FactBoxes in navigation lists perform the following steps:

1. Open Microsoft SQL Server Management Studio and connect to the SQL Server used for Dynamics GP. Enter a username and password or use Windows Authentication to connect.

2. Because of the way that Dynamics GP maintains security with SQL Server, a Dynamics GP username can't be used here. The only exception is the SQL system administrator (sa) user.

3. Click on the **New Query** button. Select the **System** database (usually **DYNAMICS**) from the drop-down box in the top-left corner. Enter the following script in the code area on the right:

```
USE DYNAMICS
GO
CREATE TRIGGER dbo.Update_SY07225_FactBoxVisible ON dbo.SY07225
AFTER INSERT
```

```
AS
  WITH
    UpdateSY07225 AS (SELECT ListDictID, ListID, ViewID, USERID
FROM inserted)
  UPDATE
    SY
  SET
    FactBoxVisible = 0
  FROM
    SY07225 SY
  INNER JOIN
    UpdateSY07225 USY ON USY.ListDictID = SY.ListDictID
      AND USY.ListID = SY.ListID
      AND USY.ViewID = SY.ViewID
      AND USY.USERID = SY.USERID
GO
```

4. Click on **Execute** to run the script. This adds a trigger to the List View Options table that sets the visible flag to false.

How it works...

Each time a user opens a navigation list for the first time an entry is added to the List View Options table in the system database. By using a trigger to set `FactBoxVisible` to `false` as the line is inserted, the Business Analyzer FactBox is not displayed to the user.

If a user wants a particular navigation list to display the FactBox, he or she can switch it back on through the interface by pressing *Ctrl + F2*.

There's more...

The trigger shown in this recipe only prevents the Business Analyzer FactBox from being displayed on navigation lists that the user opens for the first time after the trigger has been added. If a site has been using Dynamics GP for a while then the table will already be populated with entries. To update all existing entries in the List View Options table to disable the FactBox, run the following script in SQL Server Management Studio:

```
Use DYNAMICS
GO
UPDATE SY07225 SET FactBoxVisible = 0
GO
```

If you're using the Dynamics GP 2013 Named System Database functionality, make sure you change the DYNAMICS reference in the preceding script to your named system database.

See also

▸ The *Personalizing the Home page by selecting the right role* recipe in *Chapter 1, Personalizing Dynamics GP*

▸ The *Further personalizing the Home page by customizing the layout* recipe in *Chapter 1, Personalizing Dynamics GP*

▸ The *Visualizing information with Business Analyzer on the Home page* recipe in *Chapter 1, Personalizing Dynamics GP*

Preventing entry of wrong dates by closing periods

An important step in maintaining any accounting system is controlling access to financial periods. Financial period balances control how financial statements are presented. Once financial statements are complete, they shouldn't change except in very specific, controlled circumstances. If a firm doesn't properly control access to financial periods, the company's past financial statements will continue to change. In addition to the frustration of trying to compare results to a moving target, continually changing financial statements can cause SEC issues, audit problems, and a loss of confidence in the firm's financial reporting.

The way to control access to financial periods in Dynamics GP is to close financial periods that are not being used. In some systems, closing a period is a time consuming and irreversible process. This is not the case with Dynamics GP, which provides an easy way to close periods and reopen them for adjustments prior to finalizing financial statements.

Typically, companies have the current period open for transaction entry. As transactions arrive for the next period, firms typically open the next period as well to allow entry of the next period's transactions. This leaves two periods open around month end close, but otherwise only one period is open at a time. Once a period is complete, it's important to close that fiscal period to prevent further transactions.

In this recipe, we will look at the process to close fiscal periods in Dynamics GP.

How to do it...

To close a fiscal period in Dynamics GP perform the following steps:

1. Select **Administration** from the navigation pane. Select **Fiscal Periods** under the **Setup** and **Company** sections on the **Administration** area page.

2. Select the checkbox next to the period and module to close. Typically, the **Financial** series, which includes the general ledger, is the last series to be closed.

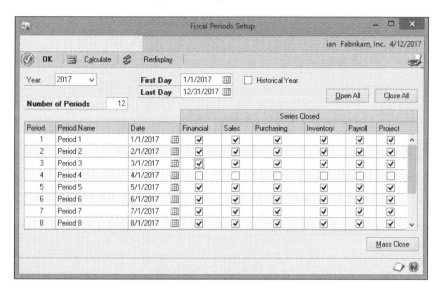

3. Unmarking the checkbox under a series reopens the period for subsequent adjusting entries.

Closing the period is an important monthly maintenance procedure. It is critical to preventing transactions from posting in the wrong period and it's an important step to ensure the correctness of the financial statements.

There's more...

By default, the fiscal period window controls posting transactions to a period for all transactions in a module. Sometimes, though, the module level is too high and companies need the ability to allow certain types of transactions to post while preventing others.

The Mass Close button

Closing fiscal periods based on series is easy. However, there are times when a company isn't ready to close an entire series, but does need to prevent the posting of certain transaction types. This can be accomplished using the **Mass Close** button on the **Fiscal Periods Setup** window.

For example, if accounts payable needs an extra day to finish cutting checks but the company wants to prevent the entry of new payable vouchers in the period, the **Mass Close** button presents a list of all of the posting transaction types and allows a user to close the period, not for a series but for one or more transaction types within that series.

To demonstrate closing only a particular transaction type for a period perform the following steps:

1. In the **Fiscal Periods Setup** window click on **Mass Close**.

2. Set the **Series** to **Purchasing**.

3. Set the **Period From** and **Period To** to **3**.

4. Scroll to **Payables Trx Entry** and check the box next to it.

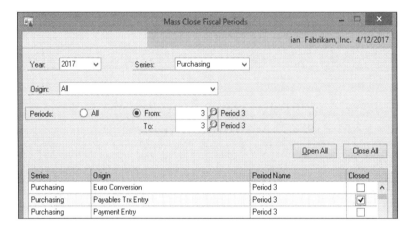

5. Click on **Save** to close the period for that transaction type.

6. Notice that the entire series is checked as closed. There is no visual cue that only part of this module has been closed.

Improving performance by adjusting the AutoComplete settings

Microsoft Dynamics GP provides auto complete functionality that remembers previous entries and displays them to users during subsequent data entry. Users can pick the appropriate item without having to type the entire text. This is a great feature but the entries are stored per user and per field. That means that each time the system saves a vendor number that has been keyed it's saved as one entry for that user. By default, Dynamics GP is set up to hold ten thousand entries, per user, for each field.

As you can imagine, over a long period of time and in organizations with heavy entry volume, the number of entries can build up, slowing down AutoComplete's performance significantly. Additionally, the number of choices presented to users can become unwieldy. For this recipe, we will look at a two-part solution to this problem. First, we will set up a maintenance routine to clean out any entries not used over the last sixty days and then we will reduce the number of results being saved per field to a more manageable one thousand.

How to do it...

To get control over AutoComplete entries perform the following steps:

1. Select **Home** from the navigation pane. Select **User Preferences** in the shortcut bar.
2. Click on the **AutoComplete** button.
3. Set **Remove Unused Entries After** to 60 days. Click on **OK** to finish.
4. Change the **Max. Number of Entries to Store per Field** setting to 1,000.

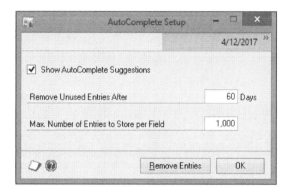

5. The new settings will take effect once the user logs out and logs in again.

How it works...

Companies can help prevent system slowdowns by controlling the volume of entries that Dynamics GP uses for AutoComplete. This setting is a per user setting so each user needs to make the change for his or her own login.

There's more...

Administrators can change the AutoComplete setting for all users with a SQL command.

Making the change for all users

Some users obviously make greater use of the AutoComplete feature than others. Consequently, companies may not want to set all users to the same settings. If a firm wants to globally set the number of days to remove unused entries after and the maximum number of entries to store per field, they can do that by executing this code in SQL Management Studio against the system database (usually DYNAMICS):

```
Update Dynamics..sy01402
Set syUSERDFSTR='TRUE-60-1000'
Where syDefaultType=30
```

The middle line turns **AutoComplete** on with the `True` setting, removes unused entries after 60 days, and sets the max number of entries to store per field to 1,000.

See also

▶ The *Cleaning up the mess by fixing Auto Complete errors* recipe in *Chapter 1, Personalizing Dynamics GP*

Cleaning up Accounts Receivable with Paid Transaction Removal

An important maintenance item that is often overlooked is the Accounts Receivable Paid Transaction Removal feature; perhaps it is overlooked because the name is somewhat misleading. Paid Transaction Removal only removes receivable transactions for companies that are not keeping receivables history. Most firms do keep history and in that case, Paid Transaction Removal only moves Accounts Receivable transactions to history rather than deleting them. This significantly reduces the number of transactions to be processed by Dynamics GP when running Accounts Receivable Aging and it can provide tremendous speed improvements to the aging process because the aging routine no longer has to work through the pile of completed paid transactions.

Once Paid Transaction Removal is run, companies can no longer "unapply" payments to a receivables invoice. Additionally, once a check is moved to history via Paid Transaction Removal it can no longer be marked as **Non-Sufficient Funds** (**NSF**). With these restrictions, it's commonly recommended that the Paid Transaction Removal process be run with a date in arrears. A misapplied invoice will typically be picked up within an invoicing cycle or two. Using a delay provides a buffer to allow for easy corrections of recent transactions while still providing the efficiency of removing completed transactions.

Companies typically run Paid Transaction Removal on a monthly basis. The routine is set to remove paid transactions older than a set date and most firms set this date thirty to ninety days before the current date. I've seen firms use time frames of six months or longer when they have significant issues with misapplied payments. The key to an efficient AR aging process isn't in the interval used, it is in running the process regularly to control the number of open receivables, which keeps the AR aging process efficient. In this recipe we'll look at how to process Paid Transaction Removal.

Getting ready

To ensure that history is being kept prior to running Paid Transaction Removal, perform the following steps:

1. In Dynamics GP select **Sales** from the navigation pane. Select **Receivables** under the **Setup** section on the **Sales** area page.

2. Check **Print Historical Aged Trial Balance** to ensure that the transaction history is kept regardless of other customer history options.

3. Click on **OK** to save.

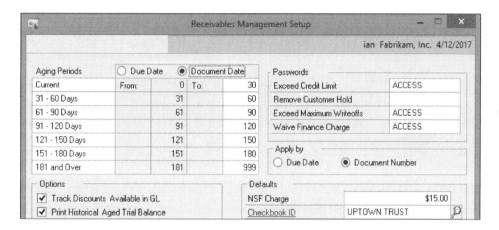

How to do it...

To run Paid Transaction Removal in Dynamics GP, perform the following steps:

1. In Dynamics GP select **Sales** from the navigation pane. Select **Paid Transaction Removal** under the **Routines** section on the **Sales** area page.

2. The process can be limited to certain customers and classes but most firms run the process for all of their customers.

3. For the sample company, change the **Cutoff Date** next to **NSF** to 2/12/2017.

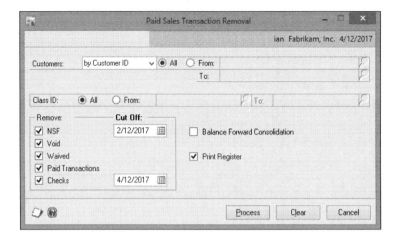

4. This **Cutoff Date** applies to all of the items from **NSF** down to the next cutoff date. This includes:

   - NSF
   - Void
   - Waived
   - Paid transactions

5. Change the **Cutoff Date** next to **Checks** to 2/12/2017.

6. Check the **Print Register** box to print the transactions being moved to history.

7. Click on **Process**. Choose to print the report and click on **Yes** to remove paid transactions.

8. A report will be printed with the specific transactions moved to history by customer.

How it works...

Regularly running Paid Transaction Removal reduces the workload on Dynamics GP when processing receivables aging. Reports based on open receivables transactions will also run faster. All of these improvements allow receivable employees to spend less time waiting for information and more time collecting open invoices.

There's more...

This process behaves differently for companies tracking receivables using the balance forward method.

The balance forward method

For companies using the balance forward balance type there are only two aging buckets, current and non-current. Most firms do not use the balance forward setting for receivables. For those firms that do use the balance forward method, the **Paid Sales Transaction Removal** window is used to consolidate balances and move current transactions to the non-current bucket.

To consolidate balances for balance forward customers, perform the following steps:

1. Select the **Balance Forward Consolidation** checkbox.

2. Uncheck the other boxes and click on **Process**.

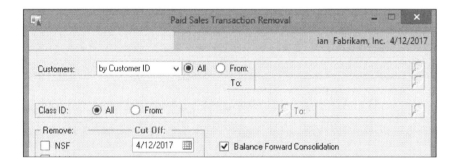

Providing correct tax information by updating 1099 information

A common problem arises at year end in the United States with vendors that were not properly set up as 1099 vendors. 1099 vendors are vendors who are required to be sent a 1099 tax form from the company. The types of transactions that can require a 1099 include rent, legal payments, and contract labor among others. The requirement is broad enough that most vendors who are not incorporated (proprietors, partners, and so on) may be due a 1099 if they are paid more than six hundred dollars in a year.

Recent changes to U.S. law have dramatically increased the number of 1099 forms that will need to be sent in the future. Essentially, all payees who receive more than $600 in payments will need to receive a 1099 in the future. As part of this legislation the fines for 1099 reporting errors have also been increased significantly. Correctly reporting 1099 information is more important than ever and this recipe can save companies a lot more than lunch money.

The specifics of 1099 requirements often means that vendors were incorrectly set up and the amounts required for tax reporting on 1099 forms were not collected for that vendor in Dynamics GP. The preferred solution is to use SmartLists or built-in reports to determine what the correct 1099 amount should have been. These amounts are then added to the vendor record so that they will print correctly on the 1099 form.

The specifics of figuring out what should be on a vendor's 1099 form are beyond the scope of this recipe. For this recipe, let's look at how to serve up correct 1099 forms in the sample company once the right amounts have been obtained.

How to do it...

To correct 1099 amounts for a vendor, perform the following steps:

1. Select **Purchasing** from the navigation pane. Select **1099 Details** under the **Cards** section of the **Purchasing** area page.

2. In the **Vendor ID** field, enter COMPUTER001 and press *Tab*.

3. Set **Tax Type** to **Miscellaneous** and **Display** to **Month**.

4. Change the **Month** to **December**.

5. In the **Amount** box next to **7 Nonemployee Compensation**, key in 1100.00 to represent the 1099 amount.

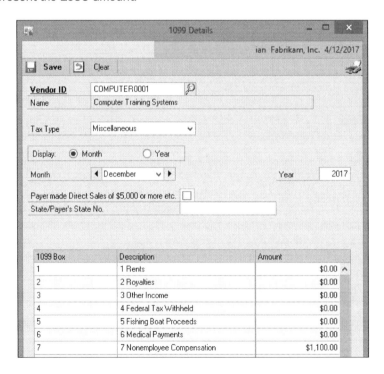

6. Entries must be made at the **Month** level. Selecting **Year** won't allow users to make an entry in the **Amount** field. When catching up vendor 1099 amounts companies can make an entry per period but most simply put the catch-up amount in the last month of the year.

How it works...

Maintaining 1099 vendors and amounts is something that many companies do a poor job of. This maintenance recipe will at least correct things at year end and provide correct 1099 amounts for tax filing. Ultimately though, better vendor setup is the answer to reducing this maintenance requirement.

There's more...

A better option to correcting 1099 amounts at year end is to get vendor setup right in the first place.

1099 vendor setup

The preferred alternative to correcting 1099 amounts is to improve vendor setup. Often the problem is that vendor setup is rushed and insufficient information is provided. A vendor's requirement for a 1099 comes to light later, after invoices have already been processed.

The key is to get control of the vendor process by placing all new vendors on hold until the vendor record contains specific information such as the vendor's tax ID number, whether or not this is a 1099 vendor and, if so, the type of 1099 expenses to be incurred. Most of the required information can be gathered by obtaining a completed W-9 form from the vendor. Vendors are happy to provide the necessary documentation if they know up front that their invoice won't be paid without it. Communicating and enforcing this policy is a step toward better 1099 reporting.

Even with proper vendor setup discipline, it is possible for someone to erroneously remove the 1099 amount from a payables voucher, but the number of vendors that need to be corrected will be dramatically reduced and this maintenance recipe becomes a simple year-end process, not an onerous one.

Maintaining updated code by rolling out service packs with Client Update

Applying service packs to Dynamics GP is an important part of maintaining the system. Service packs provide bug fixes, close potential security holes, and improve system performance. Some service packs, known as feature packs, even add new functionality. Service packs should normally be tested on a test server prior to applying them to a production environment. Service packs can negatively affect modified forms, modified reports, customizations, and third-party products so it's important to test them first.

Once service packs are tested, they should be applied to the company's server first. After that comes the burdensome process of installing service packs on each user's computer since users won't be able to log in after the service pack has been applied to the server. A better alternative is to use the Client Updates functionality for service packs in Dynamics GP 2013.

That's right, Dynamics GP provides a mechanism to make the service packs available on the server. When a user without the appropriate service pack logs in, Dynamics GP notifies the user, downloads the service pack from the server, and installs it on the user's machine, all without the intervention of an administrator. Since rolling out service packs is the focus of this recipe, let's look at how to do it.

Getting ready

Prior to rolling out service packs to users:

1. Download the service pack from CustomerSource (`http://www.microsoft.com/dynamics/customersource.mspx`) and save it to a network location accessible to Dynamics GP users.

2. Apply the service pack to the server and test to ensure that the system operates as expected.

3. For our example, we'll assume that this is service pack 1 and that we've downloaded it to a network location as `\\myserver\GPServicePacks\MicrosoftDynamicsGP-KBXXXXX-v11-ENU.msp`.

How to do it...

To roll out a service pack to Dynamics GP users perform the following steps:

1. Select **Administration** from the navigation list. Select **Client Updates** under the **System** section of the **Administration** area page.

2. In **Update Name**, name the update `Service Pack 1` to separate this from other updates.

3. Select the **Update clients at next use** checkbox.

4. Enter the update location as `\\myserver\GPServicePacks\MicrosoftDynamicsGP-KBXXXXX-v11-ENU.msp` as shown in the following screenshot.

5. Note that this requires the location to be formatted using a **Universal Naming Convention** (**UNC**). A typical `c:\mylocation` style path will not work even though the lookup button allows that.

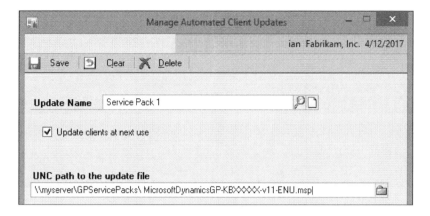

6. Click on **Save** to activate the roll out. Users will get a prompt to start the update the next time they log in.

7. Companies can set up the client update during testing and simply refrain from checking the **Update Clients at Next Use** checkbox. This saves the update until testing is complete. After that it's easy to check the box and start updating clients.

How it works...

Rolling out services packs automatically is a huge time saver in a traditional desktop environment. Administrators need to properly plan and communicate that clients will be updated since the application of a service pack can be very time consuming. A lot of complaints result when users show up on Monday morning expecting to be productive only to find that they have to wait an hour or more for a service pack to apply.

This feature isn't as important in a Citrix or Terminal server environment. Since only the Citrix or Terminal servers need to be updated in addition to the Dynamics GP server, the Client Update feature doesn't provide a big time savings over manual updates.

There's more...

It's also important to avoid the common error of removing a service pack from the server without unchecking the **Update clients at next use** checkbox.

Service pack errors

It's not unusual for someone to delete a service pack installation file from the server without unchecking **Update clients at next use**. When this happens, Dynamics GP displays an error the next time that a client computer without the service pack installed tries to log in. In that scenario, either the service needs to be returned to the download location or the **Update clients at next use** checkbox should be unchecked and the client computer updated manually.

Improving stability by managing dictionaries

Microsoft Dynamics GP uses dictionary files to hold application code, forms, and reports. Form and report modifications in Dynamics GP don't modify the underlying item; instead, modified forms and reports are modified copies of the original that are stored in the report and form dictionaries.

They key question facing companies is the placement of the dictionaries since this can impact the availability of custom forms and reports. Improper placement may mean that users don't get necessary customizations, so dictionary locations need to be set properly with each client installation of Dynamics GP.

We will look at how to set dictionary locations in this recipe.

How to do it...

To change the location of a user's forms and reports dictionary, perform the following step:

1. Select **Administration** from the navigation pane. Select **Edit Launch File** under the **Setup** section on the **Administration** area page.

2. Enter the system password if prompted.

3. Click on **Product ID 0, Product Name Microsoft Dynamics GP**. This is the main Dynamics GP application. At the bottom of the window there are three dictionary locations for **Application**, **Forms**, and **Reports**.

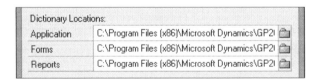

4. Changing the location of the application dictionary is not recommended since this is where the core business logic is stored and moving this file can negatively impact performance.

5. Select the **Forms** field and scroll to the right to see the full location. This is the location for custom forms. Changing this to a new location will create an empty custom forms file in the new location. If an existing custom forms field is in a different location, either enter the new location or use the file lookup to identify the new location. The same process applies to changing the location of the **Reports** dictionary.

6. Each installed product outside of the core Microsoft Dynamics GP dictionary has its own application, forms, and reports dictionaries.

7. Select the **Fixed Assets** product and notice that the dictionaries have names specific to the Fixed Asset module ID.

8. Click on **OK** to save any changes.

How it works...

Dictionary control is an important part of maintaining Dynamics GP. As new users are added and more instances are installed it's important to ensure that the dictionaries are pointed to the right place. Without this, companies end up with an incoherent mess of customized windows and reports.

The two most common placements are locally on each user's machine or centrally on a file share. Local placement was preferred for a long time since this resulted in significantly fewer incidents of dictionary corruption. Typically, a master copy of the forms and reports dictionary was maintained and copied to user machines via a network login script.

Over time, the problem of corrupt dictionaries was significantly reduced as improvements in Dynamics GP and network reliability made dictionary corruption extremely rare. This made centrally managing dictionaries much more feasible.

There are pros and cons to each approach. Locally managing dictionaries provides a type of backup. In the event of damage to a dictionary file, the file can be replaced by another user's copy. Conversely, locally managing dictionaries lets users have different customizations from their peers since each user's files can be unique. Finally, managing dictionaries locally permits forms and reports to be customized while Dynamics GP is in use.

Local placement of dictionaries does cause additional IT overhead to create and manage login scripts to update dictionaries with changes. Also, if users leave Dynamics GP logged in over several days, dictionary updates won't propagate to their machines during that time period. Finally, users could customize forms and reports locally only to have them overwritten the next day when central dictionaries are rolled out via a login script.

Central management of dictionaries provides a consistent experience for users since everyone gets the same set of customizations in their dictionaries. Backup can be centrally managed as well. Customizations can't be made directly while other users are in the system but forms and reports customizations can be exported locally, modified, and then applied to a central dictionary.

There's more...

For administrators there is another option for setting dictionary locations outside of the interface.

The Dynamics.set file

Installed dictionaries and their locations are held in the `Dynamics.set` file. This recipe shows how to set dictionary locations via the interface. This process changes the `Dynamics.set` file. The same changes could be made in the file with Notepad instead of the interface. The `Dynamics.set` file could also be copied to a user's computer (assuming that they have the same modules and dictionary locations). This process is faster and easier than changing each user via the interface.

Safeguarding data by backing everything up

Data backup may be the single most important maintenance item related to Dynamics GP. Backing up data is crucial to ensuring the long term integrity of the system. Dynamics GP provides a basic backup process designed to protect data.

The built-in Dynamics GP backup routine is not intended to be a one size fits all backup process. For example, it doesn't provide a mechanism for transaction log backups via the interface. Most companies prefer to use SQL tools to manage their backup processes. Ultimately, each company should determine a recovery plan and then work with IT professionals to create an appropriate backup process.

However, the Dynamics GP backup process is an acceptable option, especially as a preference to no backup at all. The focus of this recipe is on setting up a backup process using the Dynamics GP backup routine.

How to do it...

To set up a Dynamics GP backup routine, perform the following steps:

1. Log into Dynamics GP as the sa user.
2. Select **Microsoft Dynamics GP** at the top. Select **Maintenance | Backup** from the **Microsoft Dynamics GP** menu. Enter the system password if prompted.

3. Select the company to back up. For our example, select **Fabrikam, Inc.** and set a backup file location. The backup location needs to exist or be created using the file lookup button to the right of the field.

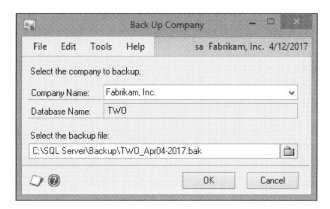

4. Click on **Save** to save the backup routine.

5. Repeat this process for other company databases and the system database.

How it works...

Backing up data is the single most important maintenance function. Companies may need to go beyond the built-in backup routine to intra-day transaction log backups for true point-in-time recovery. The built-in routine does provide at least a daily backup option for protection.

There's more...

Other files need to be backed up in addition to the databases.

Additional backups

Backing up the company and system databases provides the ability to restore a firm's information; financial statement layouts and generated reports from Management Reporter are also stored within a database on a SQL Server and should be backed up. But it's also important to back up the infrastructure around that information as well. Dictionary files hold customized forms and reports that can be extremely time consuming to restore. This also applies to integration definitions in the IMD file that stores integrations. Key items to back up include:

▶ Any files with a DIC extension.

▶ Any files with a VBA extension.

> ▶ Any files with an IMD extension from Integration Manager.

> ▶ Exports of VBA code, custom forms, and custom reports as an additional backup. These are created with the **Export** button found using the **Microsoft Dynamics GP** menu, then **Tools | Customization Maintenance**.

Resolving errors with the Check Links utility

Check Links and Reconcile are the two most commonly used utilities in Dynamics GP. Despite their common usage, their roles and outcomes are regularly misunderstood. We will look at Check Links in this recipe and move on to Reconcile for our next dish.

Check Links is a utility designed to review links between related tables for data consistency. For example, if there is a detail record, there should be a header record. The Check Links utility is able to compare header and details records and potentially rebuild damaged or missing data. When transaction data is unrecoverable, running Check Links will remove the damaged records, possibly requiring re-entry.

A transaction record can be damaged in any number of ways including lost network connectivity, poorly imported data, database level changes, and power outages. Most transactions in Dynamics GP include a header record with information about the transaction and a detail record with transaction specifics. Imagine an invoice, for example. The invoice header contains things common to the whole invoice like the invoice number, customer, and date while the invoice detail record holds the specifics of each item being purchased.

In many cases, if a header record is damaged, much of it can be repaired from the information in detail records. When possible, running the Check Links utility will rebuild the header records. Users may still need to make some adjustments but most of the data will be recovered. However, if a detail record has been damaged, often there is not enough information for the Check Links utility to recover the details. In such cases, the Check Links utility can and will delete data so it is a good idea to run a backup prior to running Check Links.

Depending on the number of transactions being checked, Check Links can take a long time to run. Since the reports generated by running Check Links are not reprintable, it's a good idea to send them to a file as well as the screen. The reports can be very large so blindly sending them to a printer is usually not a good idea. With that background, let's cook up some Check Links.

How to do it...

To run Check Links for sales order processing transactions, perform the following steps:

1. Ensure that a current backup has been created.

2. Select the **Microsoft Dynamics GP** menu and from there pick **Maintenance | Check Links**.

3. In the **Series** field select **Sales**.

4. Select **Sales Distribution** and click on **Insert** to add this item.

5. Repeat this process with **Sales History** and **Sales Work** and click on **OK**.

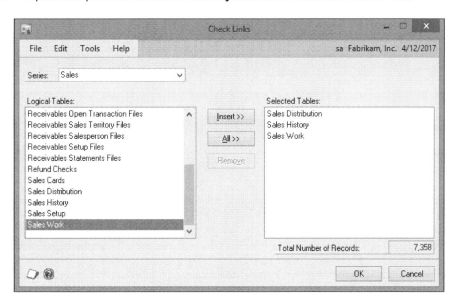

6. Select **Screen** and **File** in the **Report Destination** window. Enter a location for the file and format it as a text file.

7. Click on **OK** to run Check Links.

8. A report will print to the screen with the results, including any additions or deletions made by the utility.

How it works...

The Check Links utility works throughout Dynamics GP to validate data and connections between tables. There is still plenty of debate about whether Check Links should be run regularly to maintain the health of the system or if it is only needed when an issue has been identified. There are good arguments on both sides. As a matter of fact, I've always preferred to run Check Links only when necessary.

Since System and Company setup tables don't have dependent links in the same way that transaction tables do, Check Links typically won't solve issues with those tables. The Reconcile utility checks for data consistency among unlinked but still associated tables. Consequently, Reconcile should be used with System and Company tables in place of Check Links.

See also

▸   The *Validating balances with the Reconcile utility* recipe in this chapter

Speeding login by clearing the Menu Master table

The Menu Master table in Dynamics GP holds details of all the menu options to which users have access. Over time this table can accrue rogue entries, which can slow down the login process, or even cause errors to be displayed.

Clearing Menu Master is a fairly simple process and is often scheduled for during an upgrade, or run on an ad hoc basis if it has become corrupt and is producing error messages when a user starts GP or switches companies. This recipe will show how to clear Menu Master, which causes it to be rebuilt for each user as they log in again.

How to do it...

To clear Menu Master perform the following steps:

1.   Make a backup of Dynamics GP.

2.   Select the **Microsoft Dynamics GP** menu and from there select **Maintenance | Clear Data**.

3.   Click on **Display** on the menu and then select **Physical**.

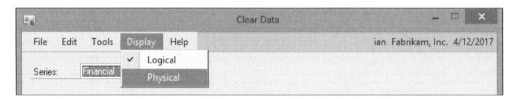

4. Select **Menu Master** and click on **Insert** to add this item.

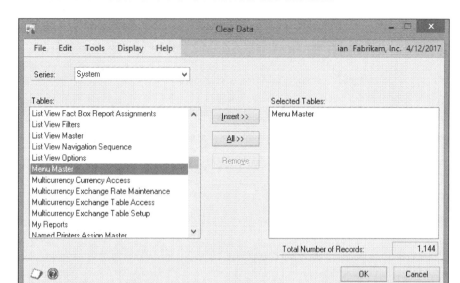

5. Click on **OK** to run Clear Data.

6. A report will be produced showing any errors that occurred.

How it works...

When **Menu Master** is cleared, the table will be repopulated with valid entries when the users log into Dynamics GP again. This has the benefit of removing both corrupt entries causing problems and also invalid entries that need to be processed even though they are not used, which improves the login speed.

Validating balances with the Reconcile utility

After Check Links, the Reconcile utility is the most commonly used utility in Dynamics GP. The job of the Reconcile utility is to replace or remove erroneous data that is related but isn't necessarily linked. For example, to improve reporting speed, Dynamics GP stores the summary totals of each account in a table. Unlike Check Links, these tables aren't related to each other, they simply hold the same information in different formats, one in detail and one in summary.

The sum total of an account should equal the sum of all of the detail transactions for an account. If it doesn't, the Reconcile utility will recalculate the totals from the detail and replace the summary total.

Like Check Links, the Reconcile utility can remove data and should be run after a backup. Additionally, any reports that are available to be printed should be printed to the screen and to a file. There is no option to reprint these reports. In this recipe, we'll look at the most common use for Reconcile, ensuring that financial summary data matches the detail.

How to do it...

To reconcile financial totals perform the following steps:

1. Make a backup of Dynamics GP.

2. Select **Financial** from the navigation pane. Select **Reconcile** under **Utilities**.

3. Check **Year**, select **Open**, and pick **2017** in the drop-down box.

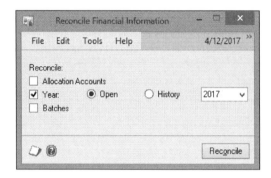

4. Unlike other Reconcile processes, no report prints when reconciling the year. Using the Reconcile utility on other parts of the system will result in a report showing changes.

How it works...

The Reconcile utility is designed to help ensure data integrity in Dynamic GP by correcting mismatched data and updating totals for summaries, batches, and headers. It is a powerful utility and shouldn't be used without a good backup. Like Check Links, there is disagreement in the Dynamics GP community over whether or not Reconcile should be run regularly. As with Check Links, my slight preference is to run it only when there is suspicion of a problem.

See also

▶ The *Resolving errors with the Check Links utility* recipe in this chapter

Troubleshooting issues with a DexSQL log

When trying to troubleshoot issues, a common request from Microsoft support and from partners is to run a DexSQL log. A DexSQL log is a file that logs commands made from Dynamics GP to the database to help understand performance issues. After creation, this file is sent to the company's partner or to Microsoft for assistance in troubleshooting.

When creating a DexSQL log, the key is to capture only the amount of data related to the problem. In this recipe, we will look at creating a DexSQL log to provide more information to Microsoft support.

For our example, we will assume that the problem relates to creating a financial batch, so that is the process that will get captured in the DexSQL log.

How to do it...

To create a DexSQL log perform the following steps:

1. Ensure that Microsoft Dynamics GP is closed.

2. Open the Notepad utility in Windows.

3. Select **File | Open** in Notepad and navigate to the location where the `Dex.ini` file for Dynamics GP is installed. By default this is `c:\Program Files\Microsoft Dynamics\GP\Data\Dex.ini`.

4. Once the `Dex.ini` file is open in Notepad, find these two lines in the file:

   ```
   SQLLogSQLStmt=FALSE
   SQLLogODBCMessages=FALSE
   ```

5. Change both lines to a value of `TRUE` and save the file. This turns on logging in Dynamics GP.

   ❑ The first line, `SQLLogSSQLStmt=TRUE`, logs all SQL statements that are sent to the server by the application.

   ❑ The second line, `SQLLogODBCMessages=TRUE`, logs all ODBC messages returned to the application by ODBC.

   ❑ Either line or both lines can be set to `TRUE`. Typically, Microsoft support asks that both lines be set to `TRUE`.

6. Start Microsoft Dynamics GP and log in. This creates a file named DexSQL.log in the same location as the Dex.ini file.

   ❑ Results will be logged to the DexSQL.log file regardless of which lines are set to TRUE.

   ❑ Any ODBC messages are prefixed by [Microsoft].

7. Select **Financial** from the navigation pane on the left. Select **Batches** under **Transactions**.

8. The DexSQL log now holds all the information related to logging in and everything done so far in this GP session. The log now needs to be cleared prior to recording the actual problem scenario.

9. To clear the DexSQL log file, find the DexSQL.log file in the same directory as the Dex.ini file. Using File Manager, select and delete the file. Once activity starts in Dynamics GP, a new file is created.

10. Return to Dynamics GP. In the open **Batch** window type TEST BATCH in the **Batch ID** field. Set the **Origin** field to **General Entry** and save the batch. Now the DexSQL.log file needs to be renamed to avoid adding unrelated data.

11. Return to the DexSQL.log file in File Manager. Right-click on the DexSQL.log file and rename it DexSQL-Batch.log.

12. Once the DexSQL log has been renamed, it's important to close Dynamics GP and turn off logging. If this doesn't happen, Dynamics GP can significantly slow down and the DexSQL log can grow to consume all of a computer's hard drive space.

13. To turn off logging, close Dynamics GP and reopen the Dex.ini file.

14. Find these lines in the Dex.ini file and change TRUE to FALSE.

    ```
    SQLLogSQLStmt=TRUE
    SQLLogODBCMessages=TRUE
    ```

15. Save the Dex.ini file and delete the leftover DexSQL.log file that was created when closing Dynamics GP.

16. What is left is the DexSQL-Batch.log file that holds specifics from right before and after the problem area. This file can be opened using Notepad to see what information is being sent to Microsoft or the company's Dynamics GP partner.

How it works...

Creating a DexSQL log file is an important maintenance process for companies to understand. Microsoft and Microsoft Partners often ask for this information when troubleshooting errors. Being able to generate a DexSQL log to facilitate problem resolution is important for maintaining a healthy Dynamics GP system.

See also

- The *Logging transactions for troubleshooting* recipe in *Chapter 11, Extending Dynamics GP with the Support Debugging Tool*

- The *Capturing and sending screenshots for support* recipe in *Chapter 11, Extending Dynamics GP with the Support Debugging Tool*

Speeding security setup with user copy

Setting up security for individual users can be a time consuming task. Dynamics GP 2010 and later provide a mechanism to copy the access from an existing user to a new user including tasks, roles, and company access. This feature provides a great way to quickly set up new users and ensure that their security is consistent.

This recipe looks at how to copy security settings from an existing user to a new user.

Getting ready

This recipe requires logging in as an sa, the system administrator. Log in to the sample company as sa to start this recipe.

How to do it...

To copy security settings to a new user performs the following steps:

1. Select **Administration** from the navigation pane. Under **Setup** and **System** on the **Administration** area page, select **User**.
2. In the **User ID** field type john.
3. Type John Doe in the **User Name** field.
4. Type Pass@word1 in the **Password** and **Confirm Password** fields.
5. Click on **Copy Access** and click on **Yes** when asked to save changes.

6. Use the lookup button (magnifying glass) to look up and select an existing user.

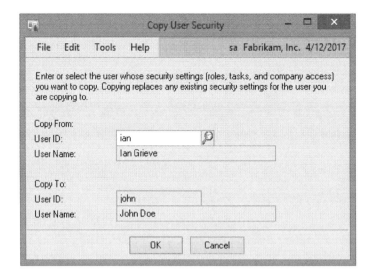

7. Click on **OK** to finish.

User **john** now has the same roles, tasks, and company access as the existing user.

11
Extending Dynamics GP with the Support Debugging Tool

In this chapter, we'll look at recipes focused on the Support Debugging Tool.

- ► Extending Dynamics GP with the Support Debugging Tool
- ► Coloring windows by company
- ► Capturing and sending screenshots for support
- ► Logging transactions for troubleshooting
- ► Executing SQL from within Dynamics GP
- ► Getting information about security resources

Introduction

It has been said that bacon is the meat that makes other meat taste better. Along those lines, the **Support Debugging Tool** is the bacon of the Dynamics GP world; it makes working with Dynamics GP better in so many ways.

The Support Debugging Tool is a free utility from Microsoft with enough features to fill several recipes. We'll do just that and spend the next several recipes looking at specific Support Debugging Tool features. The Support Debugging Tool is free, but, because of its power, it cannot be downloaded directly and has to be obtained from a Microsoft partner.

The Support Debugging Tool is the creation of Microsoft Escalation Engineer and all-round Dexterity guru David Musgrave. David, along with help from some others in the Dynamics GP community, originally created the Support Debugging Tool to improve error tracing and the tool has since morphed into an extremely handy utility for Dynamics GP.

One of the benefits of the Support Debugging Tool is that it integrates with Dynamics GP security and comes with two predefined security roles. One role, **MBS DEBUGGER USER**, provides access to standard mode features like logging and support requests; this role can safely be given to average users.

The other, more advanced, **MBS DEBUGGER ADMIN** role provides access to the more advanced sections of the tool. Finally, GP security can be used with the associated tasks to fine tune these security options.

Extending Dynamics GP with the Support Debugging Tool

Before we dig into the Support Debugging Tool, we need to install it. We will do that here and turn on the Administrator mode so that we don't have to revisit this with each new recipe.

How to do it...

To install and set up the Support Debugging Tool, perform the following steps:

1. Obtain the DEBU_1200.zip file from Microsoft via a Microsoft partner.
2. With Dynamics GP closed, right-click on the DEBU_1200.zip file, select **Extract All**, and follow the prompts to unzip the file.
3. Copy the CNK file from the new DEBU_1100 folder to the location where Dynamics GP is installed. By default this is C:\Program Files (x86)\Microsoft Dynamics\GP 2013\or C:\Program Files\Microsoft Dynamics\GP 2013\ on a 32-bit machine.
4. Start Microsoft Dynamics GP and agree to the Add New Code message. Dynamics GP may need to be run as an administrator with some versions of Windows.
5. In Microsoft Dynamics GP, select the **Microsoft Dynamics GP** menu option then **Tools | Support Debugging Tool**.
6. To turn on **Administrator settings**, select **Debugger | Dex.ini Settings**.

7. Select **Enable Debugger Advanced Mode Features** and enter the system password if prompted.

```
Support Debugging Tool Options
  ☑ Enable Debugger Advanced Mode Features
      ☐ Enable Debugger Setup Mode (Do not automatically start Triggers)
  ☐ Automatically open Support Debugging Tool main window after login
```

8. Click on **OK** to finish.

The Support Debugging Tool is now installed and we're ready for some juicy treats.

Coloring windows by company

Many companies use several company databases in Dynamics GP. This may be because they have multiple entities to account for or because they want a test and a production database. Invariably, data entry mistakes get made because users inadvertently key information to the wrong company. For some time, users have asked for a way to visually tell one company from another. One feature of the Support Debugging Tool is designed to do just this.

The Support Debugging Tool allows a user to change the window background color for a specific company. This provides a consistent visual cue to identify the company being used.

In this recipe, we will look at how to assign colors to specific companies to distinguish them from each other.

Getting ready

The Support Debugging Tool needs to be installed on each user's machine and users need access to the **MBS DEBUGGER USER** security role for the company-based color schemes to work. Additionally, the Administrator mode needs to be activated within the tool.

How to do it...

To use color to identify specific companies, perform the following steps:

1. In Microsoft Dynamics GP, select the **Microsoft Dynamics GP** menu option, then **Tools | Support Debugging Tool**.

2. In the Support Debugging Tool window select **Debugger | Administrator Settings** and enter the system password if prompted.

3. Click on the **Company** tab.

4. Select the drop-down box next to **Select Theme Colors** and set the theme to **Green**. This provides a preset green theme throughout this company.

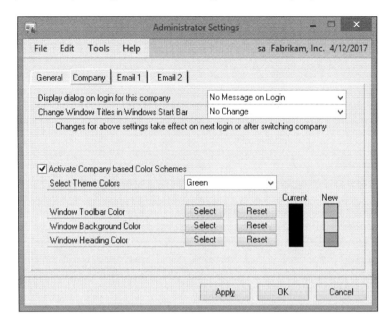

5. Click on **Apply** to see the changes. The window colors change to blue to match the theme. This setting is retained for this company.

6. Repeat this process by opening other companies and changing their window colors.

7. Colors can be controlled individually for the toolbar, background, and window heading with the selections below the theme.

How it works...

This feature of the Support Debugging Tool started out as a simple **Visual Basic for Applications** (**VBA**) add-on. Eventually, it was incorporated into the Support Debugging Tool.

Changing the background color is a great way to prevent data entry errors. I've even seen firms match the color of a company's check stock to the color of the company database to prevent check printing errors.

The following screenshots show Fabrikam, Inc. with the toolbar colored green and Fabrikam EMEA, Inc. in blue.

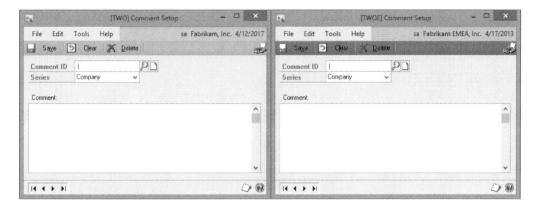

There's more...

As well as allowing the color of windows to be changed, you can also enable the **Allow Window Titles in Windows Start Bar**, which allows the Database ID, such as TWO for Fabrikam, Inc., to be prepended to the window title; this is especially useful for consultants or helpdesks to identify which database the user is logged into. This is shown in the preceding screenshots where TWO is shown for Fabruikam, Inc. and TWOE for Fabrikam EMEA, Inc.

See also...

▶ The *Ensuring entry in the correct company by warning about test companies* recipe in *Chapter 9, Preventing Errors is Dynamics GP*

Capturing and sending screenshots for support

When it comes to support, few thing are better for troubleshooting than a screenshot of what went wrong. One of the great features available in the free Support Debugging Tool from Microsoft is the ability to grab screenshots and environment files, like the Dynamics.set file, and e-mail them for support. This e-mail doesn't have to go to Microsoft; it can go to a company's Microsoft Partner, an internal support team, or almost anyone else who could help. It's also nice to be able to grab screenshots from within the Dynamics GP interface rather than relying on an external tool like the Windows Snipping Tool.

We've had a look at installing the Support Debugging Tool in the *Extending Dynamics GP with the Support Debugging Tool* recipe but I'll mention again that this free tool is available from Microsoft Dynamics Partners on request.

Installing the Support Debugging Tool adds a camera icon to the Standard toolbar. Additionally, the *Ctrl + S* key combination can be used to make it easy to grab an error message and send out for help.

In this recipe, we'll look at the Screen Capture functionality included in the Support Debugging Tool.

How to do it...

To use the Screen Capture feature of the Support Debugging Tool, perform the following steps:

1. Select **Financial** from the navigation pane. Select **General** under **Transactions**.

2. In the **Transaction Entry** window, click on the blue arrow next to **Batch ID** to open the **Batch Entry** window as well.

3. Use one of the these three options to capture the screenshot:

   ❑ Click on the camera icon in the Standard toolbar

   ❑ Press *Ctrl + S* on the keyboard

   ❑ Select the **Microsoft Dynamics GP** menu followed by **Tools | Capture Screenshots**

4. The **Support Debugging Tool ScreenShot** window will open with attached screenshots of both of the open windows. The checkboxes on the left allow specific windows to be included or excluded in a support e-mail.

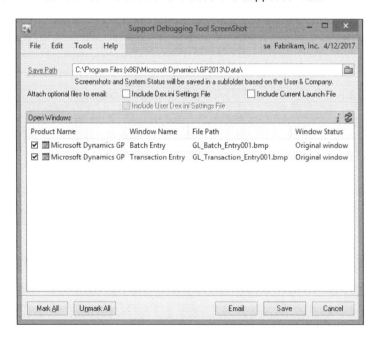

5. Next to **Attach optional files to email**, check the boxes next to **Include Current Launch File** and **Include Dex.ini Settings File**. These settings will attach the `Dynamics.set` file and `Dex.ini` file used to launch Dynamics GP.

6. Click on the **Email** button. The user's e-mail application will open with the files attached and information included in the body of the e-mail, as shown in the following screenshot:

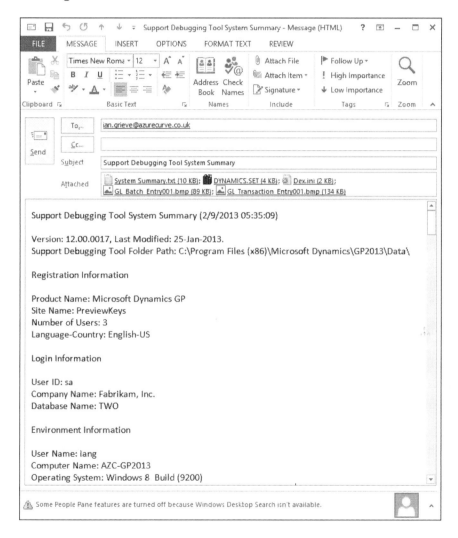

7. Users simply need to add the e-mail address of the recipient and send the e-mail.

How it works...

The Capture Screenshots feature in the Support Debugging Tool is a godsend for anyone who has had to deal with uncaptured error messages or misquoted error text. Furthermore, it provides a consistent output result for support personnel to use to review data.

There's more...

In addition to the basic settings of the Capture Screenshots feature, there are some defaults that can be set to make it even more useful.

Default settings

In the *Extending Dynamics GP with the Support Debugging Tool* recipe, we looked at turning on Administrator settings for the Support Debugging Tool. Once Administrator settings have been activated, new default settings can be created for capturing screenshots.

To change the default settings for capturing screenshots, perform the following steps:

1. In the **Support Debugging Tool** window select **Debugger | Administrator Settings**.
2. Enter the system password if prompted.
3. In the **General** tab, check the boxes next to **Include Current Launch File** and **Include Dex.ini Settings File** to include these files by default when a user takes a screenshot.

4. Click on the **Email 1** tab. Add an e-mail to the **Administrator Email** field to provide a default e-mail recipient for support requests and click on **Apply**. Do not add my e-mail address. I can't support everyone!

5. Click on the **Email 2** tab. The **Email Mode** field is used to control the type of e-mail mode. The options include using Outlook to send e-mail, using the SQL Server, or using a generic MAPI client to send support e-mails. If the SQL Server is used, other fields are exposed to allow additional setup options.

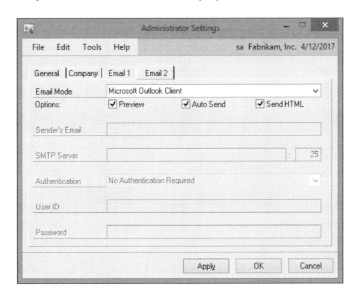

6. Finally, below the **Email Mode** field are three settings fields. The three fields and their uses are given as follows:

   - **Preview**: A preview window opens in Dynamics GP to review the e-mail before it goes out. If **Auto Send** is off, users may have the opportunity to review the e-mail again in their mail clients.

   - **Auto Send**: Sends the e-mail without the user having to press send in their e-mail clients. However, this does not override the **Preview** button if it is checked.

   - **Send HTML**: Sends the e-mail in HTML format instead of text format.

Logging transactions for troubleshooting

In the *Troubleshooting issues with a DexSQL log* recipe of *Chapter 10, Maintaining Dynamics GP* we looked at creating a DexSQL log file for use in troubleshooting. That recipe didn't require any special software but it did take a lot of back and forth to limit the contents of the file to the specific process to be logged. The free Support Debugging Tool from Microsoft not only makes this much easier, it adds a host of features and logging options to get more information for support.

How to do it...

To create a DexSQL log, perform the following steps:

1. In Microsoft Dynamics GP select **Tools | Support Debugging Tool** from the **Microsoft Dynamics GP** menu.

2. At the top of the screen, above **Microsoft SQL Server Options**, click on **Turn On Manual Logging Mode**.

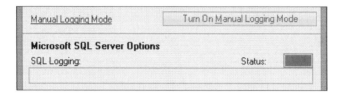

3. Select **Financial** from the navigation pane. Select **General** under **Transactions**.

4. Reopen the **Support Debugging Tool** window from the Windows taskbar and click on **Turn Off Manual Logging Mode**.

5. The DexSQL.log file now exists in the Data folder where Dynamics GP is installed.

That's it. That is the minimum amount of work necessary to create a DexSQL log with the Support Debugging Tool. Sixteen steps from the *Troubleshooting issues with a DexSQL log* recipe of *Chapter 10, Maintaining Dynamics GP* reduced to four steps with the Support Debugging Tool.

But since that is too easy, there are some additional options available on the **Dex.ini Settings** window, available from the Debugger menu, to improve DexSQL logging.

To use the additional logging features, perform the following steps:

1. Return to the **Support Debugging Tool** window and open **Dex.ini Settings** from the **Debugger** menu.

2. Prior to starting a DexSQL log, two additional options can be selected in the **Microsoft SQL Server Options** area.

3. Select the **Enable SQL Logging on next login** checkbox to debug the login process of Dynamics GP.

4. Select **Specified** to place the log file in a different location and specify the filename.

5. Return to the **Support Debugging Tool** window.
6. Under **Options**, select additional feature and click on **Administrator Settings**.
7. Select **Enable Individual Logging** Modes.
8. Click on **OK** to close the **Administrator Settings** window.
9. Click on the **Logging Options** button at the bottom of the **Support Debugging Tool** window.
10. Below the **SQL Logging** option are two similar logging options, **Dexterity Script Logging** and **Dexterity Profile Logging**. **Dexterity Script Logging** logs Dexterity events. **Dexterity Profile Logging** tracks Dexterity calls and the time it takes them to complete. Both are useful but less commonly applied than SQL logging.

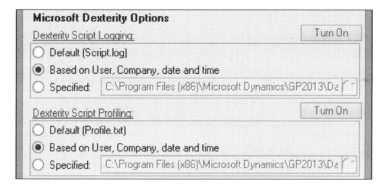

There's more...

On-demand logging just scratches the surface. The Support Debugging Tool can log events automatically and even allows the logging of SQL Profiler traces.

Automatic logging

The Support Debugging Tool can log events automatically based on the type of event to be logged.

Automatic logging is set up under **Debugger | Setup Automatic Debugger Mode** on the **Support Debugging Tool Setup** screen.

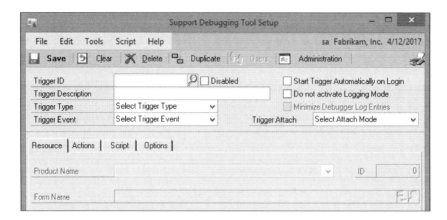

The number of options available for automatic logging is too much to cover in this recipe but this process is great for tracking down errors that are hard to reproduce. The Support Debugging Tool manual has full coverage of this feature.

Executing SQL from within Dynamics GP

Earlier in this chapter, we looked at executing SQL code from a user's machine with the free Support Administrator Console from Microsoft. Another option to execute SQL code from a user's machine is with the Support Debugging Tool.

Microsoft makes the Support Debugging Tool available to users via Dynamics GP partners. The tool is free, you just have to ask.

An advantage of the Support Debugging Tool over the Support Administrator Console is that the Support Debugging Tool is integrated into Dynamics GP and Dynamics GP security. This means that the Support Debugging Tool can be safely installed on a user's machine and access to it restricted via GP security roles. Also, as several other recipes of this chapter have shown, the Support Debugging Tool does much more than run SQL code.

It does run SQL code quite well though, and in this recipe we will look at how to accomplish that.

How to do it...

To execute SQL code via the Support Debugging Tool, perform the following steps:

1. With the Support Debugging Tool installed, select **Tools | Support Debugging Tool** from the **MS Dynamics GP** menu.

2. Select the **Options** button on the main window and click on **SQLExecute**.

3. Enter the system password if prompted.

4. Change **Execute Query in which SQL Database** to **Fabrikam, Inc**.

5. In the large white box in the center type SELECT * FROM GL00105 and click on the Execute button on the lower-right side to see the chart of accounts.

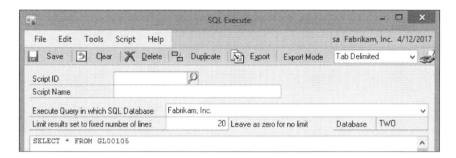

6. Click on the **Export** button to export the results to a file or e-mail. The format of the export can be changed with the **Export Mode** field to the right.

7. Click on the printer icon in the upper-right corner to print the results.

8. By default, only twenty records are returned, to prevent long running queries that might slow the system down. This can be changed in the **Limit results set to fixed number of lines** field. A setting of zero (0) indicates no limit.

9. In the **Script ID** field, enter CHART and in the **Script Name** field type Chart of Accounts. Clicking on **Save** will save this script for reuse and clear the screen.

10. Use the lookup button (magnifying glass) next to **Script ID** to reopen the **CHART** script. Click on the **Duplicate** button to make a copy of this script and allow changes.

11. When creating scripts, click on the **Tables** button to explore Dynamics GP tables to assist in writing SQL scripts.

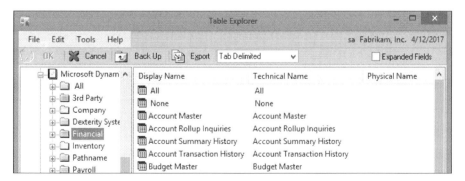

How it works...

The ability to view Dynamics GP data in the database is an important part of troubleshooting. Not having to find a machine with SQL Management Studio is important for leaving on time at night since it prevents running back and forth between machines to review query results. By integrating SQL query features into the Support Debugging Tool, troubleshooting becomes faster and easier.

One important point to remember is that the SQL queries used can potentially include far more than just selects, inserts, updates, and deletes; as well, other destructive commands can be performed through this window. It is not advised to run SQL commands against the database directly as this can have unforeseen consequences.

Getting information about security resources

Understanding security is a key piece of working with Microsoft Dynamics GP. The free Support Debugging Tool provides options to resolve security issues more easily with its Security Profiler feature. The **Security Profiler** portion of the Support Debugging Tool provides security resource specifics about any window in Dynamics GP including who has access to a resource and what role and tasks this window is assigned to.

We've covered features of the Support Debugging Tool in the last several recipes. Because of its power, the Support Debugging Tool has to be requested from a Dynamics GP partner, even though it's free.

Let's look at how to explore security with the Support Debugging Tool.

How to do it...

To understand Security Profiles with the Support Debugging Tool perform the following steps:

1. With the Support Debugging Tool installed, select **Tools | Support Debugging Tool** from the **MS Dynamics GP** menu.

2. Select the **Options** button on the main window and pick **Security Profiler**.

3. With the **Security Profiler** window still open, select **Financial** from the navigation pane. Select **General** from the **Financial** area page under **Transactions**. Opening a window populates the **Security Profiler** window.

4. In the **Security Profiler** window, highlight the line where the technical name is **GL_Transaction_Entry** and click on **Security**.

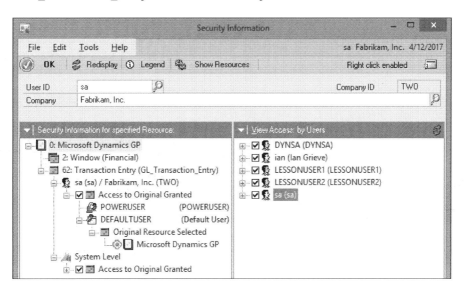

5. The **User ID** and **Company** field are displayed at the top.

6. The left pane holds role and task information. The right pane holds user IDs that can access each resource. This is extremely useful when trying to set up a user to match the access of someone else.

7. Click on the **Legend** button to get an explanation of the icons on this window.

8. The **GoTo** button in the upper-right corner opens the various security windows, allowing security settings to be changed on the fly, assuming that the logged in user has the appropriate access, of course.

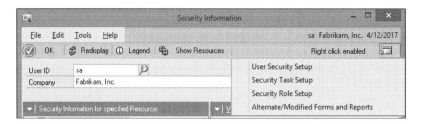

How it works...

It's not uncommon to find frustrated users trying to set security but unsure of what settings give access to a specific window. The Security Profiler feature of the Support Debugging Tool can make this process much clearer.

There's more...

The Security Profiler feature doesn't just provide resource information on request. Security information can be exported and sent by e-mail to a security administrator who can import the file for review. Also, the Security Profiler can pop up the appropriate information automatically when access to a resource is denied. This makes it easy for an administrator to adjust access at the point of the problem.

Automatic security profiles

The Security Profiler can be set up to automatically display when access to a resource is denied. To apply this, the Support Debugging Tool must be installed and Administrator access turned on.

To allow the Security Profiler to be activated automatically, users have to be added to the MBS DEBUGGER USER role in security, otherwise access to the Security Profiler window itself is denied.

To turn on automatic display of the Security Profile when access is denied to a resource, perform the following steps:

1. In the Support Debugging Tool window select **Debugger | Administrator Settings**.
2. Enter the system password if prompted.

3. In the **General** tab, set the **Automatic Open Mode** field under **Security Profiler Settings** to either **Open on Errors Only** or **Open on Errors & Warnings** and click on **OK**.

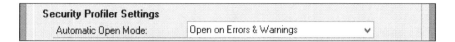

Now when access to a window is denied, the Security Profiler is activated with more information on the denied resource. This makes validating security and, if appropriate, providing security to that resource much easier.

Export/import security logs

On the **Security Profiler** window is an option to **Export** a profile to a file or e-mail. Once exported, this file can be sent to a security administrator. The administrator can then use the **Import** button to bring in the file and drill back to security to adjust the settings.

A common scenario looks like this: an employee is denied access to a resource. He or she exports the automatically opened Security Profiler information and e-mails it to his or her security administrator. The administrator imports the file and then drills back to security to review. If access should be granted, the administrator can grant the appropriate rights to the user or update the role for all related users right from that screen.

12
Extending Dynamics GP Professional Services Tools Library

In this chapter, we will look at recipes focused on the Professional Services Tools Library:

- ▶ Installing and configuring Professional Services Tools Library
- ▶ Disable a company database to prevent users from logging in
- ▶ Replicate settings and data to a new company with Company Copy
- ▶ Duplicate data between companies using Master Triggers
- ▶ Merge records with Combiner
- ▶ Change data using Modifier
- ▶ Setting a minimum PO/Receipt Number
- ▶ Preventing date errors with Doc Date Verify

Introduction

Over the years, the Microsoft Professional Services team has produced a variety of tools to meet requirements for modifying data from both customers and partners. These tools were combined into the Professional Services Tools Library and were available at a cost; as of March 2012 they became available to all for free. In this chapter, we'll take a look at how to install and configure Professional Services Tools Library as well as use some of the tools that can improve company setup and data maintenance.

Installing and configuring Professional Services Tools Library

The **Professional Services Tools Library** (**PSTL**) is a collection of tools made available by Microsoft. In this recipe, we'll take a look at installing and configuring PSTL.

Getting ready

Before PSTL can be configured for use, it must first be installed. To install PSTL, perform the following steps:

1. Ensure backups have been made of the system (usually Dynamics) and all company databases have a good backup.
2. Open **Add/Remove Programs** from the Windows Control Panel.
3. Select **Microsoft Dynamics GP** in the list and click on **Change**.
4. Click on **Add/Remove Features**.
5. Scroll down the list of available features, change **Professional Services Tools Library** to **Run from My Computer**, and click on **Next**.
6. To begin the install process, click on **Next**.
7. Once the install has finished click on **Exit**.

Make sure to log into Microsoft Dynamics GP using the sa user and log into every company; not doing this will result in users receiving errors when they log in.

How to do it...

PSTL does not appear anywhere in the menu structure by default. To configure PSTL for use, it needs to be made available manually. To make PSTL available:

1. Log into Microsoft Dynamics GP using the sa user.
2. Select a company (for configuration it doesn't matter which one).
3. Right-click on the navigation pane.
4. Click on **Add** followed by **Add Window**.

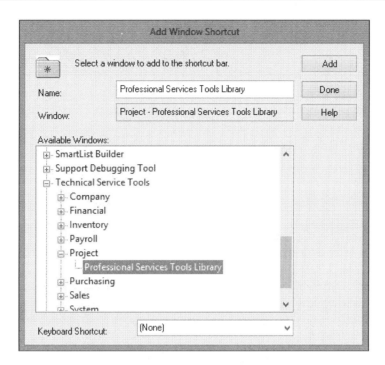

5. In the list of **Available Windows** expand **Technical Service Tools** and then expand **Project**.

6. Click on **Professional Services Tools Library** (which will auto-fill the **Name** and **Window** fields at the top of the window) .

7. Click on **Add**.

8. Click on **Done**.

9. Click on the newly created shortcut to launch PSTL, which will process through the required items and run the grant security script.

Once PSTL has had a menu item created, it can be launched with all of the features available for use.

There's more...

By default any user can create a shortcut to PSTL, but only those users with the POWERUSER security role can open it. If other users are to use PSTL, a security task needs to be created and assigned to a security role that is then assigned to the relevant users.

Disable a company database to prevent users from logging in

Out of the box, Microsoft Dynamics GP doesn't have a method for disabling access to a company. For example, if you're running an upgrade you may want to disable all companies to prevent users logging in and then enable each one as the upgrade of that database completes.

PSTL offers this functionality. In this recipe, we'll take a look at how to disable a company using Database Disabler.

How to do it...

To disable a database, perform the following steps:

1. In PSTL, select **Database Disabler** from **System Tools**.

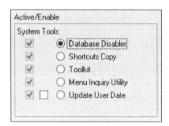

2. Click on **Next**.

3. Select the **Disable** checkbox next to the company name that is to be disabled.

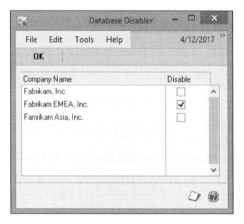

4. Click on **OK**.

How it works...

Once a database has been disabled, users who are already in that company can continue working, but users who try to log in or change company will not see the company listed for selection.

The disabled company can still be accessed by the sa user normally so there is no possibility, if you only have one company, of preventing Dynamics GP from being used.

To enable a company, simply uncheck the **Disable** checkbox and click on **OK**; users will again be able to access the company with the same security permissions as they previously had.

Replicate settings and data to a new company with Company Copy

Creating a new company can be a chore if there are a lot of modules and settings that need to be copied over to the new company, but PSTL provides a tool, Company Copy, that makes this process much easier.

Getting ready...

This tool requires the user to be logged in as a user with SQL Server administrator privileges (typically this will be the sa user) and this should be the only user logged in.

A good backup of the destination company should be made before running the tool since the copy is not reversible as it deletes tables from the destination company before creating new ones.

If there is a substantial amount of data (such as a lot of vendor records if payables is being copied) the copy can take a while to run; hence it needs to be done outside of peak hours.

A second company database needs to exist to have the settings copied into.

How to do it...

To use Company Copy, perform the following steps:

1. In PSTL, select **Company Copy** from **Misc. Tools**.

2. Click on **Next**.

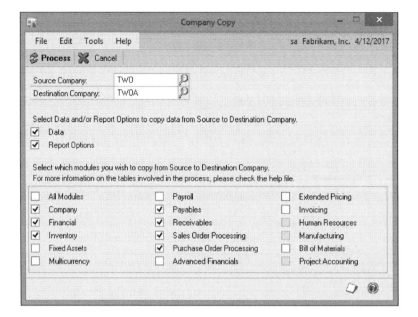

3. Enter or select the **Source Company**.

4. Enter or select the **Destination Company**.

5. Choose whether to copy across data or report options by marking the relevant checkbox:

    ❑   If **Data** is marked then **Financial** will auto-mark

    ❑   If **Report Options** is marked then **Company** will auto-mark

6. Mark the checkbox next to the module for which data should be copied to the **Destination Company**. Some modules have prerequisites that will auto-mark (such as **Inventory** when **Extended Pricing** is marked).

7. Click on **Process** to perform the copy.

When copying data, the **Destination Company** tables will be replaced so this function should only be used for newly created companies; one point to consider is that only Dynamics GP and not third-party tables and data will be copied.

How it works...

Company Copy deletes tables from the **Destination Company** and replaces them with exact copies of the Setup and Master tables in the **Source Company**. For example, if Payables is copied the following tables will be copied:

Physical name	Technical name
PM00100	PM Class Master File
PM00200	PM Vendor Master File
PM00300	PM Address Master
PM40102	Payables Document Types
PM00101	Vendor Class Accounts
PM00203	Vendor Accounts
PM40100	PM Setup File
PM40103	Payables Distribution Type

Duplicate data between companies using Master Triggers

After a new company has been created and settings replicated to it using Company Copy, it can have Master records created and updated automatically from another company using Master Triggers.

These Master Triggers are available for the general ledger, payables management, and receivables management. In this recipe, we'll take a look at using Master Triggers to create a new vendor into the Fabrikam Asia, Inc. database automatically when we create the vendor in Fabrikam, Inc.

Getting ready...

To enable Master Triggers for payables management, perform the following steps:

1. Log into the Dynamics GP company, which will be the Master database from where the information will be entered and replicated.

2. Click on the Professional Services Tools Library shortcut.

3. Select **PM Master Triggers** from **Purchasing Tools**.

4. Click on **Next**.

5. Select the destination database ID in **Replicate To DB** (in this example, **TWOA**).

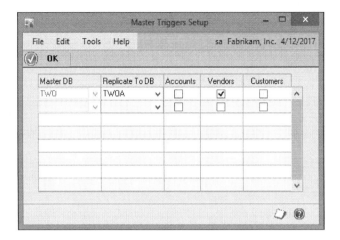

6. Mark the **Vendors** checkbox.

7. Click on **OK**.

Now that the Vendors Master Trigger has been enabled, any vendor record created or updated in Fabrikam, Inc. will be copied across to the **Replicate To DB** company

How to do it...

To use the Master Trigger to replicate a new vendor, perform the following steps:

1. Select **Purchasing** from the navigation pane. Select **Vendor** under the **Cards** section in the **Purchasing** area page.

2. Enter the new vendor information.

3. Click on **Save**.

4. Click on the **Microsoft Dynamics GP menu | User and Company**.

5. Select the company configured in the **Master Triggers**.

6. Click on **OK**.

7. Select **Purchasing** from the navigation pane. Select **Vendor** under the **Cards** section in the **Purchasing** area page.

8. Enter a value for the **Vendor ID** field created in step 2 and the new vendor created in the Master company will be displayed.

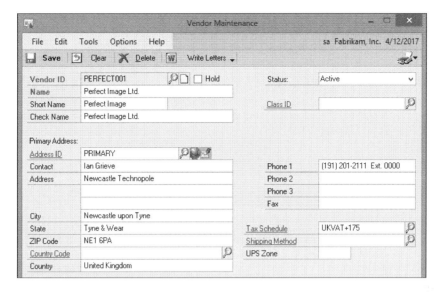

How it works...

Master Triggers work by adding SQL Triggers to the insert/update event on the tables in the SQL database to replicate the new or amended record into the destination company databases.

There's more...

Master Triggers are also available for the general ledger for replicating the chart of accounts and receivables management where they will replicate customers.

Merge records with Combiner

PSTL includes several Combiner functions that can merge records together; for example, if a duplicate customer record has been created for a returning customer, instead of the existing customer being reused, or two customers being merged, Customer Combiner can be used to combine these records together into one without losing any history.

How to do it...

To combine Pacific Digital into Aaron Fitz Electrical using Customer Combiner, perform the following steps:

1. Open PSTL and select **Customer Combiner** from Sales Tools.

2. Click on **Next**.

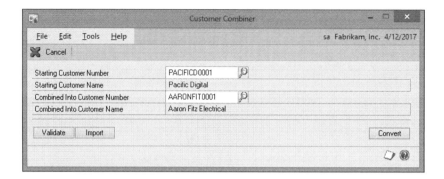

3. In the **Starting Customer Number** field, enter PACIFICD0001.

4. In the **Combined Into Customer Number**, enter AARONFIT0001.

5. Click on **Convert**.

Customer Combiner removes customer numbers and recalculates the summary records to include both customers' records so Pacific Digital will be merged into Aaron Fitz Electrical with no loss of information, leaving the combined transaction information in the system under the Aaron Fitz Electrical customer number.

There's more...

The Combiner at its most basic level allows a single record to be merged into another one but Combiner actually offers more than just this simple functionality.

Import from spreadsheet

Along with being able to combine customer numbers individually, they can also be done en masse by importing them from a spreadsheet. To do this, perform the following steps:

1. Set up a spreadsheet with two columns, the first containing the Starting Customer Number and the second containing the Combined Into Customer Number.

2. Save the spreadsheet as a tab-delimited text file.

3. Open PSTL and select **Customer Combiner** from **Sales Tools**.

4. Click on **Next**.

5. Click on **Validate**, browse to and select the tab-delimited text file.

6. When prompted, select a destination for the TA Invalid Customers report.

7. If there are errors, address them in the file and revalidate, or click on **Import**, browse to the file, and click on **OK** to process the import.

Each row of the spreadsheet will be processed and the customers combined; any errors will be reported at the end.

Other Combiner functions

Combiner functions also exist for general ledger accounts, purchasing vendors, sales territories, inventory sites, and items providing both the ability to combine records individually or en masse using imports from spreadsheets.

Change data using Modifier

Modifier functions exist in PSTL to allow record IDs to be amended. One such use might be if a non-standard Customer ID was created or if Customer Combiner has been used to combine two customer records which now has a new name and the Customer ID reflects the name. For example, if Pacific Digital was combined with Aaron Fitz Electrical, the merged company may change its name to Fitz Digital and for ease of use the Customer ID in Dynamics GP may need to be changed.

How to do it...

To change the Customer ID perform the following steps:

1. Make a backup of the SQL Server database.

2. Open PSTL and select **Customer Modifier** from **Sales Tools**.

3. Click on **Next**.

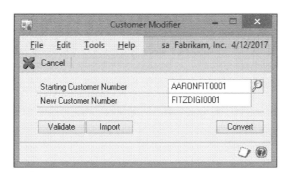

4. In the **Starting Customer Number** field, enter AARONFIT0001.

5. In the **New Customer Number** field, enter FITZDIGI0001.

6. Click on **Convert**.

7. Click on **Continue** on the warning prompt regarding having a backup of the SQL Server database.

There's more...

As with the Combiner function discussed in an earlier recipe, there is more than the single record merge available.

Customer name Modifier

Dynamics GP stores the customer name on transactions when they're created. Amendments to the customer name on the Customer Card do not roll through to the transactions.

However, the customer name stored on transactions can be modified using the Customer Name Modifier tool:

1. Open PSTL and select **Customer Name Modifier** from **Sales Tools**.

2. Click on **Next**.

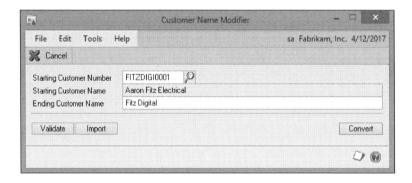

3. In the **Starting Customer Number** field, enter FITZDIGI0001.

4. In the **Ending Customer Name** field, enter Fitz Digital.

5. Click on **Convert**.

If there are a number of customers to be renamed, this can be done using the Validate/Import functions.

Import from spreadsheet

As with Customer Combiner, both Customer Modifier and Customer Name Modifier are capable of using a tab-delimited file to modify Customer Numbers in bulk.

Other Modifier functions

Combiner functions also exist for general ledger accounts, checkbooks and fiscal periods, purchasing vendors and vendor names, sales salepersons and territories, inventory sites, item numbers, items descriptions, and fixed assets providing both the ability to combine records individually or en masse using imports from spreadsheet.

Setting a minimum PO/Receipt Number

It is not unknown for Dynamics GP to set a PO or Receipt Number to an unexpectedly low number when a transaction has been deleted from the system. PSTL provides a tool which can be used to prevent this from happening by using the Minimum PO/Receipt # tool.

Getting ready

This tool differs from the ones already covered in this chapter in that it requires PSTL to be installed on each machine in which the PO/Receipt Number is to be checked. Activating the tool only needs to be done on one machine.

To switch on Minimum PO/Receipt #, perform the following steps:

1. Open PSTL and select **Customer Name Modifier** from **Sales Tools**.

2. Click on **Next**.

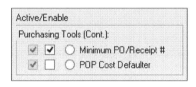

3. Mark the checkbox next to **Minimum PO/Receipt #** in the **Purchasing Tools (Cont.)** section.

How to do it...

To set a minimum PO/Receipt Number or prevent defaulting to a previous number, perform the following steps:

1. Select **Purchasing** from the navigation pane. Select **Purchase Order Processing** under the **Setup** section on the **Financial** area page.

2. Click on the **Additional** menu and then click on **Minimum PO Numbers**.

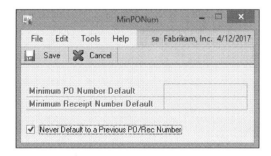

3. Enter the **Minimum PO Number Default** and **Minimum Receipt Number Default** if you want to set minimum numbers that could be used as defaults.

4. If, instead, you'd prefer that no number, previous to the Next Number, should be defaulted, mark the **Never Default to a Previous PO/REC Number** checkbox.

How it works...

The minimum PO/Receipt # tool will prevent the purchase order or **Receivings Transaction Entry** window from defaulting back to a previous number. If a minimum number has been defined then the length of the minimum number needs to be the same length as the PO Number defined in Purchase Order Processing Setup or it will be ignored.

Preventing date errors with Doc Date Verify

Microsoft previously provided a small add on for Dynamics GP called **Doc Date Verify** but this has now been added to PSTL. Doc Date Verify prevents users from entering dates in subledgers for fiscal periods that have not been set up or where the fiscal period is closed.

Without Doc Date Verify, it is possible to accidently date a payables transaction with the year 2103 instead of 2013. Since payables document dates are often different from general ledger posting dates, the transaction could post just fine but would never be selected for payment because of the odd year. It's also hard to fix because other parts of Dynamics GP validate against the fiscal period and prevent users from voiding some of these incorrectly dated transactions. Doc Date Verify rectifies this by preventing the entry of dates that don't exist in fiscal periods that have been set up.

Doc Date Verify works in core financial and distribution modules to validate date entry. In this recipe, let's look at how it works.

Getting ready

Doc Date Verify differs from most other PSTL tools in that PSTL needs to be configured on each client PC on which the Doc Date Verify tool is to check dates. To enable Doc Date Verify, perform the following steps:

1. Open PSTL and select **Customer Name Modifier** from **Sales Tools**.
2. Click on **Next**.

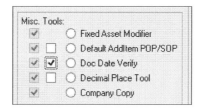

3. Mark the checkbox next to **Doc Date Verify**.

4. Close PSTL.

With the **Doc Date Verify** checkbox marked, no transactions can be entered for either a closed period or one which has not been set up.

How to do it...

To see how Doc Date Verify protects dates in Dynamics GP:

1. After Doc Date Verify has been installed, select **Purchasing** from the navigation pane. Select **Transaction Entry** under the **Transactions** section on the **Purchasing** area page.

2. In the **Doc. Date** field enter 4/12/2103.

3. Dynamics GP responds with a message that **A fiscal period for this date has not been setup**. Users must change the date to continue with the transaction.

How it works...

Doc Date Verify provides some peace of mind for core financial and distribution transactions. Other modules, like the contract portion of field service, actually needs to put dates out beyond the existing fiscal periods because of the nature of the transaction. For financial and distribution modules, Doc Date Verify does not work with quotes and orders since it is reasonable that those transactions types could affect fiscal periods not yet set up.

Index

D

validating, to ensure year-end closing 245, 246
validating, ways 246
Prepare a Letter screen 158
printer classes
any printer ID 202
company 202
manual selection 202
none 202
system 202
user 202
user & company 202
Print Options box
about 186
turning off, steps for 186, 187
processes
automating with macros 107, 108
remembering, with ad hoc workflow 82-84
Professional Services Tools Library. *See* **PSTL**
PSTL
about 304
configuring 304, 305
installing 304, 305
purchase order
closing 242
copying, steps for 196-198
partially received order, properly closing 242, 243
purchasing accounts
splitting, for improving financial reporting clarity 84, 85
Purchasing module 20

Q

Quick Links
navigation list, adding as 17-19
used, for speeding data access 17

R

reason codes
for inventory transaction 44-47
Reconcile to GL feature
using, steps for 203, 204
Reconcile utility
about 279
used, for validating balances 279, 280

record
merging, with Combiner 311, 312
recurring batches
about 234
best practices 120
setting up 229
used, for setting up accruals 118-120
used, for setting up deferrals 118-120
reminders
drilling down into 93
setting up, steps for 92, 93
using, to remember events 92
remit-to address
changing, on posted payables transaction 193
report groups
creating, steps for 97
multiple reports, running 97, 98
used, for automating reports 97
reporting control
controlling, with account rollups 79-81
report option
setting up, beginning of previous periods used 95
setting up, end of previous periods used 95
reports
adding, to My Reports 21, 22
automating, with report groups 97
Full View option 29
without options 23
Report Writer report 21
Reset History in Detail checkbox 62
revenue deferral module 121

S

sales
of discontinued inventory, preventing 249-251
Sales button 20
sales item, suggested
linking 55-57
relating 5, 56
sales order
copying, steps for 198, 199
Screen Capture feature 290

Thank you for buying
Microsoft Dynamics GP 2013 Cookbook

About Packt Publishing

Packt, pronounced 'packed', published its first book "*Mastering phpMyAdmin for Effective MySQL Management*" in April 2004 and subsequently continued to specialize in publishing highly focused books on specific technologies and solutions.

Our books and publications share the experiences of your fellow IT professionals in adapting and customizing today's systems, applications, and frameworks. Our solution-based books give you the knowledge and power to customize the software and technologies you're using to get the job done. Packt books are more specific and less general than the IT books you have seen in the past. Our unique business model allows us to bring you more focused information, giving you more of what you need to know, and less of what you don't.

Packt is a modern, yet unique publishing company, which focuses on producing quality, cutting-edge books for communities of developers, administrators, and newbies alike. For more information, please visit our website: www.PacktPub.com.

About Packt Enterprise

In 2010, Packt launched two new brands, Packt Enterprise and Packt Open Source, in order to continue its focus on specialization. This book is part of the Packt Enterprise brand, home to books published on enterprise software – software created by major vendors, including (but not limited to) IBM, Microsoft and Oracle, often for use in other corporations. Its titles will offer information relevant to a range of users of this software, including administrators, developers, architects, and end users.

Writing for Packt

We welcome all inquiries from people who are interested in authoring. Book proposals should be sent to author@packtpub.com. If your book idea is still at an early stage and you would like to discuss it first before writing a formal book proposal, contact us; one of our commissioning editors will get in touch with you.

We're not just looking for published authors; if you have strong technical skills but no writing experience, our experienced editors can help you develop a writing career, or simply get some additional reward for your expertise.

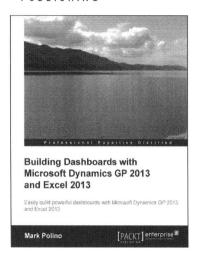

Building Dashboards with
Microsoft Dynamics GP 2013
and Excel 2013

Easily build powerful dashboards with Microsoft Dynamics GP 2013
and Excel 2013

Mark Polino

[PACKT] enterprise

Building Dashboards with Microsoft Dynamics GP 2013 and Excel 2013

ISBN: 978-1-849689-06-9   Paperback: 268 pages

Easily build powerful dashboards with Microsoft
Dynamics GP 2013 and Excel 2013

1. Build a dashboard using Excel 2013 with
   information from Microsoft Dynamics GP 2013

2. Make Excel a true business intelligence tool with
   charts, sparklines, slicers, and more

3. Utilize PowerPivot's full potential to create even
   more complex dashboards

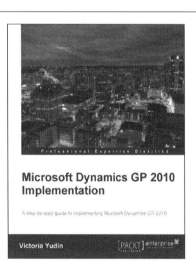

Microsoft Dynamics GP 2010
Implementation

A step-by-step guide to implementing Microsoft Dynamics GP 2010

Victoria Yudin

[PACKT] enterprise

Microsoft Dynamics GP 2010 Implementation

ISBN: 978-1-849680-32-5   Paperback: 376 pages

A step-by-step guide to implementing Microsoft
Dynamics GP 2010

1. Master how to implement Microsoft Dynamics GP
   2010 with real-world examples and guidance from
   a Microsoft Dynamics GP MVP

2. Understand how to install Microsoft Dynamics GP
   2010 and related applications, following detailed,
   step-by-step instructions

3. Learn how to set up the core Microsoft Dynamics
   GP modules effectively

4. Discover the additional tools available from
   Microsoft for Dynamics GP

Please check **www.PacktPub.com** for information on our titles

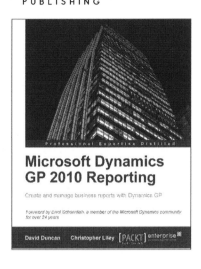
Microsoft Dynamics GP 2010 Reporting

ISBN: 978-1849682-18-3   Paperback: 360 pages

Create and manage a business reports with Dynamics GP

1. Identify the major reporting challenges facing your organization, and select the most effective reporting tool to meet those challenges

2. Empower users from top to bottom in your organization to create their own reports

3. Go beyond basic reporting by providing true business intelligence for your organization

4. Discover how to use reporting tools to mine and analyze your Dynamics GP data for maximum competitive advantage

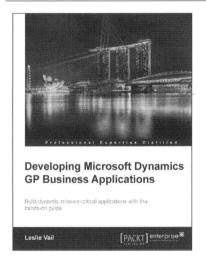

Developing Microsoft Dynamics GP Business Applications

ISBN: 9781-8-49680-26-4   Paperback: 590 pages

Build dynamic, mission-critical applications with this hands-on guide

1. Make your business more efficient with fully customizable applications

2. Develop mission-critical applications with Microsoft Dynamics GP

3. Learn how to enhance your application with sanScript

Please check **www.PacktPub.com** for information on our titles

Made in the USA
Lexington, KY
17 September 2014